Drugs, Crime, and Other Deviant Adaptations

Longitudinal Studies

LONGITUDINAL RESEARCH IN THE SOCIAL AND BEHAVIORAL SCIENCES
An Interdisciplinary Series

Series Editors:

Howard B. Kaplan, *Texas A&M University, College Station, Texas*
Adele Eskeles Gottfried, *California State University, Northridge, California*
Allen W. Gottfried, *California State University, Fullerton, California*

DRUGS, CRIME, AND OTHER DEVIANT ADAPTATIONS:
Longitudinal Studies
Edited by Howard B. Kaplan

A Continuation Order Plan is available for this series. A continuation order will bring delivery of each new volume immediately upon publication. Volumes are billed only upon actual shipment. For further information please contact the publisher.

Drugs, Crime, and Other Deviant Adaptations

Longitudinal Studies

Edited by

Howard B. Kaplan

Texas A&M University
College Station, Texas

Plenum Press • New York and London

Library of Congress Cataloging-in-Publication Data

On file

ISBN 0-306-44876-9

© 1995 Plenum Press, New York
A Division of Plenum Publishing Corporation
233 Spring Street, New York, N. Y. 10013

10 9 8 7 6 5 4 3 2 1

Printed in the United States of America

To my family:

Diane Susan, Samuel Charles, Rachel Esther

Contributors

Eleni A. Apospori, South Florida Youth Development Project, University of Miami, Coral Gables, Florida 33124.

Judith S. Brook, Department of Community Medicine, Mount Sinai School of Medicine, New York, New York 10029.

Patricia Cohen, New York State Psychiatric Institute and School of Public Health, Columbia University, New York, New York 10027.

Lori Collins-Hall, Department of Sociology, State University of New York at Albany, Hindelang Criminal Justice Research Center, Albany, New York 12222.

Kelly R. Damphousse, Department of Sociology, Texas A&M University, College Station, Texas 77843.

Andres G. Gil, South Florida Youth Development Project, University of Miami, Coral Gables, Florida 33124.

Denise B. Kandel, Department of Psychiatry and School of Public Health, Columbia University, and New York State Psychiatric Institute, New York, New York 10032.

Howard B. Kaplan, Department of Sociology, Texas A&M University, College Station, Texas 77843.

Marvin D. Krohn, Department of Sociology, State University of New York at Albany, Hindelang Criminal Justice Research Center, Albany, New York 12222.

Alan J. Lizotte, School of Criminal Justice, State University of New York at Albany, Hindelang Criminal Justice Research Center, Albany, New York 12222.

Steven S. Martin, Center for Drug and Alcohol Studies, Department of Sociology and Criminal Justice, University of Delaware, Newark, Delaware 19716.

Joan McCord, Department of Criminal Justice, Temple University, Philadelphia, Pennsylvania 19122.

Michael D. Newcomb, Division of Counseling and Educational Psychology, University of Southern California, Los Angeles, California 90007.

Cynthia A. Robbins, Center for Drug and Alcohol Studies, Department of Sociology and Criminal Justice, University of Delaware, Newark, Delaware 19716.

Alan W. Stacy, Institute for Prevention Research, Department of Preventive Medicine, University of Southern California, Los Angeles, California 90007; and Department of Psychology, University of California, Los Angeles, Los Angeles, California 90024.

Terence P. Thornberry, School of Criminal Justice, State University of New York at Albany, Hindelang Criminal Justice Research Center, Albany, New York 12222.

William A. Vega, School of Public Health, University of California, Berkeley, California 94720.

George J. Warheit, South Florida Youth Development Project, University of Miami, Coral Gables, Florida 33124.

Martin Whiteman, Columbia University, New York, New York 10027.

Ping Wu, Department of Psychiatry and School of Public Health, Columbia University, and New York State Psychiatric Institute, New York, New York 10032.

Rick S. Zimmerman, South Florida Youth Development Project, University of Miami, Coral Gables, Florida 33124.

Preface

This volume brings together a sample of the best of the studies that illustrate two recent trends in research on deviant behavior. The first of these trends is the investigation of deviant behavior in longitudinal perspective. Panels of subjects are followed over long periods of time to establish temporal relationships between deviant behavior and the antecedents and consequences of deviant behavior. The second trend in contemporary research on deviance is the recognition of the association among forms of deviant behavior such as violence, drug abuse, and theft. The recognition of the covariation among forms of deviance stimulated questions regarding the nature of the relationships among multiple forms of deviance. Is one form of deviant behavior a cause or a consequence of other forms of deviant behavior? What variables mediate and moderate such causal relationships? Do different forms of deviant behavior have common antecedents and consequences? Independent of the foregoing relationships, do particular forms of deviant behavior have unique antecedents and consequences?

The eight original research studies that, along with the introduction and overview, constitute this volume are based on data drawn from among the most influential longitudinal studies in the general area of deviant behavior. These studies variously consider common and pattern-specific antecedents and consequences, reciprocal influences, and intervening and moderating variables in causal relationships among drug use, crime, and other forms of deviance.

Earlier versions of four of the research contributions were presented as part of a panel on "Drug Abuse and Crime in Longitudinal Perspective" at the 44th Annual Meetings of the American Society of Criminology in New Orleans, in November 1992. This panel, chaired by the editor of this volume, was organized in anticipation of the preparation of this volume. These four papers, together with the other four invited research reports, have in common that they use data from longitudinal studies to address questions regarding the nature of the relationships among various forms of deviance in addition to more general questions about other psychosocial antecedents and consequences of deviant response patterns. The eight research reports use similar formats in which the theoretical and empirical bases for the research, methods, results, and discussion are presented in turn. Collectively, these contributions constitute a cumulative body of knowledge, suggest emerging trends in research on deviant behavior, and define lacunae that make up the research agenda for the coming decades concerning the nature of the relationships among drugs, crime, and other deviant adaptations to stress, and the nature of their common and pattern-specific antecedents and consequences.

Acknowledgments

The preparation of this volume was accomplished in the course of research supported by research grant R01 DA02497 and Research Scientist Award K05 DA00136 from the National Institute on Drug Abuse to the editor.

I am grateful to "Sam" McLean for her usual competence, diligence, and dedication in the preparation of this volume. I happily acknowledge also the many good services of the editorial staff of Plenum Press.

Contents

3. Stage of Drug Use, Aggression, and Theft/Vandalism: Common and Uncommon Risks.................................... 83

Judith S. Brook, Martin Whiteman, and Patricia Cohen

PART III. RECIPROCAL INFLUENCES AMONG DRUG USE, CRIME, AND OTHER FORMS OF DEVIANCE

4. Long-Term Social–Psychological Influences on Deviant Attitudes and Criminal Behavior.................................... 99

Alan W. Stacy and Michael D. Newcomb

5. Relationship between Alcohol and Crime Over the Life Course .. 129

Joan McCord

PART IV. INTERVENING VARIABLES IN CAUSAL RELATIONSHIPS AMONG DRUG USE, CRIME, AND OTHER FORMS OF DEVIANCE

PART V. MODERATORS OF THE RELATIONSHIPS AMONG DRUG USE, CRIME, AND OTHER FORMS OF DEVIANCE

PART VI. EMERGING ISSUES IN LONGITUDINAL RESEARCH ON DEVIANT BEHAVIOR

I

INTRODUCTION

1

Drugs, Crime, and Other Deviant Adaptations

Howard B. Kaplan

Introduction

Few topics have excited more interest in contemporary behavioral science than the causes of deviance. The etiology of deviance has been approached within diverse theoretical frameworks and using a range of methodological orientations. A not inconsiderable part of the literature on this topic deals with the relationships among diverse patterns of deviance: Some deviant patterns are antecedents of particular deviant outcomes, while other deviant patterns are common antecedents of a spectrum of deviant responses; some deviant patterns either have direct effects on or are influenced directly by other deviant patterns, or both affect and are affected; the influence of patterns of deviance on other patterns is often mediated by their effects on intervening variables; and deviant adaptations interact with other variables (including other deviant patterns) to moderate the influence of these adaptations on still other deviant outcomes.

The burgeoning and voluminous theoretical and empirical literature on the relationships among patterns of deviant behavior parallels the general processes that have been considered with reference to the etiology of deviance, whether from the perspective of particular theoretical orientations or more integrative approaches (Akers, 1994; Messner, Krohn, & Liska, 1989; Shoemaker, 1990).

Howard B. Kaplan • Department of Sociology, Texas A&M University, College Station, Texas 77843.

Drugs, Crime, and Other Deviant Adaptations: Longitudinal Studies, edited by Howard B. Kaplan. Plenum Press, New York, 1995.

The causal processes either clearly reflect the linear and interactive influences among deviant patterns or are interpretable in these terms. As the empirical reports and theoretical statements dealing with relationships among patterns of deviance proliferate, the etiological literature on deviance as a whole becomes more and more amenable to interpretation in terms of the common and pattern-specific direct and indirect linear, and moderating influences among patterns of deviance.

In this chapter, by way of introducing the longitudinal studies of drugs, crime, and other deviant adaptations, I propose to accomplish the following objectives: (1) discuss the nature of deviance; (2) present an integrative summary of the literature on the etiology of deviance; (3) provide an introductory overview of the empirical literature on the relationships among the patterns of deviance; (4) outline the ways in which this literature is interpretable in terms of and may contribute to the understanding of the processes that are reflected in the general literature on etiology of deviance; and (5) categorize the empirical studies that attempt to test theoretical assumptions about the causal relationships among patterns of deviance. Against this background, Chapters 2 through 9 illustrate (for the most part in longitudinal context) how deviant patterns reflect pattern-specific or common (direct or indirect) linear and interactive influences on other deviant outcomes.

Nature of Deviance

Although the behavior patterns (drugs, crime, and other deviant adaptations) that are the foci of the several contributions to this volume are widely recognized in the more inclusive society as examples of deviant behavior, the concept of deviance has more general applicability. The concept may refer to failure to conform to expectations in the context of a wide variety of interpersonal systems, including friendship groups, marital dyads, and work groups, as well as the general community. Indeed, the concept may refer to behaviors or attributes that conform to the expectations of one group but violate the expectations of another group from whose perspective the judgment of deviance is made. Deviance may refer to physical traits, social identities, experiences, behavior, or a variety of other phenomena that describe a person.

Deviance, then, refers to behaviors or attributes manifested by specified kinds of people in specified circumstances that are judged to violate the normative expectations of a specified group. Shared normative expectations refer to group evaluations regarding the appropriateness or inappropriateness of certain attributes or behaviors when manifested by certain kinds of people in certain situations.

Where deviant behavior is reflected in the presence of certain attributes or the performance of certain behaviors, the normative system expresses expectations in terms of proscribed attributes or behaviors. Where the deviant behavior is expressed in the absence of certain attributes or behaviors, the normative system expresses expectations in terms of prescriptions for particular attributes or behaviors. Being weak or sentimental might be proscribed for males, but not for females. Being gentle and courteous might be prescribed for females, but not for males.

The indication that certain patterns of behavior in certain contexts (i.e., evinced by certain kinds of people in certain situations) are socially defined as deviant is the administration of negative sanctions. Members of a group that are said to share a normative system impose these negative sanctions, which are responses that, according to the perceptions of the group, are intended to serve as a punishment for the attributes or behaviors in question. The consistent application of relatively severe sanctions in response to particular kinds of behaviors serves as indication that those behaviors are deviant according to the normative system that serves as a reference point. If the sanctions are applied only to certain kinds of people who perform the behaviors in question, then the implication is that the behaviors when performed by other kinds of people are not defined as deviant. If certain behaviors evoke negative sanctions regardless of the person's social characteristics and other situational contexts with perhaps very rare exceptions, then the implication is that the behavioral proscription is generally applicable except in extenuating circumstances. The ranking in the hierarchy of normative expectations of the evaluative standard that is violated by the behavior in context is reflected in the severity of the sanctions. Behaviors or attributes are deviant not only because they evoke negative sanctions but also because they would evoke negative sanctions if representatives of the socionormative system that defines the attributes or behaviors as deviant became aware of them.

A group that shares a normative system may evaluate the behaviors or attributes even of individuals who do not belong to the group and may apply negative sanctions for the behaviors or attributes that are judged to deviate from the normative expectations that are believed to be incumbent on even nongroup members. Depending on the group's access to sanctions that are meaningful to the nongroup members, the application of negative sanctions may have a great adverse impact on the outcomes of nongroup members.

In some cases, individuals whose behaviors or attributes appear to deviate from the normative expectations of a group to which they do not belong are not judged to be deviant because the individuals (perhaps because of their perceived inferiority) are not expected to be capable of conforming to the normative expectations. These "barbarians" or "subhumans" are judged to be deviant by virtue of not belonging to the group that evaluates them, but are not otherwise punished for failing to conform to the specific normative expectations that define the shared normative system. At worst, the failure to conform to the normative expectations is taken to be a (further) indication of their primary deviation, that is, not being part of the group that shares the normative system.

In any case, the valuation of behaviors or attributes as deviant presumes that those making the judgment have taken into account the applicability of the normative expectations to the person and, more particularly, to the circumstances in which the person finds himself or herself. It is not required that the deviant actor identify himself or herself as a group member for the group to evaluate the actor's attributes or behaviors.

The judgment that certain behaviors or attributes deviate from normative expectations may be made even if the deviant manifestations are beyond the individuals' control. Every normative system offers examples of evaluative standards that stigmatize individuals for manifesting undesirable attributes or behaviors, or for failing to manifest desirable attributes and behaviors, that are beyond their control.

The de facto deviation from the expectations of specified normative systems may be motivated or unmotivated. Motivated deviance derives from either of two sets of circumstances. In the first set, the person is a member of a group that defines the attributes or behaviors in question as deviant. Because of his experiences in the group, the person loses motivation to conform to the normative expectations and becomes motivated to deviate from the normative expectations of the group in order to serve self-enhancing functions. The manifestation of the deviant attributes or behaviors is consciously or unconsciously intended to serve such functions. In the second set of circumstances, the person is a member of a group in which the attributes or behaviors under consideration are normatively prescribed. The person is motivated to conform to the normative prescriptions as one who has been socialized in the group. The person is either unaware or considers it to be irrelevant that another group judges the attributes or behaviors to be deviant. The behavior is motivated, but the fact that the behavior or attributes are deviant does not contribute to the motivation.

Unmotivated deviance refers to instances of failure to conform to the normative expectations of the person's membership or reference groups where the failure to conform is contrary to the person's volition. The person would conform if he or she were able to. The circumstances that contribute to unmotivated deviance are discussed in some detail below.

The patterns of deviance that are the subject of the contributions to this volume generally fall into the category of motivated deviance. Unmotivated deviance is relevant as an explanatory factor, rather than as a dependent variable. The involuntary possession of traits and the involuntary performance of behaviors that are defined as deviant influence judgments of deviance, the administration of sanctions, and correlates of these phenomena that influence the onset of other deviant acts or the continuity of the deviant behaviors at a voluntary level.

An Integrative Summary of the Literature on the Etiology of Deviance

The history of the sociological study of deviant behavior has witnessed the proposal of theories that were interpreted as competing explanations of deviant behavior. The interpretation of diverse theories of deviant behavior as offering competing rather than complementary explanations has continued, to some extent, to the present. More recently, however, it has been recognized increasingly that the "competing" theories address different questions (why individuals initiate deviant behavior vs. why individuals continue to engage in deviant behavior once they have initiated the pattern) or focus on different explanatory factors that do not gainsay (but rather complement) the explanatory value of the other factors. Some theories focus on the opportunities to learn the deviant patterns; other theories focus on social or personal constraints on acting out the deviant behaviors. Recognition of these different foci has led to the offering of integrative theories that combine several different approaches. This summary is in the tradition of such treatments that combine traditional approaches to the explanation of crime or other forms of deviance including strain, social control, differential association, subcultural, social-learning, and opportunity theories (Akers, 1994; Kaplan, 1984; Messner et al., 1989; Shoemaker, 1990).

The following brief summary is offered as an initial and tentative formulation of the general relationships existing among variables that influence the onset and continuity of involvement in motivated deviance. Again, it will be apparent that this treatment subsumes a number of what have come to be accepted as classic approaches to the explanation of deviance in general or of specific forms of deviance. The summary is organized around four related issues: motivation to commit deviant acts that violate membership group norms, motivation to commit deviant acts that conform to membership group norms, acting out deviant dispositions, and continuity of deviant behavior.

Motivation to Commit Deviant Acts That Violate Membership Group Norms

In this and the following section, I consider two sets of circumstances that give rise to the motivation to commit deviant acts and two corresponding sets of satisfactions that are expected to be gained from deviant acts. In this section, I consider the circumstances surrounding the development of dispositions to perform deviant acts that involve (1) the person's earlier commitment to the normative system that judged such acts to be wrong and (2) the failure to achieve what was expected of the person according to the conventional standards. The person comes to see deviant patterns in general, or particular deviant patterns, as the only or most promising ways of satisfying his or her unresolved needs that up to now the person tried to satisfy using more conventional response patterns. In the following section, I consider the circumstances surrounding the development of dispositions to perform acts that are defined as deviant by some groups but nevertheless conform to the expectations of other groups to which the individual belongs or wishes to belong.

Conventional Failure and Deviant Dispositions

In the course of the normal socialization process one experiences, one learns to value the possession of particular attributes, the performance of certain behaviors, and particular experiences that are the outcome of the purposive or accidental responses of others toward one. These attributes, behaviors, and experiences are the basis for the individual's feelings of self-worth. If the person is unable to evaluate himself or herself positively, then the person will be motivated to behave in ways that will gain the attributes, enable the performance of the behaviors, and increase the likelihood of the experiences that will increase feelings of self-worth and decrease the feelings of psychological distress that are associated with self-rejecting attitudes. If a person perceives an inability to achieve the attributes, perform the behaviors, and enjoy the experiences he or she has been taught to value as the basis for overall positive self-evaluation through conventional behavior, then that person will be motivated to behave in deviant ways that offer promise of gaining attributes, facilitating behaviors, and enjoying experiences that will permit the person to gain a feeling of self-worth. The deviant behavior may involve using illegal means to achieve what the person has learned to value or engaging in deviant activities as a way of rejecting or avoiding the conventional standards by which the person failed and substituting deviant standards by which he or she could more easily succeed and earn feelings of self-worth.

The brief formulation of the process by which individuals become disposed to perform deviant acts that violate the moral codes of the groups in which they were raised is a reflection of a theoretical and research tradition in which motives to perform deviant acts are viewed as attempts to adjust to the psychological distress associated with failures to achieve specific values such as parental acceptance or occupational success. In the preceding synopsis and synthesis of this tradition, I merely subsumed the various specific motives that are attributed to individuals (individually or collectively) as presumed antecedents of deviant response under a more general motive—the need to avoid self-rejecting attitudes and to maintain or promote positive self-attitudes. Specific motives to attain consensually valued goals by illegitimate means are accounted for by the need to feel positively toward oneself, a prerequisite for which is the achievement of the consensually valued goals. Motivated acts that reflect contempt for the conventional value system and endorsement of values that contradict conventional value systems are intended to function in the service of the self-esteem motive by destroying the validity of the standards the person failed to meet and thereby found himself or herself making self-devaluing responses. Deviant patterns that appear to be motivated by the need to retreat (whether by decreasing contact with others or changing one's psychological state) from contact with the conventional value structure function to enhance self-attitudes by (1) avoiding further experiences of failure and rejection when measured against conventional standards or (2) avoiding recognition of such failure and rejection. The attraction of individuals who were socialized according to conventional values to groups that endorse deviant values, in addition to serving any of the foregoing self-enhancing functions, provides a new set of (deviant) standards that the person can adopt, achieve, and therefore use as a basis for positive self-evaluation (Kaplan, 1972, 1975, 1980, 1982, 1983, 1984, 1986).

Social Determinants of Conventional Failure

The failure to approximate self-evaluative standards of membership/positive reference groups may be conceptualized as *unmotivated* deviance. This concept classifies instances of failure to conform to the normative expectations of specified groups in which the failure to conform is contrary to the person's will. The person wishes to conform but is unable to do so. Thus, in effect, he deviates from the expectations of others. The unmotivated deviance may take either of two forms: the failure to possess consensually valued traits or the failure to perform consensually valued acts. In the former case, the subject has been unable to display traits within an acceptable range of values as a result of the interaction between congenital and social circumstances. Independent of or contrary to his wishes, the subject finds himself possessing physical or psychological impairments, characterized in terms of undesirable race-, ethnic-, religious-, or socioeconomic-related social categories; or falling below acceptable levels of intelligence, physical appearance, strength, or other criteria that form the basis of invidious comparisons. Since the subject, along with other group members, has internalized these values and therefore wishes to approximate them, his failure to do so constitutes one class of unmotivated deviance. The other class of unmotivated deviance comprises instances of de facto failure to *behave* so as to conform to the normative expectations of the group members, assuming the subject's desire to conform.

Unmotivated deviance is a function of three general categories of circumstances. First, individuals will fail to conform to the expectations of others when they are unaware of or mistaken about the social identities of others with whom they interact or when they are aware of the others' social positions but are unaware of or mistaken about the role expectations defining their own social identity or that of those with whom they are interacting. In the former case, the person, not knowing the social positions of those with whom he or she is interacting, is unable to identify his or her own complementary position and therefore cannot play the appropriate role. Such circumstances are most likely to arise when a person is moved to a new set of interpersonal relationships and when situational cues are vague or ambiguous or both. Members of more mobile segments of our society would be more vulnerable to these circumstances. In the latter case, the subject may know both his or her identity and the other person's identity, but have either no expectations or erroneous expectations regarding the roles that the two of them should play. Such circumstances are most likely to arise during times of rapidly changing role definitions, as a consequence of improper role models or other inadequate socialization experiences, and following life events that require the playing of unfamiliar roles.

A second category of circumstances that influence the subject's unwilling failure to perform in accordance with the expectations of others relates to the subject's having status sets or role sets that impose conflicting expectations on him or her. Although the person wishes to conform to the expectations of all the other parties with whom he or she is interacting, the nature of the conflicting expectations is such that he or she can conform to one set of expectations only at the cost of violating another set. In the case of the status set, the conflicting expectations are occasioned by the subject's simultaneously occupying two or more social positions and, in those capacities, engaging in two or more social relationships. In the case of the role set, the conflicting expectations are also occasioned by simultaneous participation in more than one relationship. In this case, however, the subject is expected to play different roles while acting in the same capacity, that is, occupying the same social position or status in each relationship. Such situations are likely to occur during periods of rapid and uneven rates of sociocultural change in diverse sectors of the more inclusive social system.

The third category of circumstances that influence unmotivated deviant behavior concerns the absence of instrumental resources to achieve legitimate goals. The absence of instrumental resources derives from (1) congenital inadequacies, as in strength, dexterity, or intelligence; (2) the failure to acquire the skills and experience necessary for adapting to or coping with the environment as a result of faulty socialization experiences, or the disruption of already acquired adaptive/coping patterns by various life events; (3) placement in inadequate social support systems; (4) the occurrence of life events that impose legitimate requirements on an individual that cannot be met by his or her heretofore adequate resources; and (5) deviant attributions by other social systems. This last set of influences on legitimate instrumental resources relates to a concept of deviance other than that of motivated and unmotivated deviance. This concept takes into account the existence of more or less inclusive and interlocking social systems. As a result of the meshing among systems, it is possible for a subject to successfully conform to the expectations of his membership group in his own view and that of other group members, and yet be judged deviant by other groups because the same behavior that conforms to the socionormative system of the membership group is judged to be deviant from the perspective of the other group's system of normative expectations. To the extent that the other group judges the subject's behavior to be deviant (and has the power to do so), it will implement negative sanctions. These negative sanctions will adversely affect the availability of legitimate instrumental resources that are required if the subject is to be able to conform to the expectations of his own membership group. In failing to conform to these expectations, against his will, the subject by definition manifests unmotivated deviance. Thus, unmotivated deviance is the indirect result of the attribution of deviance and the consequent administration of effective negative sanctions by a nonmembership/reference group for behavior by a person that is motivated and normative in the context of that person's own membership/reference group.

Motivation to Commit Deviant Acts That Conform to Membership Group Norms

The motivation to commit deviant acts is explained in part by the person's sharing with others a deviant subculture. A deviant subculture is a set of normative expectations shared by segments of a more inclusive population that include endorsements of behaviors that are defined by some specified group as deviant (whether or not the normative expectations also include prescriptions for nondeviant behaviors). In some deviant subcultures, the deviant activities are closely bound up with other aspects of group life, including language, interpersonal life, and general style of living. In other deviant subcultures, including many youth gangs, deviant activities reflect a minor portion of the more inclusive set of norms that govern the person's activities. In fact, the activity itself may have no intrinsic value except as it reflects some basic value that could be illustrated as well by nondeviant activities. In groups that share deviant standards, the deviant behaviors may promise to meet the person's needs to gain the approval of group members and other rewards associated with such approval, to behave in ways that are consistent with personal values, or to identify with a positively valued reference group.

The origin of deviant subcultures may be accounted for by the cultural diversity of groups living in the same society. The people who share a deviant subculture continue to endorse traditional values and activities, although the values and activities may have been defined as deviant by more politically influential groups. Alternatively, subcultures may develop as a collective solution to the failure to achieve conventional goals through conventional means. Individuals who share the circumstances that lead to failure as well as the fact of failure in the course of social interaction adapt to their situation by coming to accept shared values that endorse the use of illicit activities (1) to achieve conventional goals, (2) as attacks on conventional values, (3) to permit withdrawal from conventional society, or (4) as substitute standards for the measure of self-worth. The solutions either permit the achievement of values or reduce the feelings of self-rejection associated with the failure to achieve them.

Regardless of the source of the deviant subculture, its persistence depends on the transmission of the normative expectations to those who do not yet share the subcultural standards and the appropriate sanctioning of responses by those who share the subculture. The individual internalizes the culture either by being born into and reared in a group that shares a deviant subculture or by later becoming attracted to such a group and becoming emotionally committed to the subcultural standards shared by the group. The person may become attracted to the group originally because of the deviant activities that promise gratification to the person and become committed to the group because of this gratification. Alternatively, the person may become attracted to the group independent of the deviant activities but adopt the deviant subculture as a means of evoking continued identification with the group whose approval he or she needs. In any case, over time the individual learns to conform to the deviant norms because such conformity is the conventional, right, fitting, or proper way to behave in the group that shares the deviant subculture.

Acting Out Deviant Dispositions

The *motivation* to engage in deviant acts, whether generated by experiences in conventional or deviant groups, does not sufficiently explain why people *perform* deviant acts. Not all persons who are disposed or motivated to behave in deviant fashion in fact engage in those behaviors. Other factors are at work that prevent them from behaving in ways that they are disposed to behave. In particular, whether or not a person acts out the disposition to commit deviant acts will depend on (1) the relative strength of the motives to commit the act and of those not to commit the act and (2) the situational context and other opportunities to perform the act.

Counteracting Motives

While a person may see the satisfaction of certain needs as being dependent on the performance of deviant acts, and so be motivated to perform deviant acts, the person may see the satisfaction of other needs as being dependent on *not* performing deviant acts. In the latter case, the projected deviant behavior poses a threat to the satisfaction of important needs, and so the person is motivated to refrain from performing the deviant behavior. If the satisfaction of the needs that appear to be threatened by the performance of deviant behavior is more important to the person than the satisfaction of the needs that is expected to result from the deviant behavior, then the person is likely to refrain from the behavior.

Certain of an individual's needs are threatened by the mere *performance* of a particular deviant act. The need to obey the law, to do what one's parents and friends think is right, or to be a moral person are examples of needs that would be threatened by the performance of deviant behaviors and would be satisfied by refraining from deviant acts. Other needs will be threatened because of expected *consequences* of the act itself. For example, the need for the rewards granted by group members to the person might be jeopardized if the individual were known to have performed deviant acts, or the need to be in control of one's own emotions might be threatened by the use of psychoactive substances. The threats posed to the satisfaction of such needs, then, influence the likelihood of acting out deviant dispositions. This being the case, if the processes by which the person is restrained from deviant behavior are to be understood, it is important to understand the origin of the needs that motivate the individual to restrain himself or herself from yielding to impulses to perform deviant acts.

Origin of Counteracting Motives. The process by which a person comes to develop motivation to conform to the normative expectations of society—that is, the way in which one comes to need, for example, positive responses from parents, success in school, and (later) occupational success—is a complex one. The way whereby that person develops a commitment to the conventions of society is based on the infant's prolonged dependence on other human beings for the satisfaction of his or her biological needs. Since the infant's needs are satisfied by the adults in the child's immediate social circle, he or she comes to value the presence of adults. However, as the circle of people in the child's world widens, the child may note that need satisfaction is associated with certain persons and not others. By a process of association, the child comes to value those people, and less directly the traits and behaviors associated with those people, who satisfy his needs. Conversely, the child comes to disvalue the traits and behaviors that are associated in the child's mind with those persons who frustrate the satisfaction of his or her biologically given or acquired values.

A particularly important set of behaviors and attributes associated with people who ordinarily satisfy our needs are those traits and behaviors that are apparent on the particular occasions when those people satisfy our needs. Though a mother is ordinarily associated with satisfying the child's needs, there are occasions when she does not do so. Those behaviors and traits (smiles, soft words, and the like) that are associated with the occasions when the needs are satisfied come to be valued in their own right. The child is motivated to evoke those responses that he or she will later come to think of as approving responses. Conversely, those attributes or behaviors that are associated with the occasions when people who ordinarily satisfy the child's needs frustrate the satisfaction of those needs come to be regarded as undesirable in their own right. The child will be motivated to avoid such behaviors. Later, the child will come to think of such behaviors as disapproval. Thus, the person learns to value the positive and disvalue the negative attitudinal responses of others and the forms in which the attitudes are expressed—physical punishment, disapproving words, failure to reciprocate expectations.

Since people will display approving or disapproving responses depending on the individual's characteristics and behaviors, the child will come to associate certain of his or her traits and behaviors with approving responses and other traits and behaviors with disapproving responses. In this way, the child will come to evaluate behaviors and attributes as intrinsically worthy or unworthy because of their original association with approving or disapproving responses, respectively. Finally, having learned to value such traits and behaviors, the child comes to value in their own right any behavior patterns, resources, or relationships that he or she perceives to be instrumental to the achievement of these valued states. As the child's circle of significant others expands, he will come to invest with emotional significance others' traits and behaviors that are observed to evoke positive or negative sanctions.

In this way, in the ordinary course of socialization, the individual becomes emotionally attached to particular kinds of social relationships, particular attributes and behaviors that are associated with valued others, and personal attributes, behaviors, or experiences. The person has come to need the presence and approving responses of adults who have particular kinds of characteristics and behave in particular ways, and to possess the kinds of traits, perform the kinds of behaviors, and enjoy the kinds of experiences that are approved by these others. The satisfaction of these needs becomes the person's measure of self-worth. The person is motivated to behave in ways that will reflect or be instrumental in the satisfaction of these needs and, thus, to behave in ways that will evoke self-accepting attitudes. The person becomes emotionally invested in the image of self as one who has certain identities and conforms to the role expectations that are associated with those identities. If the social positions or identities are conventional ones and are defined in terms of conventional rules, then the person's self-conceptions will include images of self as not violating the law.

There are implications for both the development and the acting out of deviant dispositions in the processes by which a person (1) becomes emotionally attached to the network of relationships and the expectations of the people in those relationships regarding appropriate traits, behaviors, and experiences and (2) comes to evaluate himself in terms of conventional standards. To the extent that the person becomes attracted to and evaluates himself in terms of conventional values, he will forego engaging in deviant behaviors that threaten his needs to achieve those values. The extent to which the person evaluates himself in terms of conventional values, however, will be influenced by the degree to which he satisfies those needs by achieving conventional values. The consistent failure to achieve and to evaluate oneself positively according to conventional standards decreases emotional commitment to those standards and increases the likelihood that the person will develop dispositions to engage in deviant behaviors that promise to achieve conventional goals or to reduce the feelings of self-rejection that are the consequence of failure to do so.

Varieties of Counteracting Motives. Any of a number of motives may restrain a person from committing a deviant act that he or she is otherwise motivated to perform. The self-restraint might come from the anticipation that important needs might be satisfied by *not* performing the deviant act. For example, the person feels good about himself when he does the "right thing." The person feels an ongoing need to be law-abiding. This need is satisfied when the person resists temptations to violate the law. Alternatively, the person may be restrained from acting out deviant impulses because he or she anticipates that the performance of the deviant act will frustrate the satisfaction of important personal needs. The individual may have an ongoing need to be respected by others. He may anticipate that the satisfaction of this need (by being respected by others) will be frustrated if they find out he committed a deviant act.

The person's anticipation of the achievement or frustration of need satisfaction may be perceived by the person as being more or less directly related to the nonperformance or performance of the act. The *direct* involvement of the deviant act is perceived when the fact of not performing or of performing the deviant act provides or frustrates need satisfaction. The individual satisfies the need to be a law-abiding person or frustrates the need to conform to the expectations of his family and friends by performing the deviant act. *Less directly,* the person perceives deviant behavior as having consequences that affect the satisfaction or frustration of his or her needs. It is not the deviant behavior itself, but the consequences of the behavior, that satisfies or frustrates strong needs. Thus, the person may perceive that conformity to the law will have consequences that satisfy needs (e.g., a good job and other rewards associated with conformity) and that deviant behavior will have consequences that frustrate needs (e.g., rejection by loved ones, going to jail).

To the extent that the anticipated satisfactions associated with the act or consequences of conformity and the anticipated frustrations associated with the act or consequences of deviant behavior outweigh the projected benefits of the deviant behavior, they will prevent the person from acting out any deviant dispositions he or she might experience.

Moderating Factors. The effectiveness of counteracting motives in forestalling the acting out of deviant dispositions is moderated by two general conditions. These conditions relate to emotional attraction to the conventional order and to the ability to define the deviant act as compatible with the conventional order.

Regarding the first condition for a person to forego the performance of deviant acts because he believes it is wrong, because people he relates to think it is wrong, because it is inappropriate to his social identities, or because it will evoke informal and formal responses by others, it is necessary that the person have an emotional investment in the moral beliefs, social relationships and identities, and responses of others. If the person does not *care* about these things, they will not influence his behavior. The effectiveness of counterbalancing motives that prevent a person (who is motivated to commit a deviant act and who has the opportunity to commit a deviant act) from acting out his motivations to deviant behavior are tied up with his positive feelings about the conventional order. The individual is attracted to representatives of the conventional moral order and needs positive responses from them. Further, he respects the rightness of conventional rules and would feel guilty if he violated them. Finally, he gains gratifications from his participation in social relationships and would not like to risk the loss of present and anticipated future satisfactions that might be among the consequences of his performing deviant acts.

Whether over the short term or longer term, any of a number of factors might reduce a person's emotional attraction to the conventional world. Over the short term, any factors that influence the person's emotional and cognitive states in general and awareness of his conventional social identities in particular might reduce the effectiveness of constraints against acting out deviant dispositions. The nature of some deviant activities is such that they may reduce the constraints that might ordinarily (in the absence of these acts) prevent the acting out of *other* deviant acts. Thus, for example, while under the influence of alcohol or other substances that affect emotional and cognitive states, the person might commit crimes against property or violent acts that he might not commit in more drug-free states. Other circumstances allow the person to ignore his conventional social identities and therefore the emotional significance of conforming to the role expectations that define those identities. Such circumstances as being part of an anonymous crowd permit the individual to submerge his identity and with it his recognition that the deviant acts he is motivated to perform violate the role expectations that under less anonymous circumstances he would be motivated to honor.

Over the longer term, the emotional attraction to the representatives, moral code, and activities of the moral order depend in part on how successful the person has been in achieving what he values within conventional society. The very same experiences of failure (such as feeling rejected by family, friends, or school and failing to attain other valued attributes such as getting good grades or being popular or good looking) that make a person ready to seek satisfactions through deviant acts influence the weakening of the person's ties to the conventional system. If the person experiences failure and associates that failure with the conventional order, then he or she will simultaneously become decreasingly attracted to the conventional society and increasingly attracted to the potential satisfactions of deviant behavior. In that event, the deviant motivation will be more likely to have actual deviant behavior as an outcome.

Yet common sense tells us that people who are disposed to perform deviant acts frequently do refrain from performing such acts for the aforementioned reasons. This being the case, we must assume that the experiences of failure are rarely extreme enough to fully counteract the attachment to the social order that is associated with the individual's degree of experience with success. Although the strength of commitment to the social order may be weakened by failure, it still remains, in general, a potent force in forestalling the acting out of deviant motivations. It is only in extreme circumstances of near total failure to achieve what is expected by conventional standards that the individual's attraction to the normative order ceases to restrain deviant impulses. Short of such extreme circumstances, a number of the person's satisfactions will continue to depend on conventional norms, identities, and relationships, and the individual will tend to restrain deviant impulses.

Regarding the second condition for effectiveness of counteracting motives in forestalling the acting out of deviant dispositions, it is not enough that a person be emotionally attracted to the conventional in order for deviant impulses to be restrained. A person attracted to the social order might be motivated to do the right thing, to behave appropriately in various social capacities, to do what those with whom he interacts think is right, to elicit approving responses from others, to avoid social sanctions, and still act out a deviant disposition. All that is necessary for this to occur is that the person who is committed to the conventional moral order justify performance of the act in terms that he thinks are consistent with the conventional moral code and are acceptable to the conventional groups to which he is attracted.

A person may be able to justify illicit acts in terms of the standards that apply specifically to specific social identities or in terms of standards that are more generally applied in society. Illegal activities may be justified in terms of doing it for kicks or because it is exciting or for other reasons that may be acceptable when applied to adolescent behavior. Other illicit activities such as violence are perhaps justifiable in terms of patterns that are endorsed informally in various social institutions. Violence in legitimated form is a prevalent pattern in recreational activities (television, sports) and global political strategy (war).

Opportunities

Even if the person, on balance, expected satisfaction of important needs from the deviant behavior, the person might still not perform the deviant act because of the absence of opportunity to do so. The opportunity to perform the act includes physical, personal, and interpersonal resources as well as the situational context that provides the occasion and the stimulus for the deviant behavior. The current situation provides a number of features that may stimulate overt acts, given a predisposition to commit some form of deviant act. The opportunities presented by the person's current situation not only define the limits of what is possible but also stimulate latent dispositions, including dispositions to deviant acts. A person who is disposed to violence may be stimulated to commit a violent act at a particular time when cues for violence (e.g., a gun, television violence) are present. A person who is disposed to steal may in fact steal when an appropriate object of value becomes accessible readily and with little apparent risk.

The individual's current situation and his motivation to perform deviant acts influence each other. A person disposed to commit a deviant act may seek out situational opportunities, and the situational in which a person finds himself may stimulate a preexisting disposition to commit a deviant act. A number of factors influence opportunities to perform deviant behaviors, including generality of deviant dispositions and involvement in the conventional order.

Generality of Deviant Dispositions.   The range of opportunities that are available to the person who is motivated to perform acts defined as deviant depends in part on how general or specific the person's motives are. A person may be motivated to perform any of a range of illicit acts simply because they are illegal. The motive may stem from a history of experiences of failure and being rejected in the conventional world and from the consequent rejection of conventional morals. The motive is a general one in the sense that any of a range of deviant behaviors would satisfy the need. This being the case, the opportunities to perform any of several patterns are greater than the opportunities to perform any one of them.

Similarly, the motivation to identify with and to be accepted by a group that endorses deviant patterns can be satisfied by performing any of a range of deviant behaviors. The opportunities to perform deviant behaviors multiply as the range of behaviors that can satisfy the one's needs increases. Or, if acceptance by the group is dependent on conforming to a generally stated standard such as being daring, then any of a number of illicit activities that have a high associated risk might serve the purpose of securing group approval. Once again, as the number of deviant activities that might satisfy the person's needs multiply, so do the potential opportunities for engaging in deviant behavior. As the number of generally stated values increases, the opportunities to engage in deviant activities increase even further.

Involvement in the Conventional Order.   The involvement of the person in conventional society is relevant to availability of deviant opportunities in three ways. First, socialization in a group that shares homogeneous values may preclude conceptual awareness as well as observation of deviant adaptations. Second, such involvement increases the availability of normative response patterns that can serve the same functions as deviant patterns and so may forestall deviant behavior. If, for example, the failure to achieve the middle-class values to which one was committed leads to feelings of frustration, these feelings can be reduced by changing one's values to those of a less demanding set but one that is still acceptable within the conventional context. Third, which of a range of deviant patterns will be adopted when the person is disposed to perform deviant behavior (whether out of a need to conform to expectations that endorse deviant patterns or in response to the failure to conform to the standards of conventional society) will be affected also by the characteristic response patterns that the person learns in the course of socialization in his membership groups. Where the person is disposed to deviant responses, he is more likely to adopt those specific deviant responses that are compatible with his normal response disposition. Indeed, the deviant pattern frequently appears to be an extreme response that in a less extreme degree would be acceptable in the context of the person's membership groups. For example, certain deviant responses, particularly those involving aggressive behavior, are more appropriate as extensions of the masculine rather than the feminine role.

Continuity of Deviant Behavior

Once a deviant response has occurred, what factors then account for the stability or increase, as opposed to the decrease, of antisocial behavior over time? Is it accounted for by reinforcing social responses or the continuity of the same circumstances that led to the initial responses? Certain of the factors that determine whether early deviance will be continued or discontinued are related to the consequences of the early deviant behavior, while other influences reflect changes in the person's circumstances that are independent of the early deviant behavior (e.g., ongoing developmental processes).

Where the continuity or discontinuity of the deviant behavior is the result of consequences of the early performance of the deviant behavior, the relationship may be more or less direct. More directly, the individual may be motivated to continue or discontinue the behavior because of the immediate positive or negative consequences of the deviant behavior itself. For example, the use of illicit drugs may cause the person to feel good about himself or to feel ill. The physical abuse of another person or the destruction of property may increase the person's sense of power. Engaging in gang fights may result in physical injury. These outcomes may positively reinforce or extinguish motivation to continue the behavior. Less directly, the factors that influence continuation or discontinuation of the deviant response (whether by reinforcing or extinguishing motives to behave in this way or by influencing opportunities for deviant behavior) are mediated by other consequences of the earlier deviant behavior. Such consequences include the approving responses of deviant associates, the disapproving responses of conventional groups, and the stigmatizing effects of formal sanctions.

Determinants of Continuation

Once a person has performed deviant acts, what circumstances will lead to the continuation, repetition, or escalation of the person's degree of involvement in deviant activity? The first set of circumstances includes those that provide positive reinforcement of the need to perform deviant acts. The positive reinforcement stems from the satisfaction of important needs experienced by the person as a result of the more or less direct consequences of the deviant behavior. The second set includes those circumstances that weaken the effects of motives that previously deterred the individual from performing deviant acts. The third set of circumstances increases or establishes ongoing opportunities for the performance of deviant behavior.

Positive Reinforcement of Deviant Behavior.   Deviant behavior is self-reinforcing in two ways. First, the performance of deviant behavior may satisfy important needs for the person. Since the behavior satisfies the needs, as the needs continue or recur, the deviant behavior will continue or be repeated in the expectation that the need will still or once again be satisfied. Second, regardless of the motivation for the initial performance of the deviant behavior, the deviant behavior creates a need (specifically a need for self-justification) that is satisfied by continuation or repetition of the deviant act or by the structuring of the social environment in ways that facilitate the continuation or repetition of the deviant act. The difference between the two modes of self-reinforcement is that in the former instance, a need preceded the deviant behavior that satisfied the need. In the later case, the deviant behavior *created* a need that is satisfied by repetition or continuation of the deviant behavior.

Regarding the self-reinforcement of deviant behavior, frequently the performance of deviant acts results in the satisfaction of the individual's needs. These satisfactions reinforce motives to perform the deviant act. The various needs that the person experiences have been subsumed under the more general need for positive self-attitudes (Kaplan, 1975, 1980, 1982). It has been argued that deviant acts can help to satisfy this need in any of three ways. Deviant behavior may permit the person to (1) avoid the source of his self-devaluing attitudes, (2) attack the basis of his self-devaluing attitudes, or (3) substitute new sources of positive self-evaluation.

The *avoidance* of self-devaluing experiences as a result of deviant acts might occur through the enforced avoidance of the negative responses of people in the conventional environment. To the extent that the person spends more time with deviant peers, is incarcerated, or is otherwise excluded from interacting with conventional others, he will necessarily avoid the negative reactions that he has experienced in the conventional environment in the past.

Deviant acts that involve *attacks* on conventional institutions or the representatives of these institutions may have self-enhancing consequences by causing the individual to express his rejection of the values by which he in the past rejected himself. Deprived of self-acceptance by being unable to approximate conventional standards and, consequently, to earn group approval, the person would find rejection of the standards and of the group that rejected him to be gratifying. The deviant behavior would signify that he considers the standards by which he formerly rejected himself to be invalid.

Deviant acts provide *new routes* to positive self-evaluation. The deviant activity may involve associating with a group that endorses standards that are more easily attainable than those endorsed in the conventional environment. The individual thus gains gratification from achieving the new standards. Further, sometimes rejection by others in conventional groups stimulates the needs to be accepted by others. Toward the goal of being accepted by the group, the person behaves in ways (including deviant behaviors) that he perceives the group as endorsing. Presumably, conformity to deviant group norms will result in acceptance by the group and will positively reinforce the value of the deviant behavior that earned the acceptance. It is not even necessary for deviants to share beliefs in the rightness of their behavior for the beliefs to influence individual behavior. As long as each individual believes that the others think the behavior is correct and he is motivated to be accepted by the other members, he will continue to behave as if the group shared beliefs about the rightness of behaviors.

In addition to the gratifications that stem from conformity to the standards of deviant associates, the deviant behavior may be positively reinforced as a result of any of a number of other consequences of the substitution of deviant sources of gratification for conventional ones. For example, deviant activities may give the individual a new sense of power or control over his environment that leads him to think of himself as a more effective individual.

Regarding the relationship between the need for self-justificaiton and continuation of the deviant behavior, the initial performance of deviant acts is threatening to the satisfaction of important needs of people who were socialized in conventional society. Specifically, the person feels a need to conform to moral standards and to be accepted by the community as one who conforms to those standards. Once the person has performed deviant acts and thereby has threatened satisfaction of these needs, the person is motivated to behave in ways that reduce the distress associated with the threat to need-satisfaction. Among the ways the person can reduce the distress is, first, by justifying the act in conventional terms and, second, by transforming his or her identity in ways that justify the behavior as appropriate to the new (deviant) identity. Both sets of self-justifying responses involve the continuation, repetition, or escalation of deviant involvement. In the first case, the justification of deviant behavior in conventional terms (often facilitated by the presence of collective justifications by deviant associates or the prevalence of the deviant pattern or both) reduces the barrier to repetition or continuation of earlier deviant acts. The repetition of the deviant behavior, in turn, testifies to the person's belief in the legitimacy of the act.

In the second case, being the object of negative social sanctions causes the deviant actor to positively value deviant behaviors and identities. The person becomes attracted to deviant behavior for reasons related to the reduction of self-rejecting feelings and the affirmation of self-worth. Primarily, deviant actors evaluate deviant behavior and identities positively to "regain their identity through redefining normality and realizing that it is acceptable to be who they are" (Coleman, 1986, p. 225). Negative social sanctions influence self-conceptions of being the object of negative social sanctions and of being one who experiences intrinsically and instrumentally disvalued outcomes such as loss of income and exclusion from conventional groups. Since positive responses from others and associated resources are among the evaluative standards of self-worth, negative social sanctions lead the individual to judge himself negatively. Given the need to maintain one's self-esteem (Kaplan, 1986), the individual reevaluates the self-ascribed and other-ascribed deviant identities and behavior. The stigmatized social identity and the associated deviant acts are redefined as having positive value. At the same time, the person comes to value deviant patterns and identities because they reflect achievable standards for positive self-evaluation that replace conventional standards that cannot be achieved because the negative social sanctions exclude the deviant actor from conventional circles and restrict access to resources.

Having transformed the value of deviant behaviors and identities from negative to positive, the deviant actor is motivated to behave in ways that validate the deviant identity. Once he comes to value the identity, he is motivated to conform to its normative expectations in order to evaluate himself positively, that is, to perform deviant acts.

Loss of motivation to conform to, and acquisition of motivation to deviate from, normative expectations, as well as association with deviant peers, may facilitate the positive valuation of deviant behavior. The individual's rejection of social conventions and the loss of motivation to conform to normative expectations reduces the costs of identifying with deviant roles. Insofar as conformity to social conventions and attractive positive responses from representatives of conventional society are no longer bases for positive self-evaluation—indeed, insofar as conventional others now constitute a negative reference group—the positive evaluation of deviant behaviors and identities does not pose a threat to one's self-esteem or the possession of valued resources. Association with deviant peers facilitates acquisition of deviant identities and conformity with deviant roles by providing social support for this role and insulating the person from the experience and perception of conventional sanctions for such role performance.

Weakening of Social Controls. Social controls are weakened by circumstances that either decrease expectations of adverse consequences or decrease attraction to conventional values. Decreased expectation of adverse consequences is accounted for directly by observation that few adverse consequences of initial deviance occurred and indirectly by the circumstances surrounding stigmatization of the deviant actor following initial deviance. In the latter case, when the initial deviance is observed and harshly responded to, the person is effectively expelled from conventional society and the interaction between the individual and representatives of conventional society is thereby markedly reduced. The person may be detained in an institution or simply be denied the privileges of informal interaction with family members, neighbors, or former friends. Paradoxically, these acts of expulsion that served as negative sanctions for earlier deviance effectively preclude the observation of further wrongdoing and therefore the administration of further punishments for deviant acts. In being expelled from society, the person is removed from the surveillance of those who might prevent him from future wrongdoing by punishing the deviant acts as they are observed.

The attraction to the values of conventional society and to membership in conventional groups as a basis for positive self-evaluation is weakened both by the very same processes that influenced the person's initial motivation to perform deviant acts and by the responses of society to the initial deviance. The person's inability to succeed by conventional standards leads to negative self-attitudes and to the disposition to perform deviant acts that might lead to more positive self-feelings. At the same time, the person's association, in his own mind, between the distressful self-rejecting attitudes and the conventional standards that are the measure of his failure decreases his attraction to these standards. Hence, any impulses to deviance that the individual experiences are less likely to be restrained, as they once were, by the attraction to the conventional standards.

In addition, the early performance of the deviant acts has consequences that more or less directly lead the person to reject conventional standards that ordinarily would help to restrain deviant impulses. The informal rejection by family or school, and the stigma associated with being the object of more formal sanctions such as being arrested, reflect intrinsically distressful experiences and barriers to the achievement of other emotionally significant goals. On one hand, the shame of being punished for certain infractions leads to a self-defensive rejection of the moral standards. The person, who recognizes that the deviant behavior is an inescapable part of his public image and, over time, becomes an accepted part of his self-image, is motivated by the need to evaluate himself positively to create personal justifications for the behavior and to ally himself with those who can offer collective justifications for the behavior. On the other hand, the rejection of the person by members of conventional society deprives the person of access to resources that, aside from being intrinsically valued, are means to the achievement of other valued ends. Such resources include a good job and the trust and respect of others. As a result, the person is decreasingly attracted to the normative order. Simply put, the individual no longer cares, or does not care as much, what the representatives of the conventional order think about his behavior. Since he does not care, the attitudes of others no longer constrain him from performing a deviant act that he otherwise is motivated to perform. Rather, he becomes increasingly dependent on deviant associates for standards of self-evaluation and for the resources for achieving those standards.

Opportunities for deviance.   The early performance of deviant acts frequently has consequences that increase the individual's opportunity to perform deviant acts. As a result of the person's rejection of and by the conventional society, the person becomes increasingly attracted to deviant associates and increases the amount of social interaction with other deviants. Some of this interaction with deviant associates is the necessary result of periods of detention in custodial institutions. The increased interaction increases the opportunities to observe and learn deviant patterns and in addition provides numerous occasions that call for the enactment of the deviant behavior. With increasing interaction comes the motivation to conform to the expectations of deviant associates on whom the person depends for satisfaction of his or her day-to-day needs. As the individual becomes symbolically and physically separated from conventional society, he or she depends on deviant associates for an increasingly greater proportion of the opportunities to satisfy his or her needs.

Determinants of Discontinuation

Just as different factors influence the continuation, repetition, or escalation of deviant activity, so may any of a variety of circumstances influence the discontinuation of or decreased involvement in deviant activity.

Absence of Positive Reinforcement.   Just as people may adopt deviant values and perform deviant acts because of failure to achieve conventional values, so may people who were socialized to accept deviant behavior as proper be disposed to *reject* deviant values if they are not able to be successful according to these standards. Just as we might predict that individuals who were not successful in achieving conventional values would be more likely to commit deviant acts than those who were successful, so would we predict that individuals reared in subcultures that endorse deviant acts would be less likely to be motivated to continue performance of the deviant acts if they were unsuccessful in achieving the values. Given the opportunity to succeed according to another set of values, they would be good candidates for disengaging from the deviance-endorsing subcultures. However, as in the instance of people who become disposed to reject conventional values, continuation of the newly adopted behavior would be at risk, since the earlier set of values continues to exert some influence on the person and mitigates the tendency to continue violating the earlier set of values.

Adverse Consequences.   Not only might a person discontinue deviant behavior because he was unable to satisfy the needs (e.g., for self-esteem, to be accepted by other group members) that he anticipated would be satisfied through performing such behavior, but he might also be moved to cease deviant behaviors because of consequences that threatened the satisfaction of other needs. Among the needs that are awakened by the consequences of initial performance of the deviant acts are the discomfort experienced by the violation of conventional values to which the person continues to remain committed. A major source of motivations that counteract or mitigate the disposition to deviance is the early adoption of conventional values in the course of the socialization process. I noted earlier that individuals who have failed to achieve the values they learned in the course of the socialization process may adapt in any of a number of ways, including using deviant behaviors to achieve conventional values, withdrawing from the conventional world, and rejecting the validity of the values. However, these adaptations are potentially unstable because the actors have great difficulty in totally ridding themselves of the standards of behavior by which they were taught to evaluate themselves. It is precisely the strength of these values that makes the deviant responses unstable. As long as the person continues to feel strongly about the values he is apparently rejecting, he will feel some discomfort while performing deviant acts; given the opportunity to successfully pursue conventional values, he is likely to cease being attracted to and performing deviant acts.

Changes in Needs and Opportunities.   Since deviant behavior frequently reflects attempts to satisfy needs, it is to be expected that changes in the person's needs or the opportunities to meet those needs will make deviant behavior unnecessary. Often, the individual will experience an increase in perceived personal resources as a result of deviant behavior that might render such behavior obsolete. The successful completion of such acts might lead the individual to have faith in his own ability to achieve more conventional goals through the use of conventional means. Alternatively, a deviant act such as dropping out of school might remove the person from salient sources of self-rejection and so obviate the need for deviant responses to assuage feelings of self-rejection.

Purposive interventions may take the form of providing conventional resources to deviance-prone individuals and so reduce the motivation to perform deviant acts in order to satisfy their needs. Further, the normal process of maturation provides persons with new age-appropriate needs and the conventional means to satisfy these needs that render deviant adaptations unnecessary.

Empirical Associations among Patterns of Deviance

Perhaps the most frequently studied antecedents or consequences of particular deviant adaptations are other deviant adaptations. These include avoidance of, or inappropriate performance in, normatively defined roles or sequences (Kaplan, 1982) as well as behaviors that in fact violate normative expectations and so may be sanctioned but are contrary to the wishes of the individuals (as when the individual experiences failure in school because of the absence of ability or fails to produce children because of biological incapacity).

Concurrence of Deviant Acts

Numerous scholars in the field note concurrence of various deviant acts (e.g., Gottfredson & Hirschi, 1990, p. 93):

> Thieves are likely to smoke, drink, and skip school at considerably higher rates than nonthieves. Offenders are considerably more likely than non-offenders to be involved in most types of accidents, including household fires, auto crashes, and unwanted pregnancies. They are also considerably more likely to die at an early age.

Such concurrence is observed in a variety of nonclinical and clinical populations.

Nonclinical Populations

Among teenagers, the use of alcohol, tobacco, and other drugs has been associated with theft and interpersonal violence (Akers, 1994; Kandel, 1978). Depression is associated with use of violence among urban black adolescents (DuRant, Cadenhead, Pendergrast, Slavens, & Lindner, 1994). For a population of pregnant adolescents (Amaro & Zuckerman, 1991), compared to non-drug users, pregnant adolescents who use drugs are more likely to have a history of elective abortion and venereal diseases, to report more negative life events in the previous year, to experience violence during pregnancy, and to have a male partner who used marijuana or cocaine. At the 6-month postpartum follow-up interview, girls who used drugs were more likely than girls who did not use drugs to report that their mothers or fathers or both were current users of marijuana and cocaine. Adolescent mothers who use drugs are more likely than nonusers to report that their siblings and friends approve of their use of alcohol, marijuana, and cocaine and are more likely than nonusers to have siblings and friends who use these substances. Partners of drug users are also more likely to be perceived as approving of their drug use and are more likely to be current users of alcohol, marijuana, and cocaine.

Clinical Populations

In clinical settings, the concurrence of deviant patterns is expressed as comorbidity (Sanderson, Beck, & Beck, 1990), as in the comorbid association of substance abuse and depressive disorders (Fowler, Rich, & Young, 1986). Concurrence of substance abuse and psychiatric disorders such as conduct disorder, major depressive episode, and the combination of attention deficit, hyperactivity, and impulse disorder is observed frequently (DeMilio, 1989). Christie, Burke, Regier, Rae, Boyd, and Locke (1988), for example, report evidence of a modest but important elevation of risk for subsequent drug use or dependence among young adults who had earlier episodes of anxiety or depressive disorder.

Associations across Time

For present purposes, the more interesting relationships among patterns of deviance are associations between patterns observed at different points in time such as childhood and adulthood. In general, deviant outcomes such as crime, low occupational achievement, substance abuse, and marital instability in adults are predicted by a child's antisocial or confrontational behavior in combination with pathology in the family in which the adult was raised (pathology being reflected in violent or unpredictable child-rearing practices and parental psychiatric illness or crime) (Robins & Rutter, 1990). Differences observed between convicted and unconvicted men at age 32 replicated many differences observed at age 18, including having an unstable job record, periods of unemployment, substance-abuse-related problems, aggression, and criminal offenses (Farrington, 1989). Substance abuse in particular anticipates premarital births (Yamaguchi & Kandel, 1987), early sexual intercourse (Mott & Haurin, 1988), and marriage and conception at earlier ages, as well as divorce, marital dissatisfaction, increased psychotic thinking and violent assault, lesser education, dropping out of school, and greater job instability (Newcomb & Bentler, 1988).

In a noteworthy early study, Robins (1966) found that children referred to a guidance clinic in comparison to a control group were more likely as adults to be arrested, to get divorced, to be unemployed and on welfare, to be less likely to attend church, to have fewer friends and contacts with relatives, to use alcohol excessively, to be hospitalized for psychiatric problems, to be dishonorably discharged from the armed forces if they served, to be less likely to have children, and in general to display behavior and circumstances that would be regarded as deviant according to conventional standards. In short, referral to a guidance clinic as children anticipated the inability or unwillingness to adopt conventional roles and perform them in conventional fashion.

More recently, Eron (1987) concluded that aggression determined at age 8 anticipates social failure, psychopathology, and low educational and occupational success as well as aggression some 22 years later. Other reports suggest associations between being abused as a child and psychiatric disorders (including posttraumatic stress, anxiety, and depressive disorders as well as substance abuse) later in life (Browne & Finkelhor, 1986; Bryer, Nelson, Miller, & Krol, 1987; Evans & Schaeffer, 1987; Yandrow, 1989).

Considering substance abuse in particular, a number of childhood characteristics anticipate drug use during *adulthood* (Glantz, 1992). Thus, Lerner and Vicary (1984) reported an association between difficult temperament at age 5 and tobacco, alcohol, and marijuana use in adulthood. Kellam, Brown, Rubin, and Ensminger (1983) reported aggressiveness in combination with shyness in males to foreshadow use of these substances during adolescence. Shedler and Block (1990) reported that drug use at age 18 was foreshadowed by such characteristics as poor peer relations, little concern with reciprocity and fairness, lack of forethought, lack of dependability, lower self-confidence and self-reliance, and an inability to admit to negative feelings. Attention-deficit disorders also anticipate later substance abuse (Hartsough & Lambert, 1987).

Substance abuse, along with other deviant adaptations, is anticipated by the following experiences: a large number of experiences indicative of failure or rejection, including poor educational achievement and failure in school, social conflict and emotional tension with parents, and lack of social integration into peer groups during adolescence (Hurrelmann, 1987) and chronic role strains in other social settings such as the workplace (Mensch & Kandel, 1988) during later life stages; association with peers, siblings, or adults who model or provide the opportunities, encouragement, or occasions to engage in the deviant patterns (Brook, Whiteman, Gordon, & Brook, 1989; Kaplan, Johnson, & Bailey, 1987; Needle, Lavee, Su, Brown, & Doherty, 1988); and negative self-feelings (Kaplan, 1975). Deviant responses by others as well as personal characteristics predict drug use. Thus, drug use is associated with rejecting, cold, or inconsistent parents (Baumrind, 1985; Simcha-Fagan, Gersten, & Langer, 1986). In one study, subjects who were to use tobacco, alcohol, and marijuana at age 18 had mothers who, when the children were 5 years old, manifested cold, unresponsive, and underprotective attitudes. In addition, the mothers were performance-oriented without being supportive (Shedler & Block, 1990). Familial use of drugs and rejection of the subject are also related to drug use by the subject (Brook, Brook, Gordon, Whiteman, & Cohen, 1990).

Concurrence of Conventional Behaviors

Just as deviant attributes, behaviors, and experiences anticipate other deviant phenomena, so do changes in a more conventional direction anticipate decreased deviance in other areas. Variables that reflect the attainment of adult roles relating to marriage, parenting, and employment are reported to be inversely related to continuation of drug use, suggesting an essential incompatibility between performance of these roles and continuation of substance-abuse patterns (Bachman, O'Malley, & Johnston, 1984; O'Donnell, Voss, Clayton, Slatin, & Room, 1976; Yamaguchi & Kandel, 1985). For example, cessation of cannabis use was significantly related to establishment of adult social roles with a partner/spouse and with having children (Hammer & Vhelum, 1990; Kandel & Raveis, 1989; Yamaguchi & Kandel, 1985). The anticipation of performing these roles appears to influence cessation of unconventional activities as well, insofar as an increased tendency to stop marijuana use before marriage was noted among men and women and before parenthood among women. Further, for men, high aspirations regarding future occupational activity predicted cessation of cannabis use (Hammer & Vhelum, 1990).

The clustering of conventional patterns as well as deviant patterns is also suggested by prevention studies in which conventional interventions calculated to obviate deviant influences have the effects of reducing or forestalling deviant activities such as drug abuse (Battjes, 1988; Flay, 1985; Pentz, MacKinnon, Dwyer, Wang, Hansen, Flay, Anderson-Johnson, & Anderson-Johnson, 1989). Further, decreases in deviant activities are associated with increases in conventional attitudes. Thus, the declining use of marijuana among high school seniors since 1979 is compatible with rises in perceived risks and disapproval associated with regular marijuana use (Bachman, Johnston, O'Malley, & Humphrey, 1988). Smoking, drinking, and drug use are prevalent among adolescents when personal attitudes and perceived social support are favorable, but are relatively infrequent otherwise (Grube & Morgan, 1990). Similarly, increases in perceived risks and disapproval appear to contribute substantially to recent declines in use of cocaine (Bachman, Johnston, & O'Malley, 1990).

Etiological Significance of Associations among Patterns of Deviance

Empirical associations among patterns of deviance do not necessarily support inferences regarding causal relationships. A relationship observed between two patterns of deviance may be accounted for by their common association with other variables. Thus, this relationship may in itself have no causal significance for the association between patterns of deviance. However, when the other variables are themselves patterns of deviance, the common associations may have causal relevance. In any case, empirical associations are commonly interpreted in terms of causal relationships, and theories of deviance causation are tested by estimating theoretically informed models of the relationships among patterns of deviance.

The nature of the etiological frameworks that are used to explain empirical associations among patterns of deviance and that are tested by hypothesizing relationships among patterns of deviance is reflected in the integrative summary of the etiological literature presented above. Aspects of this framework illustrate the etiological relevance of associations among patterns of deviance. Other aspects of the integrative framework might have been cited as well to illustrate the causal relevance of patterns of deviance for explaining other patterns of deviance.

Deviance as Experiences of Failure and Rejection

The failure to conform to the expectations of others (whether motivated or unmotivated) as well as the ensuing experiences of punitive responses by others constitutes deviance. The experiences of self-rejection that follow on self-awareness of having engaged in deviance and of being the object of punitive responses by valued others are associated in the subject's mind with the conventional environment in which the subject experienced deviance, punitive responses, and distressing self-rejecting feelings. As a consequence, the person loses motivation to conform and becomes motivated to engage in deviant acts that promise to enhance self-esteem through facilitating the avoidance of conventional contacts, rejection of the punitive conventional environment, substitution of alternative deviant standards that are more easily attainable than conventional standards, or attainment of conventional goals through unconventional means. The loss of motivation to conform facilitates acting out the deviant dispositions that stem from earlier failures to conform to the expectations of significant others.

Consistent with this theoretical orientation are reports of relationships between deviant behaviors and other deviant phenomena, including experiences of failure, negative self-feelings, and negative social sanctions.

Experiences of Failure

Poor academic attainment, among other self-devaluing experiences, has been associated with onset of substance use (Brunswick & Messeri, 1984; Kandel, 1978). Poor academic performance reflects failure to accomplish conventionally valued goals, low educational aspirations and achievement orientation, low commitment to school and concomitant ineffective conventional incentives and sanctions, and dispositions to seek alternative self-enhancing mechanisms, such as substance abuse, that could assuage self-derogation and provide opportunities (such as by deviant peer associations) to enhance self-attitudes.

As a further illustration, Ross (1994) reports data consistent with the conclusion that the relationship between being overweight and depression is accounted for, in part, by the positive association between being overweight and dieting, and between dieting and depression: "Dieting to lose weight as an attempt to fit norms that equate attractiveness to thinness is more distressing than being overweight per se" (p. 72). One form of deviance (obesity) has the effect of imposing new standards for achievement, that is, successful dieting, that the subject may fail to achieve. Such failure may lead to depression.

Negative Self-Feelings

Self-derogation as the outcome of experiences of failure and rejection has been associated with the onset of drug use (Kaplan, Martin, & Robbins, 1982), as well as with other forms of deviant behavior. Consistent with these observations, negative affect reflected in measures of depression and pessimism as well as apathy have been associated with the onset of drug abuse (Powers, 1987).

At the same time, negative self-feelings are influenced by drug abuse and other deviant patterns. Generally, substance abuse appears to have short-term effects of reducing self-derogation and depression but long-term effects of increasing these states (Bentler, 1987; Newcomb & Bentler, 1988). Substance abuse as a coping device may provide the short-term gratification of assuaging negative self-feelings, but over the long term may forestall the development of socially acceptable and effective coping mechanisms, with the end result that the individual will maintain or exacerbate chronic self-rejecting feelings. The momentary experiences of gratification may be sufficient to blind the person to the recognition of the long-term consequences of the deviant adaptation. Indeed, adverse consequences such as social stigmatization may increase the need for momentary reduction of negative self-feelings. Consistent with this possibility, Johnson (1988) reported a positive association between punitive consequences and subsequent use. Possibly, the self-enhancing effect of substance use is most likely to occur during earlier levels of immaturity when the person is less able to see the long-term consequences of the behavior. It would not be surprising to find that individuals who use drugs to assuage subjective distress tend to be impulsive individuals who are unable to delay gratification or recognize the long-term effects of using drugs.

Negative Social Sanctions

Negative social sanctions are associated with subsequent drug use even after controlling on earlier drug use (Kaplan, Johnson, & Bailey, 1988). These sanctions for earlier drug use frequently have the effects of alienating the individual from the conventional social order, increasing association with substance-abusing subgroups that reinforce these patterns, and motivating the individual to identify with the substance-abusing role and to employ this pattern in order to assuage or adapt to the stigmatization associated with initial drug use.

Inadequate Resources and Deviance

The failure to conform to the expectations of others, that is, the experience of self-rejection and failure, is itself the outcome of other motivated or unmotivated deviant behaviors or attributes. Such behaviors or attributes either reflect the absence of resources (e.g., congenital inadequacies, socially deprived identities) or result in the deprivation of resources that is a concomitant of being the object of negative social sanctions for the *initial* failure to conform to the expectations of others. The deprivation of resources is in itself intrinsically disvalued and, further, decreases the person's ability to conform to still other normative expectations. Thus, certain race- or ethnicity-related identities reflect the absence of social resources, lead to social rejection because of the absence of resources, and impede the approximation of socially valued standards relating, for example, to the attainment of education and occupational upward mobility.

Congruent with these theoretical considerations, among the characteristics of drug abusers are histories of being unable to fulfill personal goals including the possession of and appropriate role performance associated with valued social identities. Correlated with these outcomes are socioculturally defined barriers in the form of paucity of resources and role conflicts that preclude simultaneous performance of valued social roles. Thus, drug abuse will be characterized in terms of the absence of fulfillment of valued social roles and social–psychological and sociocultural conditions that preclude the fulfillment of personal goals. Such characteristics include racial, ethnic, and socioeconomic identities. For example, for African-American men, increasing educational level was associated with cessation of using illicit drugs rather than maintaining use at a controlled level (Brunswick, Messeri, & Titus, 1992). In general, indicators of certain social identities in the more inclusive social system, such as lower socioeconomic status (Kleinman, 1978), are associated with higher rates of drug use. The adoption of deviant patterns, a consequence of inadequate resources, in turn adversely affects resources, as when drug use between adolescence and young adulthood may hinder the development of appropriate interpersonal skills (Baumrind & Moselle, 1985) and may have adverse effects on health (Brunswick & Messeri, 1984).

Deviance and Personal Controls

Engaging in deviant acts affects personal controls that might forestall the performance of other deviant acts. Thus, acts of substance abuse might permit the person to commit acts of violence that that person might not commit in non-intoxicated states. Substance abuse might reduce the subjective emotional significance of such deterrents as fear of punishment, feelings of guilt, and the emotional attachment of the child to his parents. On the other hand, some drug use patterns might assuage the intense negative affect that disposes the person to engage in violent acts (see Chapter 8).

For example, characteristics of substance abusers relating to modes of psychopathology, self-destructive behavior, and sensation-seeking may reflect consequences of drug use insofar as drug abuse increases impulsiveness and decreases deliberate planning (in the case of self-destructive consequences) or induces cognitive impairment (perhaps with regard to consequences for psychotic episodes). Particularly among men, substance abuse has a deleterious effect with regard to suicidal ideation, and major depression and substance abuse constitute independent and interactive risk factors for suicidal ideation and suicide attempts (Levy and Deykin, 1989).

Deviance and Opportunities for Deviance

The performance of deviant acts frequently increases the opportunities to learn and to become motivated to perform deviant acts. A person's deviant acts often have consequences (negative social sanctions) that publicly identify the person as a deviant. This public identification makes the person attractive to those who have been similarly stigmatized. At the same time, the person's experience of negative social sanctions alienates that person from the conventional social world and makes him or her amenable to overtures from other deviant individuals who offer promise of fulfilling heretofore unsatisfied needs. The increased association with deviant peers increases the occasions for performing deviant acts, the opportunities to learn new deviant patterns, and the resources that are required to engage in deviant activities. Increased association with deviant peers is particularly facilitated when punitive responses to earlier deviance impose interaction with such peers (incarceration) or decrease interaction with more conventional peers (through suspension or expulsion from school). Consistent with these propositions, association with drug-using peers is frequently observed to be related to the initiation of drug use (Elliott, Huizinga, & Ageton, 1985; Kaplan et al., 1988; Swaim, Oetting, Edwards, & Beauvais, 1989).

Nonsymbolic Effects of Deviance on Other Deviant Patterns

Deviant behaviors, experiences, or attributes may have nonsymbolic effects on other deviant behaviors, experiences, or attributes through the mediation of physiological or physical pathways. Drug use may cause other forms of deviant behavior, not only by reducing internal controls, as when judgment is impaired, but also by impairing cognitive functions in such a way that violation of expectation inevitably occurs, as when drinking leads to traffic accidents due to the effect of the substance on reaction time. Drug abuse affects clinical depression either through the toxic effects of the drug or through the dysphoria induced by withdrawal. The linkage between cocaine use and depression may be mediated by the effects of cocaine on dopamine receptors in the central nervous system (Hyman & Nestler, 1993). By way of further illustration, the relationship between being overweight and depression is explained in part by the negative association between being overweight and perceived physical health and the negative association between physical health and depression (Ross, 1994).

Deviant Behavior by Others

Deviant behavior by others influences the likelihood of the subject's engaging in deviant responses. Others' deviant responses serve as models for imitation when the others are admired. Further, whether or not the others are admired, when the subject is motivated to engage in deviant responses, the visible deviant acts of others instruct the subject in how to perform the act. When the subject is alienated from the conventional environment, for example, and so is motivated to engage in some form of deviance, the observation of a particular deviant act makes conceivable what up to that time was inconceivable. When the person is disposed to engage in a particular deviant act, the observation of that act may stimulate the person to perform a similar act. Thus, reports of the relationship between exposure to violence and the use of violence among urban black adolescents are consistent with the cultural-transmission theory that proposes that violence is learned in intimate primary groups and other environments for modeling such behavior (DuRant et al., 1994).

In addition, the deviant acts of others provide social support for performing an act that the subject might otherwise have hesitated to perform. Social support for deviance also implies the absence of social control mechanisms that might have inhibited the adoption of, for example, substance-abuse patterns, as well as the presence of subcultures that may provide social support for such patterns and influence the traffic in drugs. Through these mechanisms, new methods of drug administration and supplies of drugs become available (Woody, Urschel, & Alterman, 1992).

Nowhere is the effect of others' deviant patterns on the subject's deviance more apparent than in the study of cross-generational influences. Multigeneration patterns of substance abuse of other deviant adaptations have been observed frequently (Farrington, 1989; Kandel, 1990; Roehrich & Gold, 1988). The multigeneration patterns may be accounted for by linear and interactive effects of the earlier-generation experiences on the later-generation outcomes or by common antecedent causes that result in similar outcomes for both generations. The causal influences on second-generation substance abuse and other deviant adaptations, and on the precursors and consequences of these adaptations, may act via substance-abuse and other deviant behavior of the earlier generation or (independent of their effects on parental deviance) via other psychosocial influences. Parental drug use or other deviant behavior may affect the child's health, as well as other outcomes widely regarded as precursors of deviant adaptations.

Drug use during pregnancy has been associated with a variety of adverse physical and psychological consequences for the neonate, including developmental retardation (Chasnoff, 1988; Livesay, Erlich, & Finnegan, 1987). Adolescents with substance-abusing parents experience more stress than teens from nonsubstance-abusing families (Brown, 1989). Adolescents with substance-abusing parents reported more negative life events and rated the events more undesirable. Substance-abusing parents are less able to provide social support to children in their times of need (Holden, Brown, & Mott, 1988).

The adoption of maladaptive coping patterns such as substance abuse by parents provides social models for the adoption of this pattern by children (Patterson, 1986), perhaps due in part to the implied or actual endorsement of the patterns (Brook, Whiteman, Gordon, & Cohen, 1986). Punitive discipline methods and disagreement among spouses about discipline are related to reports of children behaving in problematic ways. Authoritarian and permissive styles were inversely associated with grades, while authoritative style (expectations of mature behavior from the child and clear settings of standards by parents) was positively associated with grades (Dornbusch, Ritter, Leiderman, Roberts, & Fraleigh, 1987).

Parental rejection was associated with adolescent delinquency even after controlling for potentially confounding family factors such as family conflict and family control (Simons, Robertson, & Downs, 1989). Family disruption (Kalter, Riemer, Brickman, & Chen, 1985; Peterson & Zill, 1986) and the nature and effectiveness of parental social controls have been associated with second-generation substance abuse.

Parents who delay having children may have the most trouble rearing them in the child's teenage years because of the older mother's inability to relate to the adolescent and emotional problems associated with coping with recognition of her own aging, thereby reducing emotional accessibility to the child (Rossi, 1980). Mother's age at first birth was positively related to the daughter's perception of affection, mediated by number of siblings and level of parental marital happiness, while the relationship between father's age at first birth and perceived closeness to the father by the son was mediated by the parents' marital happiness (Heuvel, 1988). Parents with higher self-esteem communicated better with their children, while parents with lower self-esteem were more likely to exert their control by punishment and making decisions for the children (Small, 1988). Economic stress influences distressful self-feelings, which in turn influence negative attitudes toward the father (Elder, Nyugen, & Caspi, 1985). The failure to monitor children contributes to subsequent drug use by permitting association with deviant peers and other failure to detect and intervene against the drug use (Dishion, Patterson, & Reid, 1988).

The relationships simultaneously reflect a number of circumstances, including distressful experiences that adversely influence self-attitudes and motivate the adoption of deviant patterns (including substance abuse), attenuated social control over dispositions to engage in substance abuse (where family norms eschew substance-abuse patterns), and opportunities to learn or reject substance-abuse patterns. Acceptance or rejection of substance-abuse patterns depends on the interaction of the family's attitude toward and patterns of substance abuse with the child's attitude toward the family (rebellious attitudes toward the family that approved of substance abuse would lead to the child's rejection of use, while rebellious attitudes toward a family that disapproved of substance abuse might lead to the child's adoption of the substance-abuse pattern). In short, familial factors operate as influences on the distressful self-feelings of the subject that may motivate adoption of substance-abuse patterns and through the provision of occasions and models for substance-abuse patterns. Parental drug use may also reflect the subject's stressful experience of membership in a stigmatized social unit whether or not it also reflects genetic transmission of dispositions to use drugs.

Testing Causal Models of Relationships among Deviant Patterns

The estimation of models that specify causal relations among diverse patterns of deviance tends to take the form of some combination of four categories of study. These categories of study variously specify: (1) common and pattern-specific correlates of multiple modes of deviance, (2) causal relationships between two patterns of deviance whereby any one pattern may be a cause of consequence of the other, (3) variables that mediate the causal relationships between two or more patterns of deviance, and (4) variables that moderate the causal relations between two or more patterns of deviance.

Common and Pattern-Specific Correlates of Deviance

A number of models specify both common and pattern-specific correlates among diverse deviant patterns.

Common Correlates

The causal models may specify diverse deviant antecedents of a common deviant outcome, or diverse deviant outcomes of a common antecedent, or both. In each case, multiple common antecedents or outcomes may be specified in the same model.

Diverse Deviant Outcomes. The frequently observed correlation between diverse substance-use patterns or between substance abuse and other forms of deviance (Bukstein, Brent, & Kaminer, 1989; Fernandez-Pol, Bluestone, & Mizruchi, 1988; Shaffer, Nurco, Hanlon, Kinlock, Duszynski, & Stephenson, 1988) is consistent with hypothesized common pathways. It is possible that the association between substance abuse and other forms of deviance is accounted for by the fact that they share common antecedents such as a disposition to engage in short-term pleasures, in conjunction with the absence of personal and social restraints against acting on such dispositions. Both drug use and other forms of deviance such as theft and violence are common outcomes of such antecedent circumstances. Other common antecedents that lead to drug use and other forms of deviant behavior encompass deviant peer influences and compatibility of the deviant behaviors with adolescent values such as risk-taking.

Models that specify common antecedents of diverse deviant outcomes are not unlike those that specify different patterns of deviance as multiple indicators of underlying constructs (Donovan & Jessor, 1985; Kaplan, 1972). For example, using three waves of self-reports about heavy alcohol use, marijuana use, other illicit drug use, dangerous driving, and other criminal behavior for a nationally representative sample of high school seniors, Osgood, Johnston, O'Malley, and Bachman (1988) observed that a relatively stable general involvement in deviance accounted for virtually all associations among the different types of deviance. However, while each behavior was in part a manifestation of a more general tendency, in part each behavior was a unique phenomenon with its own causes and consequences. Consistent with this view, Gottfredson and Hirschi (1990, p. 93) conclude:

> In our view, the relation between drug use and delinquency is not a causal
> question. The correlates are the same because drug use and delinquency are

both manifestations of an underlying tendency to pursue short-term, immediate pleasure.

Lack of self-control may be manifested in many ways, including the absence of concern over the feelings of others, impulsiveness, the inability to form deep and persistent attachments to others, poor judgment, low levels of anxiety and distress associated with deviant acts, extrapunitive tendencies, and unwillingness to assume personal responsibility for failure. Any of a number of deviant acts may be the outcome of lack of self-control. According to Gottfredson and Hirschi, (1990, p. 91):

> Our image of the "offender" suggests that crime is not an automatic or necessary consequence of low self-control. It suggests that many noncriminal acts analogous to crime (such as accidents, smoking, and alcohol use) are also manifestations of low self-control. Our image therefore implies that no specific act, type of crime or form of deviance is uniquely required by the absence of self-control.

Just as diverse deviant patterns manifested by the same people may have common antecedents, so may similar deviant patterns manifested by different people or groups have common antecedents. Thus, frequently observed intergenerational continuities (Sebald, 1986) may be accounted for in terms of common antecedents as well as intergenerational influences. Among these common influences are: normative life changes, including change of schools, onset of puberty, and dating, as well as geographic mobility and changes in family structures (Simmons, Burgeson, Carlton-Ford, & Blyth, 1987), which may have adverse effects on self-esteem and academic grade point average, indicating difficulty in coping caused by these changes; stages of development of the self that are characterized in terms of particular contents of self-concepts, relevant reference groups, and centrality of particular qualities of self (Leahy, 1985); and challenges by developmental tasks that include developing a self-identity in light of physical changes, developing a gender identity, gaining independence from parents, accepting/rejecting family values, shaping up to an occupational or unemployed role, and developing and extending friendships (Tolan, 1988).

Diverse Deviant Antecedents.   Many different deviant states may lead to a common deviant outcome. Thus, cocaine abuse might be a consequence of attempts to medicate depressive states, attempts by subjects with attention-deficit hyperactivity disorders to assuage restlessness and increase their attention span, preexisting antisocial dispositions, or a need for status enhancement (Weiss & Mirin, 1986). A common antecedent of both smoking and depression, or of (for women) alcoholism and depression, may be a genetic predisposition (Kendler, Heath, Neale, Kessler, & Eaves, 1993; Kendler, Neale, MacLean, Heath, Eaves, & Kessler, 1993).

Pattern-Specific Correlates

The existence of common antecedents (or consequences), however, does not preclude the presence of unique correlates. Structural differences may be expected with regard to which pattern of deviance is involved, above and beyond what the multiple patterns of deviance share. In one study, differential associations exhibited the strongest path effect to marijuana use (Johnson, 1988). Specific substance-abuse patterns may be associated with particular kinds of symptoms. Positive associations were found between cocaine use and low energy and interest, impaired motivation, impaired affect, and lack of purpose in life (Newcomb, Bentler, & Fahy, 1987). These data support the hypothesis that dysphoria may induce use of stimulant drugs such as cocaine in particular. While each pattern of deviance may share antecedents and consequences with other deviant patterns, each pattern may still be a unique phenomenon with its own causes and consequences (Osgood et al., 1988).

Reciprocal Influences

Another category of studies encompasses estimates of models in which one deviant pattern is specified as a cause or consequence, or both, of another pattern. In some studies, the reciprocal relationship is modeled in the same analysis. In other instances, the reciprocal nature of the relationship is apparent only when considering several studies in some of which a particular pattern is the dependent variable and in others of which the pattern is the independent variable. Studies of the influence of one mode of deviance on another are illustrated by investigations of the relationship between substance abuse and theft or violence, depression and substance abuse, and psychopathology and physical or sexual abuse.

Substance-abuse patterns cause violence and theft by reducing inhibitions that in the absence of drugs would restrain the individual from acting on his or her violent and acquisitive impulses, or by motivating the acquisition of money to buy drugs to support a habit. Conversely, involvement in theft causes drug use by leading drug users to interact with other teenagers who get into trouble and who are engaged in other deviant acts such as substance abuse. Through interaction with these individuals, whether by a process of socialization or of modeling, patterns of substance abuse are learned.

Depression and drug use are often hypothesized to be causally related. Depression may motivate the use of drugs in order to provide symptomatic relief (Khantzian, 1985). Conversely, drug use may influence depression either through the toxic effects of the drugs or through the dysphoric effects of withdrawal.

Being physically or sexually abused has been hypothesized to influence subsequent onset of clinical anxiety, depression, and substance abuse (Browne & Finkelhor, 1986; Evans & Shaeffer, 1987; Yandrow, 1989). Psychopathological outcomes, in turn, may influence the practice of abusive child-rearing patterns.

Mediating Variables

In some studies, the relationship between patterns of deviance is explained, wholly or in part, in terms of theoretically informed mediating variables. As noted earlier, the deviant patterns of parents may affect their children's delinquency via the effects of parental deviance on the child's health, the child's experience of psychological distress, the paucity of parental social support, initiation of maladaptive coping patterns, implied endorsement by the parents of such patterns, and ineffective parental controls.

Specifically, in one study, the relationship between parents' stressful life events and adolescents' depressed mood is mediated by parents' depressed mood and consequent disruption of skillful parenting practices (Ge, Conger, Lorenz, & Simons, 1994). In another study, Kessler and Magee (1994) report that the effect of childhood family violence on the recurrence of depression is mediated by chronic interpersonal stress in adulthood. Finally, the lower likelihood of drug abuse among black youths reported by some investigators appears to be mediated by the tendency for black youths to be much less likely to report substance abuse by friends, to be more likely than white youths to perceive that drug use involves high risks, and to be more likely to disapprove of drug use (Bachman et al., 1990).

Moderating Variables

The relationships between patterns of deviance are moderated by a number of variables. Thus, Kessler and Magee (1994) report that family violence during childhood magnifies the effect of chronic adult interpersonal stress on the recurrence of depression and that, in the absence of chronic adult interpersonal stress, there is no association between family violence during childhood and recurrence of depression during adulthood.

The influence of first-generation deviant experiences on second-generation patterns is moderated by a number of variables that frequently are conceptualized as protective factors (Brook et al., 1990), but may exacerbate relationships as well. Social-bonding variables have been found to be more strongly associated with delinquency among rural youths than among urban youths (Gardner & Shoemaker, 1989) and in later adolescent years than in earlier adolescent years (Krohn, Skinner, Zielinski, & Naughton, 1990). An aspect of the mother's life course such as subsequent fertility may affect a child's behavior problems during the preschool years, but not later on; marital status may be related to behavioral problems and delinquency in adolescence, but not to preschool behavior problems (Furstenberg, Brooks-Gunn, & Morgan, 1987). Data from the Kauai longitudinal study (Werner, 1989) indicate that at ages 2, 10, and 18, prenatal and perinatal complications resulting in impairment of physical or psychological development are exacerbated when children grow up in chronic poverty and are raised by parents with little education in a family environment troubled by parental conflict, alcoholism, or mental illness. Among the protective factors in the first two years of life that are important in counterbalancing stress, deprivation, and disadvantage (but are not important among children in the absence of such circumstances) are good health, autonomy and self-help skills (for males), a positive social orientation (for females), and emotional support provided by alternative caregivers in the family. Ability to maintain important family rituals intact even in the face of severe parental drinking is protective with regard to transmission to the next generation (Bennett, Wolin, & Reiss, 1988). Healthy psychological development in the face of detrimental psychosocial living conditions is in large measure an outcome of the support of the provision of constant and reliable care provided by an available, stable, and beneficial reference person (Tress, Reister, & Gegenheimer, 1989). For certain populations, such as severely economically disadvantaged ones (Werner & Smith, 1982), older mothers are more likely to have a son with serious learning or behavioral problems at age 10 or delinquency or mental health problems by age 18.

Parts II through V present two studies to illustrate each of the four kinds of models that estimate, respectively: (1) common and pattern-specific correlates of deviance; (2) reciprocal influences among patterns of deviance; (3) variables that mediate influences of certain patterns of deviance on other patterns; and (4) variables that moderate the nature of the relationships among patterns of deviance. In Part VI (Chapter 10), I explore and summarize the contemporary themes and emerging directions in longitudinal studies of the relationships among patterns of deviance.

ACKNOWLEDGMENTS.   This work was supported by research grant DA02497 and Research Scientist Award DA00136 to the author from the National Institute on Drug Abuse.

References

Akers, R. L. (1994). *Criminological theories: Introduction and evaluation.* Los Angeles: Roxbury Publishing.

Amaro, H., & Zuckerman, B. (1991). Psychoactive substance use and adolescent pregnancy: Compounded risk among inner city adolescent mothers. In M. E. Colten & S. Gore (Eds.), *Adolescent stress: Causes and consequences* (pp. 223–236). New York: Aldine de Gruyter.

Bachman, J. G., Johnston, L. D., O'Malley, P. M., & Humphrey, R. H. (1988). Explaining the recent decline in marijuana use: Differentiating the effects of perceived risks, disapproval, and general lifestyle. *Journal of Health and Social Behavior, 29*, 92–112.

Bachman, J. G., Johnston, L. D., & O'Malley, P. M. (1990). Explaining the recent decline in cocaine use among young adults: Further evidence that perceived risks and disapproval lead to reduced drug use. *Journal of Health and Social Behavior, 31*, 173–184.

Bachman, J. G., O'Malley, P. M., & Johnston, L. D. (1984). Drug use among young adults: The impacts of roles, status, and social environment. *Journal of Personality and Social Psychology, 47*, 629–645.

Battjes, R. J. (1988). Prevention of adolescent drug abuse. *International Journal of the Addictions, 20*, 1113–1134.

Baumrind, D. (1985). Familial antecedents of adolescent drug use: A development perspective. In C. Jones & R. J. Battjes (Eds.)., *Etiology of drug abuse* (NIDA Drug Research Monograph No. 56) (pp. 13–44). Rockville, MD: National Institute on Drug Abuse.

Baumrind, D., & Moselle, K. A. (1985). A developmental perspective on adolescent drug abuse. *Advances in Alcohol and Substance Abuse, 4*, 41–67.

Bennett, L. A., Wolin, S. J., & Reiss, D. (1988). Cognitive, behavioral, and emotional problems among school aged children of alcoholics. *American Journal of Psychiatry, 145*, 185–190.

Bentler, P. M. (1987). Drug use and personality in adolescence and young adulthood: Structural models with nonnormal variables. *Child Development, 58*, 65–79.

Brook, J. S., Brook, D. W., Gordon, A. S., Whiteman, M., & Cohen, P. (1990). The psychosocial etiology of adolescent drug use: A family interactional approach, *Genetic, Social, and General Psychology Monographs, 116*(2), 111–267.

Brook, J. S., Whiteman, M., Gordon, A. S., & Brook, D. W. (1989). The role of older brothers in younger brothers' drug use viewed in the context of parent and peer influences. *Journal of General Psychology, 151*, 59–75.

Brook, J. S., Whiteman, M., Gordon, A. S., & Cohen, P. (1986). Some models and mechanisms for explaining the impact of maternal and adolescent characteristics on adolescent stage of drug use. *Developmental Psychology, 22*, 460–467.

Brown, S. A. (1989). Life events of adolescents in relation to personal and parental substance abuse. *American Journal of Psychiatry, 146*, 484–489.

Browne, A., & Finkelhor, D. (1986). Impact of child sexual abuse: A review of the literature. *Psychological Bulletin, 99*, 66–77.

Brunswick, A. F., & Messeri, P. A. (1984). Causal factors in onset of adolescents' cigarette smoking: A prospective study of urban black youth. *Advances in Alcohol and Substance Abuse, 3*, 35–52.

Brunswick, A. F., Messeri, P. A., & Titus, S. P. (1992). Predictive factors in adult substance abuse: A prospective study of African American adolescents. In M. Glantz & R. Pickens (Eds.), *Vulnerability to drug abuse* (pp. 419–472). Washington, DC: American Psychological Association.

Bryer, J., Nelson, B., Miller, J. B., & Krol, P. (1987). Childhood physical and sexual abuse as factors in adult psychiatric illness. *American Journal of Psychiatry, 144*, 1426–1430.

Bukstein, O. G., Brent, D. A., & Kaminer, Y. (1989). Comorbidity of substance abuse and other psychiatric disorders in adolescents. *American Journal of Psychiatry, 146*, 1131–1141.

Chasnoff, I. J. (1988). *Drugs, alcohol, pregnancy and parenting*. Boston: Kluwer Academic.

Christie, K. A., Burke, J. D., Jr., Regier, D. A., Rae, D. S., Boyd, J., & Locke, B. Z. (1988). Epidemiological evidence for early onset of mental disorders and higher risk of drug abuse in young adults. *American Journal of Psychiatry, 145*, 971–975.

Coleman, L. M. (1986). Stigma: An enigma demystified. In S. C. Ainlay, G. Becker, & L. M. Coleman (Eds.), *The dilemma of difference: A multidisciplinary view of stigma* (pp. 211–232). New York: Plenum Press.

DeMilio, L. (1989). Psychiatric syndromes in adolescent substance abusers. *American Journal of Psychiatry, 146,* 1212–1214.

Dishion, T. J., Patterson, G. R., & Reid, J. R. (1988). Parent and peer factors associated with drug sampling in early adolescence: Implications for treatment. In E. R. Rahdert & J. Grabowski (Eds.), *Adolescent drug abuse: Analysis of treatment research* (NIDA Research Monograph 77) Washington, DC: U.S. Government Publications Office.

Donovan, J. E., & Jessor, R. (1985). Structure of problem behavior in adolescence and young adulthood. *Journal of Consulting and Clinical Psychology, 53,* 890–904.

Dornbusch, S. M., Ritter, P. L., Leiderman, P. H., Roberts, D. F., & Fraleigh, M. J. (1987). The relation of parenting style to adolescent school performance. *Child Development, 58,* 1244–1257.

DuRant, R. H., Cadenhead, C., Pendergrast, R. A., Slavens, G., & Lindner, C. W. (1994). Factors associated with the use of violence among urban black adolescents. *American Journal of Public Health, 84,* 612–617.

Elder, G. H., Jr., Nyugen, T. V., & Caspi, A. (1985). Linking family hardship to children's lives. *Child Development, 56,* 361–375.

Elliott, D., Huizinga, D., & Ageton, S. (1985). *Explaining delinquency and drug use.* Beverly Hills: Sage Publications.

Eron, L. (1987). The development of aggressive behavior from the perspective of a developing behaviorism. *American Psychologist, 42,* 435–442.

Evans, S., & Schaeffer, S. (1987). Incest and chemically dependent women: Treatment implications. *Journal of Chemical Dependency Treatment, 1,* 141–173.

Farrington, D. P. (1989). Later adult life outcomes of offenders and nonoffenders. In M. Brambring, F. Lösel, & H. Skowronek (Eds)., *Children at risk: Assessment, longitudinal research, and intervention* (pp. 220–244). New York: Aldine de Gruyter.

Fernandez-Pol, B., Bluestone, H ., & Mizruchi, M. S. (1988). Inner-city substance abuse patterns: A study of psychiatric inpatients. *American Journal of Drug and Alcohol Abuse, 14,* 41–50.

Flay, B. R. (1985). Psychosocial approaches to smoking prevention: A review of findings. *Health Psychology, 4,* 449–488.

Fowler, R. C., Rich, C. L., & Young, D. (1986). San Diego suicide study. II. Substance abuse in young cases. *Archives of General Psychiatry, 43,* 962–965.

Furstenberg, F. F., Jr., Brooks-Gunn, J., & Morgan, S. P. (1987). *Adolescent mothers in later life.* New York: Cambridge University Press.

Gardner, L., & Shoemaker, D. J. (1989). Social bonding and delinquency: A comparative analysis. *Sociological Quarterly, 30,* 481–500.

Ge, X., Conger, R. D., Lorenz, F. O., & Simons, R. L. (1994). Parents' stressful life events and adolescent depressed mood. *Journal of Health and Social Behavior, 35,* 28–44.

Glantz, M. (1992). A developmental psychopathology model of drug abuse vulnerability. In M. Glantz & R. Pickens (Eds.), *Vulnerability to drug abuse* (pp. 389–418). Washington, DC: American Psychological Association.

Gottfredson, M. R., & Hirschi, T. (1990). *A general theory of crime.* Stanford, CA: Stanford University Press.

Grube, J. W., & Morgan, M. (1990). Attitude–social support interactions: Contingent consistency effects in the prediction of adolescent smoking, drinking, and drug use. *Social Psychology Quarterly, 53,* 329–338.

Hammer, T., & Vhelum, P. (1990). Initiation, continuation or discontinuation of cannabis use in the general population. *British Journal of Addiction, 85,* 899–909.

Hartsough, C. S., & Lambert, N. M. (1987). Pattern and progression of drug use among hyperactives and controls: A prospective short-term longitudinal study. *Journal of Child Psychology and Psychiatry, 28,* 543–553.

Heuvel, A. V. (1988). The timing of parenthood and intergenerational relations. *Journal of Marriage and the Family, 50,* 483–491.

Holden, M. G., Brown, S. A., & Mott, M. A. (1988). Social support network of adolescents: Relation to family alcohol abuse. *American Journal of Drug and Alcohol Abuse, 14,* 487–498.

Hurrelmann, K. (1987). The limits and potential of social intervention in adolescence: An exemplary analysis. In K. Hurrelmann, F. Kaufmann, & F. Lösel (Eds.), *Social intervention: Potential and constraints* (pp. 219–328). New York: Aldine de Gruyter.

Hyman, S. E., & Nestler, E. J. (1993). *The molecular foundations of psychiatry.* Washington, DC: American Psychological Association Press.

Johnson, V. (!988). Adolescent alcohol and marijuana use: A longitudinal assessment of a social learning perspective. *American Journal of Drug and Alcohol Abuse, 14,* 419–439.

Kalter, N., Riemer, B., Brickman, A., & Chen, J. W. (1985). Implications of parental divorce for female development. *Journal of the American Academy of Child Psychiatry, 24,* 538–544.

Kandel, D. B. (1978). Convergences in prospective longitudinal surveys of drug use in normal populations. In D. B. Kandel (Ed.), *Longitudinal research on drug use: Empirical findings and methodological issues* (pp. 3–38). Washington, DC: Hemisphere-Wiley.

Kandel, D. B. (1990). Parenting styles, drug use, and children's adjustment in families of young adults. *Journal of Marriage and the Family, 52,* 183–196.

Kandel, D. B., & Raveis, V. H. (1989). Cessation of illicit drug use in young adulthood. *Archives of General Psychiatry, 46,* 109–116.

Kaplan, H. B. (1972). Toward a general theory of psychosocial deviance: The case of aggressive behavior. *Social Science & Medicine, 6,* 593–617.

Kaplan, H. B. (1975). *Self-attitudes and deviant behavior.* Pacific Palisades, CA: Goodyear.

Kaplan, H. B. (1980). *Deviant behavior in defense of self.* New York: Academic Press.

Kaplan, H. B. (1982). Self-attitudes and deviant behavior: New directions for theory and research. *Youth and Society, 14,* 185–211.

Kaplan, H. B. (1983). Psychological distress in sociological context: Toward a general theory of psychosocial stress. In H. B. Kaplan (Ed.), *Psychosocial stress: Trends in theory and research* (pp. 195–264). New York: Academic Press.

Kaplan, H. B. (1984). *Patterns of juvenile delinquency.* Beverly Hills: Sage Publications.

Kaplan, H. B. (1986). *Social psychology of self-referent behavior.* New York: Plenum Press.

Kaplan, H. B., Johnson, R. J., & Bailey, C. A. (1987). Deviant peers and deviant behavior: Further elaboration of a model. *Social Psychology Quarterly, 50,* 277–284.

Kaplan, H. B., Johnson, R. J., & Bailey, C. A. (1988). Explaining adolescent drug use. *Psychiatry, 51,* 142–163.

Kaplan, H. B., Martin, S. S., & Robbins, C. A. (1982). Applications of a general theory of deviant behavior: Self-derogation and adolescent drug use. *Journal of Health and Social Behavior, 23,* 274–294.

Kellam, S. G., Brown, C., Rubin, B., & Ensminger, M. (1983). Paths leading to teenage psychiatric symptoms and substance use: Developmental epidemiological studies in Woodlawn. In S. Guze, F. Earls, & J. Barrett (Eds.), *Childhood psychopathology and development* (pp. 17–51). New York: Raven Press.

Kendler, K. S. Heath, A. C., Neale, M. C., Kessler, R. C., & Eaves, L. J. (1993). Alcoholism and major depression in women. *Archives of General Psychiatry, 50,* 690–698.

Kendler, K. S., Neale, M. C., MacLean, C. J., Heath, A. C., Eaves, L. J., & Kessler, R. C. (1993). Smoking and major depression: A causal analysis. *Archives of General Psychiatry, 50,* 36–43.

Kessler, R. C., & Magee, W. J. (1994). Childhood family violence and adult recurrent depression. *Journal of Health and Social Behavior, 35,* 13–17.

Khantzian, E. J. (1985). The self-medication hypothesis of addictive disorders: Focus on heroin and cocaine dependence. *American Journal of Psychiatry, 142*, 1259–1264.

Kleinman, P. H. (1978). Onset of addiction: A first attempt at prediction. *International Journal of the Addictions, 13*, 1217–1235.

Krohn, M. D., Skinner, W. F., Zielinski, M., & Naughton, M. (1990). Elaborating the relationship between age and adolescent cigarette smoking. *Deviant Behavior, 10*, 105–129.

Leahy, R. L. (1985). The development of the self: Conclusions. In R. L. Leahy (Ed.), *The development of self* (pp. 295–304). New York: Academic Press.

Lerner, J. V., & Vicary, J. R. (1984). Difficult temperament and drug use: Analyses from the New York longitudinal study. *Journal of Drug Education, 14*, 1–8.

Levy, J. C., & Deykin, E. Y. (1989). Suicidality, depression, and substance abuse in adolescence. *American Journal of Psychiatry, 146*, 1462–1467.

Livesay, S., Erlich, S. M., and Finnegan, L. P. (1987). Cocaine and pregnancy: Maternal and infant outcome. *Pediatric Research, 21*, 387.

Mensch, B. S., & Kandel, D. B. (1988). Do job conditions influence the use of drugs? *Journal of Health and Social Behavior, 29*, 169–184.

Messner, S. F., Krohn, M. D., & Liska, A. E. (1989). *Deviance and crime: Problems and prospects*. Albany: State University of New York Press.

Mott, F. L., & Haurin, R. J. (1988). Linkages between sexual activity and alcohol and drug use among American adolescents. *Family Planning Perspectives, 20*, 128–136.

Needle, R. H., Lavee, Y., Su, S., Brown, P., & Doherty, W. (1988). Familial, interpersonal and intrapersonal correlates of drug use: A longitudinal comparison of adolescents in treatment, drug-using adolescents not in treatment, and non-drug-using adolescents. *International Journal of the Addictions, 23*, 1125–1143.

Newcomb, M. D., & Bentler, P. M. (1988). *Consequences of adolescent drug use: Impact on the lives of young adults*. New York: Sage Publications.

Newcomb, M. D., Bentler, P. M., & Fahy, B. (1987). Cocaine use and psychopathology: Associations among young adults. *International Journal of the Addictions, 22*, 1167–1188.

O'Donnell, J., Voss, H. L., Clayton, R. R., Slatin, G., & Room, R. (1976). *Young men and drugs: A nationwide survey* (NIDA Research Monograph 5). Rockville, MD: National Institute on Drug Abuse.

Osgood, D. W., Johnston, L. D., O'Malley, P. M., & Bachman, J. G. (1988). The generality of deviance in late adolescence and early adulthood. *American Sociological Review, 53*, 81–93.

Patterson, G. R. (1986). Performance models for antisocial boys. *American Psychology, 41*, 432–444.

Pentz, M. A., MacKinnon, D. P., Dwyer, J. H., Wang, E. Y. I., Hansen, W. B., Flay, B. F., Anderson-Johnson, P., & Anderson-Johnson, C. (1989). Longitudinal effects of the Midwestern Prevention Project on regular and experimental smoking in adolescents. *Preventive Medicine, 18*, 304–321.

Peterson, L., & Zill, N. (1986). Marital disruption and behavior problems in children. *Journal of Marriage and the Family, 48*, 295–308.

Powers, R. J. (1987). Stress as a factor in alcohol use and abuse. In E. L. Gottheil, K. A. Druley, S. P. Pashko, & S. Weinstein (Eds.), *Stress and addiction* (pp. 248–260). New York: Brunner/Mazel.

Robins, L. (1966). *Deviant children grown up*. Baltimore: Williams & Wilkins.

Robins, L. N., and Rutter, M. (1990). *Straight and devious pathways from childhood to adulthood*. New York: Cambridge University Press.

Roehrich, H., & Gold, M. S. (1988). Familial addiction in cocaine abusers. *Journal of Clinical Psychiatry, 49*, 326.

Ross, C. E. (1994). Overweight and depression. *Journal of Health and Social Behavior, 35*, 63–78.

Rossi, A. S. (1980). Aging and parenthood in the middle years. In P. B. Baltes & O. G. Brim (Eds.), *Life span development and behavior* (pp. 138–205). New York: Academic Press.

Sanderson, W. C., Beck, A. T., & Beck, J. (1990). Syndrome comorbidity in patients with major depression or dysthymia: Prevalence and temporal relationships. *American Journal of Psychiatry, 147*, 1025–1028.

Sebald, H. (1986). Adolescents' shifting orientation toward parents and peers: A curvilinear trend over recent decades. *Journal of Marriage and the Family, 48*, 5–13.

Shaffer, J. W., Nurco, D. N., Hanlon, T. E., Kinlock, T. W., Duszynski, K. R., & Stephenson, P. (1988). MMPI-168 profiles of male narcotic addicts by ethnic group and city. *Journal of Clinical Psychology, 44*, 292–298.

Shedler, J., & Block, J. (1990). Adolescent drug use and psychological health: A longitudinal inquiry. *American Psychologist, 45*, 612–630.

Shoemaker, D. J. (1990). *Theories of delinquency: An examination of explanations of delinquent behavior*, 2nd ed. New York: Oxford University Press.

Simcha-Fagan, O., Gersten, J. C., & Langner, T. (1986). Early precursors and concurrent correlates of patterns of illicit drug use in adolescence. *Journal of Drug Issues, 16*, 7–28.

Simmons, R. G., Burgeson, R., Carlton-Ford, S., & Blyth, D. A. (1987). The impact of cumulative change in early adolescence. *Child Development, 58*, 1220–1234.

Simons, R. L., Robertson, J. R., & Downs, W. R. (1989). The nature of the association between parental rejection and delinquent behavior. *Journal of Youth and Adolescence, 18*, 297–310.

Small, S. A. (1988). Parental self-esteem and its relationship to childrearing practices, parent adolescent interaction, and adolescent behavior. *Journal of Marriage and the Family, 50*, 1063–1072.

Swaim, R. C., Oetting, E. R., Edwards, R., & Beauvais, F. (1989). Links from emotional distress to adolescent drug use: A path model. *Journal of Consulting and Clinical Psychology, 57*, 227–231.

Tolan, P. H. (1988). Delinquent behaviors and male adolescent development: A preliminary study. *Journal of Youth and Adolescence, 17*, 413–427.

Tress, W., Reister, G., & Gegenheimer, L. (1989). Mental and physical resiliency in spite of a stressful childhood. In M. Brambring, F. Lösel, & H. Skowronek (Eds.), *Children at risk: Assessment, longitudinal research, and intervention* (pp. 173–185). New York: Aldine de Gruyter.

Weiss, R. D., & Mirin, S. M. (1986). Subtypes of cocaine abusers. *Psychiatric Clinics of North America, 9*, 491–501.

Werner, E. E. (1989). Vulnerability and resiliency: A longitudinal perspective. In M. Brambring, F. Lösel, & H. Skowronek (Eds.), *Children at risk: Assessment, longitudinal research, and intervention* (pp. 157–172). New York: Aldine de Gruyter.

Werner, E. E., & Smith, R. S. (1982). *Vulnerable but invincible: A longitudinal study of resilient children and youth*. New York: Aldine de Gruyter.

Woody, G. E., Urschel, H. C., III, & Alterman, A. (1992). The many paths to drug dependence. In M. Glantz & R. Pickens (Eds.), *Vulnerability to drug abuse* (pp. 491–507). Washington, DC: American Psychological Association.

Yamaguchi, K., & Kandel, D. B. (1985). Dynamic relationships between premarital cohabitation and illicit drug use: A life event history analysis of role selection and role socialization. *American Sociological Review, 50*, 530–546.

Yamaguchi, K., & Kandel, D. B. (1987). Drug use and other determinants of premarital pregnancy and its outcome: An analysis of competing life events. *Journal of Marriage and the Family, 49*, 257–270.

Yandrow, B. (1989). Alcoholism in women. *Psychiatric Annals, 19*, 243–247.

II

COMMON AND PATTERN-SPECIFIC ANTECEDENTS AND CONSEQUENCES OF DRUG USE, CRIME, AND OTHER FORMS OF DEVIANCE

Investigations of deviant behavior have frequently studied multiple modes of deviance simultaneously as causes or consequences of other modes of deviance. In these investigations, the researchers variously observed that (1) particular deviant patterns have consequences for several other deviant patterns, (2) several deviant patterns have a common deviant outcome, or (3) a particular deviant pattern has a unique deviant antecedent or consequence that is not shared by other deviant patterns. Any combination of these circumstances may be observed in the same study where diverse deviant patterns are modeled as both causes and consequences.

The two studies that constitute Part II illustrate such studies. In Chapter 2, Wu and Kandel study intergenerational behavioral transmission by examining the common and pattern-specific effects of smoking and delinquency by mothers and fathers on the same behaviors by their sons and daughters. Although the data from 201 mother–father–child triads were collected in the course of a longitudinal study, the analyses rest on cross-sectional data from which a causal order between parental socialization practices and the child's functioning is inferred. The linear structural relations models manifest both common effects (father's criminal record has a direct effect on the son's smoking and delinquency; mother's smoking has an indirect effect on son's smoking and delinquency by reducing norm-setting) and specific effects (father's criminal record has a direct effect on daughter's delinquency, but not on daughter's smoking). This study is also noteworthy in that it illustrates analyses that specify variables that mediate (parental socialization practices) and moderate (gender) the effects of parental deviance on the child's deviance and so anticipates the kinds of studies to be considered in Part IV and Part V, respectively.

In Chapter 3, Brook, Whiteman, and Cohen use a "net regression" technique on data collected from a cohort of children interviewed up to four times between 1975 and 1992 to document both specific and common antecedents for different components of problem behavior. In multivariate context, risk factors measured during middle and late adolescence are observed to have a pervasive effect on different problem behaviors (aggression, drug use, theft/vandalism) measured during young adulthood. Rebellion and school rejection (suggesting rejection of conventional social roles) anticipate all three deviant outcomes. At the same time, certain psychosocial variables are uniquely associated with each outcome. For example, peer deviance anticipates vandalism, but not drug use or aggression, and low father identification and mother's use of alcohol predicts drug use, but not aggression or vandalism.

These studies clearly demonstrate the importance of simultaneously considering multiple patterns of deviance as antecedents and consequences of other patterns. To fail to do so might preclude identifying those antecedents and consequences that are common to multiple modes of deviance found in a broad array of unconventional attributes and behaviors, and differentiating them from antecedents and consequences that are uniquely associated with one deviant pattern.

2

The Roles of Mothers and Fathers in Intergenerational Behavioral Transmission
The Case of Smoking and Delinquency

Ping Wu and Denise B. Kandel

Introduction

Continuity across generations has been observed for different behaviors, from nondeviant to deviant, including domains as diverse as occupational choice, television watching, educational attainment, religious practices, personality characteristics, alcoholism, psychiatric disorders, and childbearing in adolescence (Caspi & Elder, 1991; Clark, Worthington, & Danser, 1988; Davies & Kandel, 1981; Kahn & Anderson, 1992; Plomin, 1986; Plomin, Corley, DeFries, & Fulker, 1990; Rutter, Macdonald, Le Couteur, Harrington, Bolton, & Bailey, 1990; Webster, Harburg, Gleiberman, Schork, & DiFrancesico, 1989). The majority of studies on familial influences focus on mothers and fail to take fathers into account; they rely on children's perceptions of parental behaviors rather than on parental self-reports. The respective roles of mothers and fathers in intergenerational behavioral continuity remain to be elucidated.

Smoking and delinquency constitute two interesting cases for the study of intergenerational behavior transmission because of contrasting sex-specific prevalence for each behavior. Delinquent participation is much more prevalent among males than among females, while sex differences in the prevalence of

Ping Wu and **Denise B. Kandel** • Department of Psychiatry and School of Public Health, Columbia University, and New York State Psychiatric Institute, New York, New York 10032.

Drugs, Crime, and Other Deviant Adaptations: Longitudinal Studies, edited by Howard B. Kaplan. Plenum Press, New York, 1995.

cigarette smoking have diminished among adults (Fiore, Novotny, Pierce, Hart-ziandreu, Patel, & Davis, 1989), and females actually report slightly higher rates of smoking than males among high school seniors (Johnson, O'Malley, & Bachman, 1992). In this chapter, we investigate the potential transmission of cigarette smoking and delinquent participation across generations in adolescence, the relative influence of mothers and fathers in each domain, the potential occurrence of crossover parental effects on the child from one domain to the other, and selected processes underlying parental influences. Intergenerational transmission is inferred from similarity between mothers and fathers and their adolescent children.

Processes of Intergenerational Transmission

Similarity between parent and child can be accounted for by three processes, which are not mutually exclusive. Similarity can be due to modeling and imitation of the parent by the child, to socialization of the child by the parent, and to a genetic predisposition. With the data at our disposal, the third genetic hypothesis cannot be assessed and differentiated from modeling. We may conclude that a familial effect is present if the impact of parental behavior persists with controls for other factors.

Parental and Child Similarity

Associations between parents' and children's smoking, and between parental criminality and child delinquency, have previously been reported. Integrating the results of these investigations is difficult because they are based on different types of samples, they rarely collect independent data from both mothers and fathers, they use various definitions of the behaviors of interest and different analytical techniques, they do not always collect data separately for boys and girls, and even when they do so, they do not always report results for each sex separately.

The majority of studies that have examined the influence of parents' smoking on children's smoking are based on the children's reports of parental behaviors, rather than on parental self-reports. We have identified 12 studies that collected independent data from parents. Six studies obtained data from only one parent (Bewley & Bland, 1977; Brook, Gordon, & Brook, 1986; Foshee & Bauman, 1992; Gfroerer, 1987; Green, Macintyre, West, & Ecob, 1990; Pulkkinen, 1983), and six obtained independent data from both parents. Of these latter six studies, two found the mother's smoking to have a stronger influence on the child's smoking than the father's smoking (Rossow, 1992; Melby, Conger, Conger, & Lorenz, 1993), although in the later study the zero-order correlation observed between mother and son became nonsignificant in a multivariate model. One study found fathers to be more important than mothers (Tildesley, Lichtenstein, Ary, & Sherman, 1990). Two investigators found same sex-specific effects, with mothers more important for daughters and fathers more important for sons (Banks, Bewley, Bland, Dean, & Pollard, 1978; Murray, Kiryluk, & Swan, 1985). One study found no parental effect (Annis, 1974). The highest odds ratios, as calculated by us from data published by the authors (Banks et al., 1978; Bewley & Bland, 1977; Murray, et al., 1985), or adjusted odds as reported by the author (Rossow, 1992), are observed for mother–daughter pairs and range from 3 to 4.

Similarly, child delinquency has been found to be related to parental criminality (for reviews, see Loeber & Stouthamer-Loeber, 1986; McCord, 1991a). Variations in definitions of constructs and in samples are greater in studies of parental influences on child delinquency than on smoking. Some investigators include alcoholism, in addition to officially recorded criminal records, in the definition of parental deviance (e.g., Laub & Sampson, 1988). The majority of studies have examined the impact of fathers on sons and have defined parental delinquent activity according to official court records. Six major studies can be highlighted (Farrington, Gundry, & West, 1975; Glueck & Glueck, 1962; McCord, 1991a; Robins, 1966; Robins, West & Herjanic, 1975; Simcha-Fagan & Schwartz, 1992), with Laub and Sampson (1988) carrying out a reanalysis of the Gluecks' data. The risk of a child committing an officially recorded offense increases approximately twofold for males with a criminal father (Farrington, Gallagher, Morley, Ledger, & West, 1988; McCord, 1991a; Robins, et al., 1975; Simcha-Fagan & Schwartz, 1992). However, with controls for quality of parenting, Laub and Sampson (1988) found no direct effects of parental criminality (or drunkenness) on officially identified delinquents.

Parental Socialization Practices and Child Behaviors

Besides imitation of the parent by the child, similarity between parent and child on smoking or delinquency can be due to attributes of the parents, such as personality characteristics and child-rearing socialization practices, which are related to the parents' own behaviors and would in turn foster smoking or delinquency by the child. Socialization practices are of particular interest; they include two different domains. One pertains to the quality of the interactions between parent and child; the second consists of social reinforcement, or the setting of norms that define the appropriate behaviors and values concerning specific arenas. Two major dimensions of parent–child interactions have been consistently identified as important correlates or predictors, or both, of children's psychosocial functioning: warmth and control (Maccoby & Martin, 1983; Patterson, 1982; Rollins & Thomas, 1979). The warmth dimension emphasizes closeness, affection, nurturance, and acceptance of the child by the parent. The control dimension has more recently been differentiated into disciplinary methods, that is, the manners in which parents exercise control over the child, reward the child for positive behaviors and provide negative reinforcements for negative behaviors (Patterson, 1982), and monitoring, that is, the degree of parental involvement in the child's life, supervision of the child's activities, and firmness in setting controls and limits (Patterson, 1982). Theoretical models of parental socialization influences have been more extensively developed for delinquent and acting-out behavior than for drug use and have been extended from the former to the latter (Elliott, Huizinga, & Ageton, 1985; Hawkins, Catalano, and Associates, 1992; Loeber & Stouthamer-Loeber, 1986; Patterson & Dishion, 1985; Patterson, DeBaryshe, & Ramsey, 1989; Simcha-Fagan & Schwartz, 1992). Theoretical models are particularly lacking in studies of smoking. Important exceptions include the work of Krohn and Conger and their colleagues (Krohn, Massey, Skinner, & Laver, 1983; Melby et al., 1993).

A substantial body of research has documented the role of parental socialization practices on children's delinquent behavior and drug involvement, although relatively little research has been conducted on parents' socialization practices specifically as they relate to children's smoking. Similar practices are important for both delinquency and drug use. Delinquent participation and drug use, including smoking, by children and adolescents are related to lack of affection between parent and child, conflict, poor child identification with the parent, lack of supervision of the child's activities, explosive discipline, and inconsistent parenting (e.g., Barnes, 1990; Barnes & Farrell, 1992; Block, Keyes, & Block, 1986; Brook & Cohen, 1992; Brook, Whiteman, Nomura, Gordon, & Cohen, 1988; Brook, Brook, Gordon, Whiteman, & Cohen, 1990; Castro, Maddahean, Newcomb, & Bentler, 1987; Coombs & Landsverk, 1988; Dishion, Patterson, & Reid, 1988; Dishion, Ray, & Capaldi, 1992; Elliott et al., 1985; Hawkins, Lishner, & Catalano, 1985; Hawkins et al., 1992; Huba & Bentler, 1980; Hundleby & Mercer, 1987; Jacob & Leonard, 1991; Kandel, Kessler, & Margulies, 1978; Leonard, 1990; McCord, 1991a,b; Melby et al., 1993; Mercer & Kohn, 1980; Simcha-Fagan & Schwartz, 1992; Simons, Conger, & Whitbeck, 1988; Skinner, Massey, Krohn, & Lauer, 1985; Zucker & Noll, 1987).

More empirical evidence exists regarding the consequences of child-rearing practices than those of norm-setting, and more regarding the consequences of smoking than those of delinquent participation. With rare exceptions (Krohn, Skinner, Massey, & Akers, 1985; McAlister, Krosnick, & Milburn, 1984), several studies report a direct impact of perceived parental attitudes on either initiation or maintenance of children's smoking behavior (Brook, Whiteman, Gordon, & Brook, 1983; Brook, et al., 1986; Chassin, Presson, Bensenberg, Corty, Olshavsky, & Sherman, 1981; Krosnick & Judd, 1982; Murray et al., 1985; Neukirch & Cooreman, 1983; Palmer, 1970). Nolte, Smith, and O'Rourke (1983) found that parental attitudes exerted a greater impact than parental behaviors.

Much remains to be learned regarding the extent of parental influence and the underlying mechanisms. To the best of our knowledge, no report has yet appeared in the literature comparing intergenerational transmission for more than one behavior at a time and from the perspective of both mothers and fathers. In addressing the issue of the intergenerational transmission of smoking and delinquency in adolescence, we are interested in three issues: (1) What is the impact of parents on their children's smoking and delinquency? Is there a differential impact of mothers and fathers, and does parental impact vary according to the behavioral domain and to the sex of the child? (2) In addition to specific effects, are there crossover effects of parental behavior in one domain on child behavior in the other domain? (3) What processes account for the transmission of behaviors from parent to child? We investigate the degree of similarity between parent and child in a sample of mother–father–child triads. We include socialization measures in a causal model to assess whether the effects of parental smoking and delinquency are direct or are indirect through parental socialization practices. If there are different effects, we conclude that parental influences is consonant with a familial role modeling (as well as a genetic) effect.

Methods

Sample and Data

The analyses are based on a sample of 201 mother–father–child triads, in which the child is the firstborn and aged 9–17. One parent is the focal member of a longitudinal cohort that has been followed for 19 years since age 15–16.*

---

*The cohort constitutes a representative sample of former adolescents enrolled in grades 10 and 11 in New York State public high schools in 1971–1972 and was selected from a stratified sample of 18 high schools throughout New York State (Kandel, Single, & Kessler, 1976). The target population for the adult follow-up was drawn from the enrollment list of half the homerooms from grades 10 and 11 and included students who were absent from school at the time of the initial study. The inclusion of these former absentees assures the representativeness of the sample and the inclusion of the most deviant youths (Kandel, Raveis, & Kandel, 1984).

Respondents were first contacted in 1971 and were reinterviewed in 1980, 1984, and 1990. The 1160 adults reinterviewed in 1990 represent 72% of the original target adolescents enrolled in the sample schools.

In 1990, additional personal interviews were conducted with spouses and partners, when there was at least one child aged 6–17 in the household and up to two children aged 9–17. The completion rate for spouses/partners was 82.4% and for the firstborn child 87%. The analyses presented in this chapter are based on the sample of 201 triads in which both parents and the firstborn child were interviewed. This sample includes 66% of all the firstborns in that age group; the remaining 34% either lived in single-parent families or are cases in which either parent or the child was not interviewed. Data from all respondents were obtained through structured personal interviews, which took on the average 1½ hr to complete for the adults and 1 hr for the children. Two slightly different interview schedules were developed for younger children aged 9–10 and older children aged 11 and over.

Males represent 46.2% of all focal respondents and 56.2% of spouses/ partners. In order to carry out the analyses for mothers and fathers, male and female parents among focals and spouses/partners were combined across each sample. Because females marry at an earlier age than males, 63.7% of mothers in the triads were from the focal sample and 36.3% from the spouse/partner sample. The converse distribution characterizes fathers in the triads. The mean age of mothers was 34.4 years (S.D. = 2.3), of fathers 35.8 years (S.D. = 4.35), and of the children 12.6 years (S.D. = 2.5) at the time of the interview.

Behavioral Measures of Parents' and Children's Cigarette Smoking and Delinquent Participation

Parental Behaviors

For cigarette smoking, parents were classified into one of four categories that took into account lifetime and past-year smoking as well as information about the number of packs of cigarettes consumed the last month the parent smoked within the past years. The categories were: never smoked, smoked but not within the past year, smoked less than a pack a day within the past year, and smoked at least a pack a day.

Two measures of deviance were constructed. A measure of official contact with the criminal justice system was based on whether the parent had ever ex- perienced any one or more of the following: been convicted, been arrested, or appeared in front of a juvenile court. An additional variable consisted of the total number of delinquent acts that adults reported to have committed within the last 12 months* out of a list of 15 items.[†]

Children's Behaviors

Two measures of children's smoking were based on questions that asked them whether they had ever smoked and how many times they had smoked within the past year. The precoded response categories ranged from 1 or 2 times to 40 or more times.

Two measures of delinquent participation were the total scores for items committed lifetime and in the past 6 months, based on a list of 11 items[‡] common to the items administered to the 9 to 10-year-olds and to the older children aged 11 and over.

Measures of Parental Socialization Practices

The socialization measures cover quality of parenting and norm-setting and include those identified in prior research to be important correlates and predictors of child's conduct problems, delinquency, and involvement in drugs (see above). Identical questions were included in the interview schedules for focal respondents, spouses, and children. For most items, the children were asked first about their mothers and then about their fathers. The measures were developed on the basis of psychometric analyses carried out separately for children, fathers, and mothers. The measures included in the analyses are based on reports from two or three informants: either each parent's report about his or her parenting practices, and the child's report about that parent; or the mother, father, and child

---

*A measure of lifetime delinquent participation was available only for focal respondents, 127 mothers and 73 fathers, and is not included in the analysis.

†The 15 items were (1) got into a serious fight in school or at work; (2) took something not belonging to you worth under $50; (3) broke into some house or place of business; (4) set fire to someone's property on purpose; (5) got into trouble with the police because of something you did; (6) hurt someone badly enough to need bandages or a doctor; (7) damaged property at school or at work on purpose; (8) took something from a store without paying for it; (9) hit an instructor or supervisor; (10) took or used a car without permission of the owner; (11) took part in a fight where a group of your friends were against another group; (12) took something not belonging to you worth over $50; (13) used a knife, gun, or some other weapon, such as a club, to get something from a person; (14) forged or passed bad checks; (15) sold drugs.

‡The 11 items were: (1) ran away from home; (2) skipped classes or school without excuse; (3) carried a hidden weapon; (4) was rowdy in a public place; (5) tried/committed arson; (6) avoided paying for things; (7) tried to go/went into a building to steal something; (8) took something from a store without paying; (9) snatched a purse or wallet/picked a pocket; (10) took something from a car that did not belong to you; (11) threw objects at people.

reports, when children were not asked to differentiate between their mothers and their fathers. Multiinformant measures are advantageous because they reduce measurement error in the variables (Bank, Dishion, Skinner, & Patterson, 1990; Melby et al., 1993).

Measures of Quality of Parenting

The questions were designed to measure three broad parenting dimensions: (1) closeness, (2) discipline, and (3) supervision. Specific factors for discipline included discipline for negative behaviors (punitive, physical, love withdrawal, and cognitive discipline) and consistency of discipline. Each respondent was asked how frequently the parent engaged in specific interactions with the child relevant to each dimension.

Measures of Norm-Setting

To obtain information about parental norms, we asked parents what rules they had for the child. One of the 12 items specifically pertained to rules against smoking cigarettes.

Factor analyses of the parenting items were conducted for six multiitem scales that were subsumed under closeness, discipline for negative behaviors, and supervision. Consistency of discipline consists of the mean value on two four-category items. Rule against smoking included a single dichotomous item. With rare exceptions, the resulting factor structures were identical in the different samples.* Based on the results of the factor analyses and the reliabilities, eight parent–child relationships scales were retained for the present analyses. Multiinformant parent-specific scales were created, which aggregated the parent and child reports for that parent or the mother–father–child reports, when children were not asked to differentiate between mothers and fathers. Alpha values, calculated over the total range of items included in the multiinformant scales (mother and child, father and child, mother–father–child), ranged from 0.40 to

---

*The factor structures obtained from the different data sets are very similar for closeness and supervision. The structure regarding discipline for negative behaviors is less parallel across the different samples. The results of factor analyses of four of the data sets (children's reports of their mothers in all families, children's reports of mothers and of fathers in intact families, and fathers' self-reports in intact families) indicated that four factors underlie the items regarding discipline for negative behaviors (punitive discipline, cognitive discipline, physical discipline, and love withdrawal). The results of the other three data sets (all children's reports of their fathers, focal mothers' self-reports, and mothers' self-reports in intact families) indicated that items in both punitive and cognitive discipline load on a single punitive–cognitive factor.

0.76. Details about the scales, including items included and reliabilities, are presented in Table A in the Appendix.

Other Variables

The models included two other variables found in prior research to be related to adult or to child smoking: (1) mean years of education completed by both parents (range: 9.5–20 years); (2) child's age.

Analytical Strategies

The analytical strategies we pursued were designed to answer the three basic questions outlined above and to do so most efficiently by including as small a number of factors as possible. In a first step, in order to establish the relevance of the different socialization practices to the children's behaviors of interest, correlations partialing out the child's age were run between each of the eight socialization scales and the parent and child measures of lifetime and recent smoking and delinquency. In a second step, to get an understanding of the processes that underlie parental influence, causal models were estimated through LISREL (Jöreskog & Sörbom, 1989). First, two parallel causal models were run to estimate domain-specific parental effects on child smoking and child delinquency. One behavior-specific model predicted the child smoking within the past year, the second predicted the child delinquent participation within the past 6 months. A third model was tested in which both outcomes were considered simultaneously in order to identify potential crossover effects. Details of the models are provided in the Results section. Because of the small sample size, we attempted to include as few factors as possible, sacrificing potential symmetry in the inclusion of mother- and father-specific variables. Each behavior-specific model included two demographic variables, the relevant mother's and father's domain-specific behavior (i.e., smoking or criminal record) and socialization practices found to be significantly related to the child behaviors in the partial correlations outlined above. These models allowed us to select a reduced number of significant variables that were included in a third causal model that was designed to identify crossover effects and that considered both child outcomes simultaneously. Since the third model included relevant measures of parental behaviors in both domains, we could assess specificity vs. generality of parental influence. For these final models, the equality of paths between boys and girls was systematically tested through the multigroup analysis feature of LISREL. The causal models allowed us to evaluate the influence of parental smoking or criminality on the quality and nature of parenting as well as on each child outcome and the mediating role of parenting on the outcomes.

Results

Distribution of Parents' and Children's Behaviors

The behaviors of parents in these intact families follows the sex-specific patterns characteristic of males and females in the United States population. The prevalence of lifetime and former smoking is identical among males and females, although among smokers, males are heavier smokers than females. Of each sex, 20% had never smoked; 42.8% of mothers and 44.3% of fathers had smoked within the past year; 72.7% of fathers who had smoked within the past year, compared with 58.1% of mothers, smoked at least a pack of cigarettes a day.

Adult males are also more extensively involved in delinquency, especially serious delinquency involving some type of official contact with the criminal justice system, than females. Almost three times as many fathers (30.3%) as mothers (10.9%) have at some time had an official contact with the criminal justice system; 19.6% of fathers reported having committed an act within the past year and 8% of mothers did so; 10.1% and 1.5%, respectively, had committed two or more acts.

As regards the children, a slightly higher proportion of girls than boys have smoked cigarettes: 29.7% of girls and 25.7% of boys have smoked at some time; 20.9% and 16.5%, respectively, have smoked within the past year. By contrast, more boys than girls reported delinquent participation at some time: 43.1% and 31.5%, respectively, reported having ever committed at least one delinquent act in their lives, and 22.5% and 10.2% having ever committed at least two acts; 29.7% and 22.5% reported having committed any act within the last 6 months, 15.8% of boys and 6.8% of girls having committed at least two acts.

Similarity between Parents and Children

Smoking

As a first step in the analysis, we examined the distribution of the children's behaviors in each domain as a function of each parent's parallel behavior.

Children whose parents smoke are themselves more likely to smoke (Table 1). The influence of mothers is stronger than the influence of fathers. Similarity between child and mother appears only when mothers are currently smoking heavily, while for fathers, the same pattern appears whether he is currently

Table 1. Children's Cigarette Smoking by Parents' Lifetime, Past Year, and Quantity Cigarette Smoking, by Child's Sex (Mother–Father–First Born Child Triads)

Children who smoked	Mother's smoking				Father's smoking			
	Never smoked (%)	Smoked, not past year (%)	Smoked past year		Never smoked (%)	Smoked, not past year (%)	Smoked past year	
			< pack/day (%)	≥ pack/day (%)			< pack/day (%)	≥ pack/day (%)
Total								
Lifetime	15.0	17.6	22.2	56.0***	14.6	28.6	29.2	34.4
Past year	10.0	9.5	11.1	44.0***	9.8	21.4	25.0	18.8
N	40	74	36	50	41	70	24	64
Boys								
Lifetime	17.4	17.0	29.4	50.0*	12.5	23.4	38.5	30.3
Past year	13.0	8.5	11.8	40.9**	0.0	14.9	38.5	18.2*
N	23	47	17	22	16	47	13	33
Girls								
Lifetime	11.8	18.5	15.8	60.7***	16.0	39.1	18.2	38.7
Past year	5.9	11.1	10.5	46.4***	16.0	34.8	9.1	19.4
N	17	27	19	28	25	23	11	31

*p ≤ .05; **P ≤ .01; ***p ≤ .001 (chi-square test)

smoking or not. Almost four times as many children have ever smoked or are currently smoking when their mother currently smokes at least a pack of cigarettes a day or more compared with children whose mothers have never smoked. Twice as many smoke when their father has smoked at some time, whether or not he has smoked within the past year.

Furthermore, there is a same-sex effect, especially with respect to mothers and daughters. The association between mother and child is stronger for mother–daughter pairs than for mother–son pairs. The association between father and child is stronger for father–son than for father–daughter pairs.

Delinquent Participation

There is a statistically significant parental effect on children's delinquency, but only for fathers and only when they have had an official contact with the criminal justice system, that is, have ever been arrested (except for a driving violation), convicted, or had contact with a juvenile court (Table 2). Children of fathers with such experiences are more likely to report having committed delinquent acts than are children of fathers with no such experiences. There is a slight trend in the same direction for mothers, but with respect to sons and not daugh-

Table 2. Children's Delinquent Behavior Lifetime and in the Past 6 Months by Parents' Formal Contact with the Criminal Justice System[a], by Child Sex (Mother–Father–First Born Child Triads)

| Children who commited 2 + acts | Parents' formal contact with criminal justice system | | | |
| | Mother | | Father | |
	No (%)	Yes (%)	No (%)	Yes (%)
Total				
Lifetime	15.9	23.8	12.0	27.6*
Past 6 months	11.2	14.3	6.8	22.4**
N	170	21	133	58
Boys				
Lifetime	19.8	45.5[†]	19.2	31.0
Past 6 months	14.4	27.3	11.1	27.6
N	91	11	73	29
Girls				
Lifetime	11.4	0.0	3.3	24.1**
Past 6 months	7.6	0.0	1.7	17.2*
N	79	10	60	29

[a]Ever convicted of a crime, arrested (excluding traffic violation), or appeared in court as a juvenile.
*p ≤ .05; [†]p ≤ .10; **p ≤ .01 (chi-square test)

ters. The differences are not as statistically significant for mothers as for fathers, probably because of the small number of mothers who ever had a contact with the criminal justice system. Daughters of mothers with a criminal record are less likely to report having committed two or more acts (Table 2), although they are more likely to have committed one act (data not shown). The small number of delinquent mothers, however, creates instability in the results.

The sex-specific patterns are opposite to those observed for smoking. The relationships between father and child are stronger for father–daughter than for father–son pairs.

The relationships between child delinquency and parental self-reported delinquency are weaker and do not reach statistical significance (Table 3). There are too few mothers who report any delinquent participation in the past year to yield any reliable results.

These data support the existence of intergenerational continuity in behaviors between parents and children, with certain sex specificity. The mother's behavior is more important for the child's smoking of cigarettes, and the father's officially recorded deviance is more important for the child's self-reported delinquent participation. In both domains, the link between parent and child is stronger for daughters than for sons.

Table 3.   Children's Delinquent Behavior Lifetime and in the Past 6 Months by Parents' Past-Year Delinquent Participation, by Child Sex (Mother–Father–First Born Child Triads)

| Children who committed 2 + acts | Parents' past-year delinquent participation | | | |
| | Mother | | Father | |
	No (%)	Yes (%)	No (%)	Yes (%)
Total				
Lifetime	16.1	25.0	15.7	21.6
Past 6 months	11.6	12.5	10.5	16.2
N	173	16	152	37
Boys				
Lifetime	20.0	66.7*	19.8	33.3
Past 6 months	14.9	33.3	13.8	23.8
N	94	6	80	21
Girls				
Lifetime	11.4	0.0	11.1	6.3
Past 6 months	7.6	0.0	6.9	6.3
N	79	10	72	16

*p < .01 (chi-square test)

Parents' Behaviors, Children's Behaviors, and Parenting

As we noted earlier, intergenerational similarity can be due to imitation (or genetic susceptibility) as well as to the social environment created by the parent for the child. Parents' socialization styles may foster negative psychosocial development in their children. It must be stressed that associations observed at one point in time cannot truly separate the effects of parenting on the children's behaviors from the effects of children's behavior on parents' treatment of them.

Parents' Behaviors and Parenting

First, we examined the relationships between each parent's smoking and delinquent behaviors and quality of parenting with control for the child's age, since parenting is highly related to the child's age. We present data for one measure each in each domain for parents and children.

As expected, parental smoking and parental contact with the criminal justice system (Table 4) are related to specific parenting styles. In general, parents who smoke and those who are deviant exhibit less positive parenting than nonsmokers or nondelinquents. The relationships appear to involve somewhat different dimensions of parenting for mothers and fathers, and in some cases for sons compared with daughters.

For mothers, smoking is related to decreased rule-setting toward boys and girls and decreased supervision and closeness toward boys. A criminal record is related to increased use of negative disciplinary strategies, such as love withdrawal and harsh discipline in addition to reduced supervision and norm-setting toward boys, and reduced physical discipline and consistency in discipline toward daughters. Fathers' behaviors show fewer relationships than mothers' to socialization practices. Fathers who smoke are less likely to exert physical discipline toward their sons and daughters and to be consistent disciplinarians. To the extent that paternal parenting is related to deviant behavior, fathers who report a formal contact with the criminal justice system are less likely to supervise their daughters and are more likely to use cognitive forms of discipline toward their sons.

Children's Behaviors and Parenting

The patterns of relationships observed among parents are magnified among children. The relationships between parental socialization and children's behaviors are more extensive and stronger than those observed with parental behaviors. The patterns regarding norm-setting and supervision are similar, whether the child is smoking or has engaged in delinquent acts (Table 5). Closeness, supervision, and norm-setting are the important domains of parenting. High

Table 4. Partial Correlations of Parents' Smoking and Self-Reported Deviance with Parents' Socialization Practices[a] among Boys and Girls, Controlling for Child's Age (Mother–Father–First Born Child Triads)

Socialization practices	Parents' life/last-year quantity cigarette smoking[a]				Parents' contact with criminal justice system			
	Mother socialization		Father socialization		Mother socialization		Father socialization	
	Boys	Girls	Boys	Girls	Boys	Girls	Boys	Girls
Quality of parenting								
Warmth								
Closeness	−0.17†	−0.10	0.01	0.03	−0.06	0.15	−0.07	0.13
Discipline								
Punitive discipline	0.12	−0.13	0.00	−0.07	0.18†	−0.15	0.07	0.13
Physical discipline	−0.03	−0.14	−0.16†	−0.18†	0.17†	−0.21*	−0.02	0.01
Love withdrawal	0.08	−0.16	0.06	0.02	0.22*	−0.12	−0.06	0.17
Cognitive discipline	−0.04	−0.02	0.07	0.10	−0.04	−0.09	−0.05	0.29**
Consistency of discipline	−0.14	−0.15	−0.11	−0.18†	−0.09	−0.30**	0.02	0.06
Supervision	−0.27**	0.15	−0.08	0.11	−0.31***	0.13	−0.21*	0.08
Norm-setting								
Rules against cigarette smoking	−0.20*	−0.22*	−0.04	−0.11	−0.27**	0.05	−0.02	0.09
Total N ≥	104	90	107	91	104	91	107	91

[a]Measures were based on combined parent and child reports.

[b]Four categories: never smoked cigarettes; yes, but not past year; past year, less than a pack/day; past year, a pack or more/day.

†p ≤ .10; *p ≤ .05; **p ≤ .01; ***p ≤ .001

63

Table 5. Partial Correlations of Child's Self-Reported Smoking and Deviance with Parents' Socialization Practices[a] among Boys and Girls, Controlling for Child's Age (Mother–Father–First Born Child Triads)

Socialization practices	Children's frequency of last-year cigarette smoking[b]				Children's past 6 months delinquency			
	Mother socialization		Father socialization		Mother socialization		Father socialization	
	Boys	Girls	Boys	Girls	Boys	Girls	Boys	Girls
Quality of parenting								
Warmth								
Closeness	−0.04	−0.42***	−0.15	−0.22*	−0.04	−0.19†	−0.19†	0.01
Discipline								
Punitive discipline	0.07	0.07	−0.05	0.05	0.20†	0.10	0.00	0.01
Physical discipline	−0.02	−0.09	−0.11	0.04	0.12	0.04	0.02	−0.09
Love withdrawal	0.07	0.00	0.09	0.10	0.20*	−0.01	0.23*	−0.03
Cognitive discipline	−0.04	−0.03	−0.04	−0.14	0.14	0.02	0.02	0.09
Consistency of discipline	−0.12	−0.07	−0.11	−0.07	−0.05	−0.04	0.02	−0.18†
Norm-setting								
Supervision	−0.29**	−0.06	−0.34***	−0.09	−0.26**	−0.15	−0.23*	−0.12
Rules against cigarette smoking	−0.38***	−0.38***	−0.39***	−0.35***	−0.29**	−0.12	−0.21*	−0.12
Total $N \geq$	104	90	107	91	97	88	101	88

[a]Measures were based on combined parent and child reports.
[b]Four categories: never smoked cigarettes; yes, but not past year; past year, less than a pack/day; past year, a pack or more/day.
†p ≤ .10; *p ≤ .05; **p ≤ .01; ***p ≤ .001

scores on these dimensions are associated with reduced rates of smoking and delinquency by the children, with closeness more significant for daughters and supervision for sons. Disciplinary methods designed to control negative behaviors, in particular love withdrawal and punitive discipline, are related to sons' delinquency. A major difference in the relationships between parenting and children's delinquency and smoking is the more frequent use of negative discipline methods by both parents, in particular love withdrawal, when the child participates in delinquent activities than when the child smokes.

Domain-Specific Parental Effects

Causal models were estimated to predict the child's smoking and delinquent participation, for boys and girls separately. As noted earlier, because of small sample sizes, we included as few variables as possible. We excluded variables that were of theoretical interest if they showed no statistically significant age-partialed correlations with the child outcome. On the basis of the partial correlations reported in Tables 4 and 5, especially those that pertain to children's behaviors (Table 5), a reduced set of parental socialization practices was included in each model. Although a different set of practices was included for smoking and for delinquency, for each domain, identical variables were included in the models for girls and boys. Separate measures of each parent domain-specific behavior, parental educational level, and child age were also included in each model. The effects of the latter variable are not displayed. We assumed initially that each parent could affect only his or her own parenting, as well as those dimensions, such as supervision and norm-setting, for which the child answered for both parents jointly. The paths to the spouse's specific parenting measures were fixed to zero. This restriction needed to be relaxed in some cases. The figures display significant and nonsignificant standardized path coefficients that were estimated. The sex-specific correlation matrices are presented in Table B in the Appendix.

Children's Smoking

Four socialization measures were included in the smoking model; separate measures of mother and father closeness, parental supervision, and parental rules against smoking. The last two were entered as joint parental descriptions because the child was not asked to differentiate between the two parents.

The model (Figures 1 and 2) provides a good fit to the data both for boys and for girls (for boys, $\chi^2 = 0.60$, $df = 2$, $p = 0.739$; for girls, $\chi^2 = 1.17$, $df = 2$, $p = 0.557$) and explains 41% of the variance in the children's smoking. Direct positive effects of parental behavior on children's smoking appear only

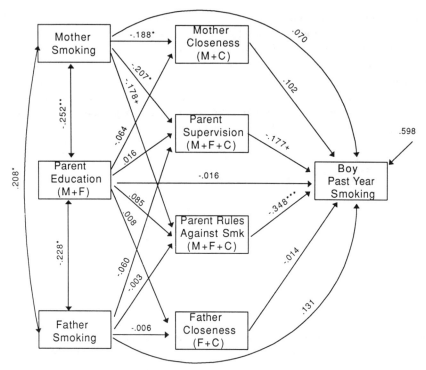

Figure 1. Model of the impact of parents' smoking on boys' smoking (N = 104 intact families). The boy's age is controlled for in the model; paths are not shown. Correlations of error terms for parenting variables are not shown. $^{\dagger}p \leq 0.10$; $^{*}p \leq 0.05$; $^{**}p \leq 0.01$; $^{***}p \leq 0.001$. Standardized coefficients. χ^2 = 0.60; df = 2; p = 0.739.

for mothers toward girls, an effect, however, that barely reaches statistical significance ($p < 0.10$). In addition to a direct effect, maternal smoking also has a strong indirect effect through norm-setting for girls and, especially, for boys. Mothers who smoke are less likely to have rules against smoking, and such household rules reduce children's smoking. Parental rules against smoking have the strongest (negative) effect on a boy's smoking of any of the variables included in the model. Father's smoking is negatively related to girls' and positively related to boys' smoking, although the coefficients do not reach statistical significance. In addition, the relevant dimensions of parenting differ between boys and girls, except for the consistent restraining influence of norm-setting, which is most important for both. Closeness between mother and child is a strong protective factor for girls, while parental supervision is a weaker protective factor for sons.

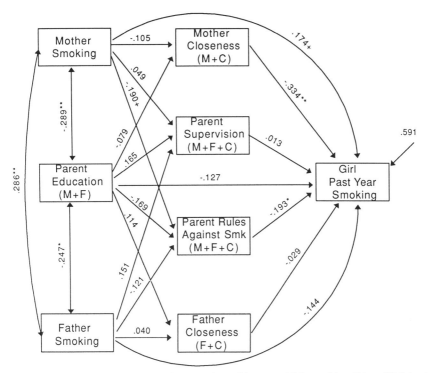

Figure 2. Model of the impact of parents' smoking on girls' smoking ($N = 90$ intact families). The girl's age is controlled for in the model; paths are not shown. Correlations of error terms for parenting variables are now shown. $^{†}p \leq 0.10$; $^{*}p \leq 0.05$; $^{**}p \leq 0.01$. Standardized coefficients. $\chi^2 = 1.17$; $df = 2$; $p = 0.557$.

The correlations among the exogenous variables reflect similarity between spouses in smoking and the well-known negative correlation between education and smoking.

Delinquency

Parental formal contact with the criminal justice system was entered as the exogenous measure of parental deviant behavior.

Reflecting the greater complexity of the correlations between parenting and child delinquency than of those between parenting and smoking, a larger number of socialization practices were included in the model. Similar factors for closeness and love withdrawal were included for both mothers and fathers, but punitive discipline was entered for mothers and consistency of discipline for fathers.

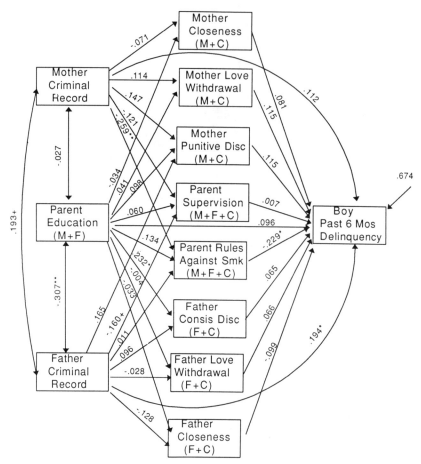

Figure 3. Model of the impact of parents' deviance on boys' deviance (N = 97 intact families). The boy's age is controlled for in the model; paths are not shown. Correlations of error terms for parenting variables are not shown. $^{\dagger}p \leq 0.10$; $^*p \leq 0.05$; $^{**}p \leq 0.01$. Standardized coefficients. χ^2 = 9.16; df = 12; p = 0.690.

The model explains less of the variance in child delinquency (Figures 3 and 4) than in the child smoking, 33% for boys and 26% for girls, compared with about 40% for smoking. Furthermore, contrary to our initial hypothesis, the modification indices indicated that a path from father's official criminal record to maternal punitive discipline needed to be freed for girls. For symmetry, this path was estimated both for girls and for boys. The fit of the final model is

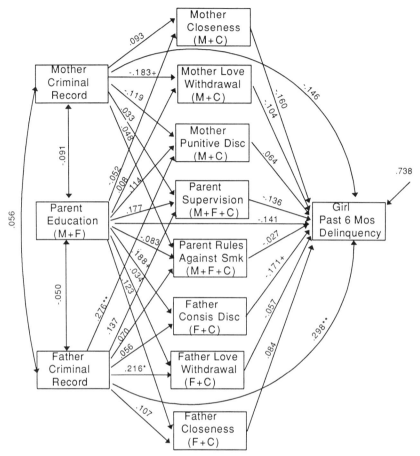

Figure 4. Model of the impact of parents' deviance on girls' deviance (N = 89 intact families). The girl's age is controlled for in the model; paths are not shown. Correlations of error terms for parenting variables are not shown. $^{\dagger}p \leq 0.10$; $^{*}p \leq 0.05$; $^{**}p \leq 0.01$. Standardized coefficients. χ^2 = 14.44; df = 12; p = 0.273.

weaker for girls (χ^2 = 14.44, df = 12, p = 0.273) than for boys (χ^2 = 9.16, df = 12, p = 0.690).

The results are the mirror images of those obtained with respect to children's smoking. The important parental behavior is that of the father. The father's criminal record has a highly significant direct effect on the child's self-reported delinquency. The mother's criminal record has an indirect impact through parental rules against smoking. Mothers with such records are less likely to be part of households with such rules. Parental rules against smoking have a strong (negative) effect on sons' delinquency. Fathers' consistency in discipline, which is positively related to educational level, reduces daughters' delinquency.

In contrast to the sex-specificity of maternal effect on children's smoking, paternal criminality has a potentiating effect both on daughters and on sons, with the effect actually stronger on daughters than on sons.

Unexplained differences between boys and girls appear in the correlations among the exogenous variables. Similarity between parents on criminal behavior, which is lower than for smoking, is zero for girls' parents and significant only at $p \leq 0.10$ for boys' parents. A negative correlation between fathers' deviance and education appears only for boys' fathers. We attribute the sex-specific differences to random sample fluctuations due to small sample sizes.

Crossover Effects

From these two models, a reduced set of statistically significant factors was selected for inclusion in a third model (Figs. 5 and 6) in which both child outcomes were included simultaneously in order to determine the specificity of the effects of parental behaviors on the child (see Table B in the Appendix). Does maternal smoking affect children's smoking exclusively, and does paternal criminality affect children's delinquency exclusively? Or are there crossover effects of one behavior on the other? Crossover effects would suggest that the significant direct paths from parental behaviors to child do not reflect a modeling effect exclusively, but some additional familial process, which is captured by the behavioral measure but is independent of it.

The models fit the data (for boys, $\chi^2 = 2.20$, $df = 4$, $p = 0.699$; for girls, $\chi^2 = 4.0$, $df = 4$, $p = 0.406$). As reflected in the contrasting significance of the correlation between the error terms of the two child outcomes, the model accounts for all the common variance between smoking and delinquency among girls, but not for that among boys. In this more complex model, the barely significant effect of maternal smoking on daughters disappears. The most significant direct paternal behavioral effect is that of father's deviance on sons' and daughters' delinquency. For sons, there is also a crossover effect of the father's criminal record on the son's smoking, although the effect is not as significant as the direct effect on the son's delinquency. The path from mother's smoking to the child's delinquency is positive but not significant. Hierarchical tests comparing these models with ones in which the crossover paths from each parental behavior to the child's behaviors in the other domain were successively fixed at zero in-

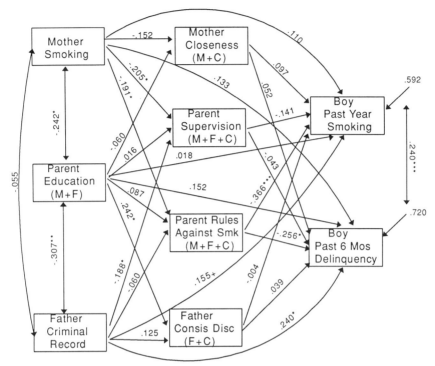

Figure 5. Model of specific and crossover effects of parental behaviors on boys' smoking and deviance (N = 97 intact families). The boy's age is controlled for in the model; paths are not shown. Correlations of error terms for parenting variables are not shown. $^{\dagger}p \leq$ 0.10; $^{*}p \leq 0.05$; $^{**}p \leq 0.01$; $^{***}p \leq 0.001$. Standardized coefficients. χ^2 = 2.20; df = 4; p = 0.699.

dicate that only in the case of father's deviance to son's smoking does freeing the path improve the fit of the model at $p \leq 0.10$ (χ^2 = 4.15, df = 5, p = 0.529 compared with χ^2 = 6.94, df = 6, p = 0.326, with no crossover effect either from mother or father).

Parental norm-setting is highly statistically significant, and in the case of sons reduces both smoking and delinquent participation. Parental rules against smoking are determined by the mother's smoking. Thus, the crossover parental effects on the son's smoking involve the direct effect of the father's criminal behavior and the indirect effect of the mother's smoking in decreasing socialization practices that reduce negative behaviors in the children.

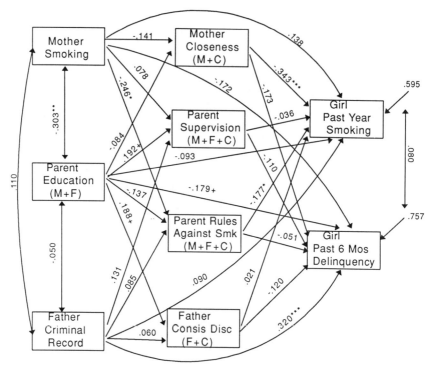

Figure 6. Model of specific and crossover effects of parental behaviors on girls' smoking and deviance (N = 89 intact families). The girl's age is controlled for in the model; paths are not shown. Correlations of error terms for parenting variables are not shown. $^{\dagger}p \leq$ 0.10; $^*p \leq 0.05$; $^{**}p < 0.01$; $^{***}p < 0.001$. Standardized coefficients. χ^2 = 4.00; df = 4; p = 0.406.

The pattern for daughters is somewhat different from that for sons. Two commonalities involve (1) the direct positive effect of the father's criminal record on the daughter's delinquent participation and (2) the indirect positive effect of the mother's smoking on the daughter's smoking through lack of rules against smoking. Two other effects appear only among girls: a strong negative effect of maternal closeness on the daughter's smoking and a direct negative effect of parental education on the daughter's delinquency. These two paths are statistically significantly different for boys and girls.

While parental supervision of sons is negatively affected by the fathers' criminal record and maternal smoking, supervision has no direct statistically significant impact on the boys' behaviors. By contrast, parental supervision of daughters is independent of parental behaviors.

Discussion and Conclusion

The simultaneous examination of two different behavioral domains in a sample of intact families in which the behaviors of mothers and fathers could be examined jointly provides novel insights into processes of intergenerational behavioral transmission from parents to their preadolescent and adolescent children. There are domain-specific and sex-specific effects of same-sex parents on the same-sex child, as well as some crossover effects. As noted earlier, smoking and delinquent participation provide particularly interesting contrasts for such analyses because of the differential extent of participation of males and females in each domain. Males are consistently more delinquent than females. Not only have sex differences in smoking disappeared among adults, but also, in adolescence, the prevalence of smoking is slightly higher among females than among males. Our analyses have identified direct effects of parental behaviors on their children as well as intervening socialization practices that underlie parental influence.

We find that parents have effects for the domain in which their own sex has highest prevalence, but that both mothers and fathers have a stronger impact on daughters than on sons. Controlling for other covariants, mothers' smoking impacts their daughters' smoking but not their sons', while fathers' criminal record impacts both their sons' and their daughters' delinquency, the latter more than the former, although the difference is not statistically significant. There is a direct crossover effect of a father with a criminal record on his daughter's smoking and an indirect crossover effect of a mother's smoking on her son's delinquency through rules against smoking. Thus, the crossover parental behavioral effects appear for children of the opposite sex.

Most parental effects are direct. The impact of socialization practices depends on the behavioral domain and on the child's sex. The explicit prescription of rules against smoking reduces the risk of the child's smoking as well as of the child's committing delinquent acts for children of both sexes. This explicit norm is more influential than supervision of the child, as reflected in parents' attempts at monitoring the child's activities and contacts. Different dimensions of parenting are important for boys and girls. For girls, closeness with mothers is most important, with closeness reducing the girls' risk of smoking. By contrast, boys seem to be more responsive to specific limit-setting, with rules against smoking important in reducing not only boys' smoking but also their delinquency.

As we stressed earlier, although we are inferring a causal order between parental socialization practices and the child's functioning, the cross-sectional data could reflect as much the child's impact on the parent as the parent's impact on the child. However, the findings we report are consistent with those reported by other investigators who have examined separately the predictors of delinquent participation or various forms of drug use in a longitudinal framework (e.g., Brook & Cohen, 1992; Dishion, et al., 1992; McCord, 1991a).

There is intergenerational transmission of smoking from mother to daughter and of delinquent tendencies from father to daughters and sons. Both smoking and delinquent participation by children clearly have a familial component. With our data, imitation and role-modeling effects cannot be clearly differentiated from a genetic effect. A genetic effect could lead to personality and temperamental differences in the parent that would be associated with differential socialization practices and to similar differences in the child—for example, greater irritability, impulsiveness, risk-taking, hostility—that are known precursors to delinquent participation and smoking. Furthermore, personality and life-style characteristics in the parents, which are related to smoking or deviant behaviors or both, could be imitated by the child, which would increase the child's own propensity to smoke or participate in delinquent acts or both.

The model that we have estimated is not assumed to represent an exhaustive model of the determinants of the behaviors under consideration. Other factors omitted from the analysis that are influenced by familial behaviors, such as association with deviant peers (Brown, Mounts, Lamborn, & Steinberg, 1993; Dishion et al., 1988; Elliott et al., 1985; Kandel, 1986), are known to be important influences on children's smoking and delinquency (Melby et al., 1993). However, these additional variables were purposefully excluded from the analysis in order to focus on the specific questions regarding intergenerational transmission that were of concern to us.

While our analyses have confirmed the importance both of role models and of socialization practices in the development of deviant behavior in children previously highlighted by other researchers, the joint examination of two different behaviors, by mothers and fathers, and their respective influence on sons and daughters separately advances our understanding of intergenerational transmission in novel directions. Such transmission and underlying mechanics depend on the nature of the behavior, the sex of the adult parental role model, and the sex of the child.

ACKNOWLEDGMENTS.   This work was supported in part by research grants DA03196, DA04866, and DA02867 and Research Scientist Award DA00081 to D.B.K. from the National Institute on Drug Abuse. Partial support for computer costs was provided by Mental Health Clinical Research Center Grant MH30906 from the National Institute on Mental Health to the New York State Psychiatric Institute. The research assistance of Christine Schaffran is gratefully acknowledged.

Appendix

Table A.   Parenting Scales: Items and Reliabilities

Identical scales were created for mothers and fathers. Except for parental rules, identical questions were asked about mothers and fathers and were included in each parent's and child's instruments. Each scale is scored as the mean of the component items, except as indicated. The number of items listed for each scale refers to each respondent.

Items	Mother/ child	Father/ child	Mother/ father/ child
Closeness (4 items): parent gives praise or encouragement [1 (never) to 5 (every day)]; child depends on parent for advice [1 (not at all) to 5 (completely)]; how close parent feels to child/child feels to parent [1 (not at all) to 5 (extremely)]; how often they do things together [1 (never) to 5 (every day)].	0.73	0.76	—
Punitive discipline (4 items): sends child to room; yells; takes away child's privilege; does not let child go out of the house [1 (never) to 4 (very often)].	0.68	0.60	—
Physical discipline (2 items): spanks or slaps; beats child [1 (never) to 4 (very often)].	0.58	0.57	—
Love withdrawal (3 items): makes fun of child; acts cold and unfriendly; ignores [1 (never) to 4 (very often)].	0.40	0.42	—
Cognitive discipline (2 items): talks about what child did wrong; tells child not to do it again [1 (never) to 4 (very often)].	0.51	0.46	—
Consistency of discipline (2 items): how often punishes child when child does not listen to warnings [1 (never) to 4 (very often)]; how often child can change parent's decision about punishment [1 (very often) to 4 (never)].	0.54	0.53	—
Supervision (6 items asked about both parents together): child leaves house without telling parent [1 (very often) to 4 (never)]; parent knows where child is when away; knows who child is with; tells child the time to be back; child knows how to get in touch with parents; child tells when he/she will be back [1 (never) to 4 (very often)].	0.72	0.69	0.72
Rules against smoking (1 item) (1 = yes): Child was asked about both parents together. (Additive score.)	0.51	0.62	0.62

Table B. Zero-Order Correlations among Variables in Path Models, for Boys ($N \geq 101$) and Girls ($N \geq 89$)

Girls	Child age	Child past yr smoking	Child past 6 mos delinquency	Parent educ	Mother Smoking	Mother Criminal record	Mother Closeness
Child age	—	0.47***	0.39***	−0.25**	0.21*	−0.08	−0.42***
Child past yr smoking	0.44***	—	0.59***	−0.21*	0.30**	0.11	−0.23*
Child past 6 mos delinq.	0.22*	0.28**	—	−0.09	0.24*	0.20*	−0.20*
Parent education	−0.28**	−0.21*	−0.22*	—	−0.23*	−0.03	0.08
Mother smoking	0.36***	0.37***	0.01	−0.30**	—	0.16†	−0.24*
Mother criminal record	0.26*	0.23*	−0.07	−0.09	0.25*	—	−0.02
Mother closeness	−0.44***	−0.53***	−0.26*	0.07	−0.24*	0.2	—
Mother love withdrawal	0.15	0.07	0.02	−0.02	−0.09	−0.07	−0.24*
Mother punit. discip.	−0.07	0.03	0.08	0.12	−0.15	−0.16	−0.06
Father smoking	0.21*	0.02	0.13	−0.25*	0.29**	0.11	−0.05
Father criminal record	0.13	0.12	0.30**	−0.05	0.09	0.06	−0.04
Father closeness	−0.55***	−0.40***	−0.11	0.25*	−0.30**	−0.04	0.48***
Father love withdrawal	0.07	0.12	−0.01	−0.01	0.07	0.10	−0.13
Father consist discip.	−0.16	−0.14	−0.21†	0.23*	−0.07	−0.19†	0.22*
Parental supervision	−0.11	−0.19†	−0.19†	0.14	0.02	0.03	0.31**
Parental rules against smoking	−0.08	−0.31**	−0.07	−0.07	−0.21*	0.04	0.28**

†$p \leq .10$; *$p \leq .05$; **$p \leq .01$; ***$p \leq .001$

	Mother		Father						
	Love withdrawal	Punitive discipline	Smoking	Criminal record	Closeness	Love withdrawal	Consistency discipline	Parental supervision	Parental rules against smoking
	-0.01	-0.04	0.08	-0.01	-0.43***	0.13	-0.20*	-0.45***	-0.40***
	0.06	0.04	0.19*	0.17†	-0.32***	0.14	-0.19†	-0.50***	-0.53***
	0.18†	0.16†	0.10	0.20*	-0.33***	0.26**	-0.06	-0.36***	-0.39***
	0.01	0.05	-0.22*	-0.29**	0.11	-0.05	0.23*	0.16†	0.23*
	0.08	0.11	0.21*	-0.02	-0.06	0.15	-0.14	-0.31***	-0.25*
	0.22*	0.18†	0.06	0.17†	0.05	0.10	-0.05	-0.12	-0.21*
	-0.11	-0.05	-0.05	0.01	0.47***	-0.12	0.07	0.39***	0.31***
	—	0.07	0.06	-0.07	-0.17†	0.45***	-0.23	-0.14	-0.14
	0.26*	—	0.08	0.17†	0.08	0.02	0.36***	-0.06	0.11
	0.06	-0.00	—	0.19*	-0.02	0.07	-0.12	-0.12	-0.08
	-0.01	0.24*	0.25*	—	-0.06	-0.06	0.03	-0.15	-0.06
	-0.04	-0.03	-0.09	0.04	—	-0.33***	0.29**	0.48***	0.28**
	0.31**	0.13	0.03	0.18†	-0.23*	—	-0.37***	-0.34***	-0.30**
	-0.10	0.27*	-0.21†	0.04	0.04	-0.05	—	0.34***	0.20*
	-0.30**	-0.13	0.12	0.11	0.20†	0.05	0.07	—	0.45***
	-0.15	-0.06	-0.13	0.08	0.20†	-0.12	0.08	0.17	—

Boys

References

Annis, H. M. (1974). Patterns of intra-familial drug use. *British Journal of Addiction, 69,* 361–369.

Bank, L., Dishion, T. J., Skinner, M., & Patterson, G. R. (1990). Method variance in structural equation modeling: Living with GLOP. In G. R. Patterson (Ed.), *Aggression and depression in family interactions.* Hillsdale, NJ: Lawrence Erlbaum.

Banks, M. H., Bewley, B. R., Bland, J. R., Dean, S., & Pollard, V. (1978). Long-term study of smoking by secondary schoolchildren. *Archives of Disease in Childhood, 83,* 12–19.

Barnes, G. M. (1990). Impact of the family on adolescent drinking patterns. In R. L. Collins, K. E. Leonard, & J. S. Searles (Eds.), *Alcohol and the family: Research and clinical perspectives* (pp. 137–161). New York: Guilford Press.

Barnes, G. M., & Farrell, M. P. (1992). Parental support and control as predictors of adolescent drinking, delinquency, and related problem behaviors. *Journal of Marriage and the Family, 54,* 763–776.

Bewley, B. R., & Bland, J. M. (1977). Academic performance and social factors related to cigarette smoking by schoolchildren. *British Journal of Preventive and Social Medicine, 31,* 18–24.

Block, J., Keyes, S., & Block, J. H. (1986). Childhood personality and environmental antecedents of drug use: A prospective longitudinal study. Paper presented at the meeting of the Society for Life History Research in Psychopathology, Palm Springs, CA, March.

Brook, J. S., & Cohen, P. (1992). A developmental perspective on drug use and delinquency. In J. McCord (Ed.), *Facts, frameworks, and forecasts* (pp. 231–251). New Brunswick, NJ: Transaction Publishers.

Brook, J. S., Whiteman, M., Gordon, A. S., & Brook, D. W. (1983). Fathers and sons: Their relationship and personality characteristics associated with the son's smoking behavior. *Journal of Genetic Psychology, 142,* 271–281.

Brook, J. S., Gordon, A. S., & Brook, D. W. (1986). Fathers and daughters: Their relationship and personality characteristics associated with the daughter's smoking behavior. *Journal of Genetic Psychology, 148,* 31–44.

Brook, J. S., Whiteman, M., Nomura, C., Gordon, A. S., & Cohen, P. (1988). Personality, family, and ecological influences on adolescent drug use: A developmental analysis. In R. H. Coombs (Ed.), *The family context of adolescent drug use* (pp. 123–160). New York: Haworth Press.

Brook, J. S., Brook, D. W., Gordon, H. S., Whiteman, M., & Cohen, P. (1990). The psychosocial etiology of adolescent drug use: A family interactional approach. *Genetic, Social, and General Psychology Monographs, 116,* (2), 111–267.

Brown, B. B., Mounts, N., Lamborn, S. D., & Steinberg, L. (1993). Parenting practices and peer group affiliation in adolescence. *Child Development, 64,* 467–482.

Caspi, A., & Elder, G. H. (1991). Emergent family patterns: The intergenerational construction of problem behavior and relationships. In R. Hinde & J. Stevenson-Hinde (Eds.), *Relationships within families—Mutual influences* (pp. 218–240). Oxford: Oxford University Press.

Castro, F. G., Maddahean, E., Newcomb, M. D., & Bentler, P. M. (1987). A multivariate model of the determinants of cigarette smoking among adolescents. *Journal of Health and Social Behavior, 28,* 273–299.

Chassin, L., Presson, C. C., Bensenberg, M., Corty, E., Olshavsky, R. W., & Sherman, S. J. (1981). Predicting adolescents' intentions to smoke cigarettes. *Journal of Health and Social Behavior, 22,* 445–455.

Clark, C. A., Worthington, E. L., Jr., & Danser, D. B. (1988). The transmission of religious beliefs and practices from parents to firstborn early adolescent sons. *Journal of Marriage and the Family, 50,* 463–472.

Coombs, R. H., & Landsverk, J. (1988). Parenting styles and substance use during childhood and adolescence. *Journal of Marriage and the Family, 50,* 473–482.

Davies, M., & Kandel, D. B. (1981). Parental and peer influences on adolescents' educational plans: Some further evidence. *American Journal of Sociology, 87,* 363–387.

Dishion, T. J., Patterson, G. R., & Reid, J. R. (1988). Parent and peer factors associated with drug sampling in early adolescence: Implications for treatment. In E. R. Rahdert & J. Grabowski (Eds.), *Adolescent drug abuse: Analyses of treatment research* (pp. 69–93). Rockville, MD: National Institute on Drug Abuse.

Dishion, T. J., Ray, J., & Capaldi, D. (1992). Parenting precursors to male adolescent substance use. Presented at the symposium on Family Processes and Adolescent Substance Use at the Society of Research in Adolescence, Washington, DC, March.

Elliott, D. S., Huizinga, D., & Ageton, S. S. (1985). *Explaining delinquency and drug use.* Beverly Hills: Sage Publications.

Farrington, D. P., Gundry, G., & West, D. J. (1975). The familial transmission of criminality. *Medicine, Science and the Law, 15,* 177–186.

Farrington, D. P., Gallagher, B., Morley, L., Ledger, R. J., & West, D. J. (1988). Cambridge study in delinquent development: Long-term follow-up. Final Report to the Home Office, November. Institute of Criminology, Cambridge University.

Fiore, M., Novotny, T. E., Pierce, J. P., Hatziandreu, E. J., Patel, K. M., & Davis, R. M. (1989). Trends in cigarette smoking in the United States. *Journal of the American Medical Association, 261,* 49–55.

Foshee, V., & Bauman, K. E. (1992). Parental and peer characteristics as modifiers of the bond–behavior relationship: An elaboration of control theory. *Journal of Health and Social Behavior, 33,* 66–76.

Gfroerer, J. (1987). Correlation between drug use by teenagers and drug use by older family members. *American Journal of Drug and Alcohol Abuse, 13,* 95–108.

Glueck, S., & Glueck, E. (1962). *Family environment and delinquency.* Boston: Houghton Mifflin.

Green, G., Macintyre, S., West, P., & Ecob, R. (1990). Do children of lone parents smoke more because their mothers do? *British Journal of Addiction, 85,* 1497–1500.

Hawkins, J. D., Lishner, D. M., & Catalano, R. F., Jr. (1985). Childhood predictors and the prevention of adolescent substance abuse. In C. L. Jones & R. J. Battjes (Eds.), *Etiology of Drug Abuse: Implications for prevention* (pp. 75–226). Washington, DC: Superintendent of Documents, U.S. Government Printing Office.

Hawkins, J. D., Catalano, R. F., Jr., & Associates. (1992). *Communities that care: Action for drug prevention.* San Francisco: Jossey-Bass.

Hops, H., Tildesley, E., Lichtenstein, E., Ary, D., & Sherman, L. (1990). Parent–adolescent problem-solving interactions and drug use. *American Journal of Drug and Alcohol Abuse, 16,* 239–258.

Huba, G. J., & Bentler, P. M. (1980). The role of peer and adult models for drug taking at different stages in adolescence. *Journal of Youth and Adolescence, 9,* 449–465.

Hundleby, J. D., & Mercer, G. W. (1987). Family and friends as social environments and their relationship to young adolescent's use of alcohol, tobacco, and marijuana. *Journal of Marriage and the Family, 49,* 151–164.

Jacob, T., & Leonard, K. (1991). Family and peer influences in the development of adolescent alcohol abuse. Prepared for NIAAA supported conference, working group on the development of alcohol-related problems in high-risk youth: Establishing linkages across biogenetic and psychosocial domains. November 14–18, Washington, DC.

Johnston, L. D., O'Malley, P. M., & Bachman, J. G. (1992). *Smoking, drinking, and illicit drug use among American secondary school students, college students, and young adults, 1975–1991.* Rockville, MD: National Institute on Drug Abuse.

Jöreskog, K. G., & Sörbom, D. (1989). *LISREL 7 user's reference guide*. Mooresville, IN: Scientific Software.

Kahn, J . R., & Anderson, K. E. (1992). Intergenerational patterns of teenage fertility. *Demography, 29*, 39–57.

Kandel, D. B. (1986). Processes of peer influences in adolescence. In R. K. Silbereisen, K. Eyferth, & G. Rudinger (Eds)., *Development as action in context* (pp. 203–227). Berlin: Springer-Verlag.

Kandel, D. B., Single, E., and Kessler, R. (1976). The epidemiology of drug use among New York State high school students: Distribution, trends and change in rates of use. *American Journal of Public Health, 66*, 43–53.

Kandel, D. B., Kessler, R., & Margulies, R. (1978). Adolescent initiation into stages of drug use: A developmental analysis. In D. Kandel (Ed.), *Longitudinal research on drug use: Empirical findings and methodological issues* (pp. 73–99). Washington, DC: Hemisphere-Wiley.

Kandel, D. B., Raveis, V. H., & Kandel, P. I. (1984). Continuity in discontinuities: Adjustment in young adulthood of former school absentees and school dropouts. *Youth and Society, 13*, 325–352.

Krohn, M. D., Massey, J. L., Skinner, W. F., & Lauer, R. M. (1983). Social bonding theory and adolescent cigarette smoking: A longitudinal analysis. *Journal of Health and Social Behavior, 24*, 337–349.

Krohn, M. D., Skinner, W. F., Massey, J. L., & Akers, R. L. (1985). Social learning theory and adolescent cigarette smoking: A longitudinal study. *Social Problems, 32*, 455–473.

Krosnick, J., & Judd, C. (1982). Transitions in social influence at adolescence: Who induces cigarette smoking? *Developmental psychology, 18*, 359–368.

Laub, J. H., & Sampson, R. J. (1988). Unraveling families and delinquency: A reanalysis of the Gluecks' data. *Criminology, 26*, 355–380.

Leonard, K. E. (1990). Summary: Family processes and alcoholism. In R. L. Collins, K. E. Leonard, & J. S. Searles (Eds.), *Alcohol and the family: Research and clinical perspectives* (pp. 272–281). New York: Guilford Press.

Loeber, R., & Stouthamer-Loeber, M. (1986). Family factors as correlates and predictors of juvenile conduct problems and delinquency. In M. Tonry & N. Morris (Eds.), *Crime and justice*, vol. 7 (pp. 29–149). Chicago: University of Chicago Press.

Maccoby, E. E., & Martin, J. A. (1983). Socialization in the context of the family: Parent–child interaction. In E. M. Hetherington (Ed.), *Handbook of child psychology*, Vol. 4, *Socialization, personality, and social development* (pp. 1–101). New York: John Wiley.

McAlister, A. L., Krosnick, J. A., & Milburn, M. A. (1984). Causes of cigarette smoking: Test of a structural equation mode. *Social Psychology Quarterly, 47*, 24–36.

McCord, J. (1991a). The cycle of crime and socialization practices. *Journal of Criminal Law and Criminology, 82*, 211–228.

McCord, J. (1991b). Family relationships, juvenile delinquency, and adult criminality. *Criminology, 29*, 397–417.

Melby, J. A., Conger, R. D., Conger, K. J ., & Lorenz, F. O. (1993). Effects of paternal behavior on tobacco use by young male adolescents. *Journal of Marriage and the Family, 55*, 439–454.

Mercer, G. W., & Kohn, P. M. (1980). Child-rearing factors, authoritarianism, drug use attitudes, and adolescent drug use: A model. *Journal of Genetic Psychology, 136*, 159–171.

Murray, M., Kiryluk, S., & Swan, A. V. (1985). Relation between parents' and children's smoking behavior and attitudes. *Journal of Epidemiology and Community Health, 39*, 169–174.

Neukirch, F., & Cooreman, J. (1983). Influence des parents sur le tabagisme de leurs enfants. *Social Science Medicine, 17*, 763–769.

Nolte, A. E., Smith, B. J., & O'Rourke, T. (1983). The relative importance of parental attitudes and behavior upon youth smoking behavior. *Journal of School Health, 53,* 264–271.

Palmer, A. B. (1970). Some variables contributing to the onset of cigarette smoking among junior high school students. *Social Science and Medicine, 4,* 359–366.

Patterson, G. R. (1982). *Coercive family process: A social learning approach,* Vol. 3. Eugene, OR: Castalia.

Patterson, G. R., & Dishion, T. J. (1985). Contributions of families and peers to delinquency. *Criminology, 23,* 63–79.

Patterson, G. R., DeBaryshe, B. D., & Ramsey, E. (1989). A developmental perspective on antisocial behavior. *American Psychologist, 44,* 329–335.

Plomin, R. (1986). *Development, genetics, and psychology.* Hillsdale, NJ: Lawrence Erlbaum.

Plomin, R., Corley, R., DeFries, J. C., & Fulker, D. W. (1990). Individual differences in television viewing in early childhood: Nature as well as nurture. *Psychological Science, 1,* 371–377.

Pulkkinen, L. (1983). Youthful smoking and drinking in a longitudinal perspective. *Journal of Youth and Adolescence, 12,* 253–283.

Robins, L. N. (1966). *Deviant children grown up.* Baltimore: Williams & Wilkis.

Robins, L. N., West, P. A., & Herjanic, B. L. (1975). Arrests and delinquency in two generations: A study of black urban families and their children. *Journal of Child Psychology and Psychiatry, 16,* 125–140.

Rollins, B., & Thomas, D. (1979). Parental support, power, and control techniques in the socialization of children. In W. Burr, R. Hill, F. I. Nye, & I. Weiss (Eds.), *Contemporary theories about the family,* (Vol. 1). New York: Free Press.

Rossow, I. (1992). Additive and interactional effects of parental health behaviors in adolescence: An empirical study of smoking and alcohol consumption in Norwegian families. Presented at Youth and Drug Conference, Larkollen, Norway, April.

Rutter, M., Macdonald, J., Le Couteur, A., Harrington, R., Bolton, P., & Bailey, A. (1990). Genetic factors in child psychiatric disorders. II. Empirical findings. *Journal of Child Psychology and Psychiatry, 31,* 39–83.

Simcha-Fagan, O., & Schwartz, J. E. (1992). Familial socialization and the transmission of antisocial behavior. Presented at the Fourth Biennial Meeting of the Society for Research on Adolescence.

Simons, R. L., Conger, R. D., and Whitbeck, L. B. (1988). A multistage social learning model of the influences of family and peers upon adolescent substance abuse. *Journal of Drug Issues, 18,* 293–315.

Skinner, W. F., Massey, J. L., Krohn, M. D., & Lauer, R. M. (1985). Social influences and constraints on the initiation and cessation of adolescent tobacco use. *Journal of Behavioral Medicine, 8,* 353–376.

Webster, D. W., Harburg, E., Gleiberman, L., Schork, A., & DiFranceisco, W. (1989). Familial transmission of alcohol use. I. Parent and adult offspring alcohol use over 17 years—Tecumseh, Michigan. *Journal of Studies on Alcohol, 50,* 557–566.

Zucker, R. A., & Noll, R. A. (1987). The interaction of child and environment in the early development of drug involvement: A far ranging review and a planned very early intervention. *Drugs and Society, 1,* 57–97.

3

Stage of Drug Use, Aggression, and Theft/Vandalism

Shared and Unshared Risks

Judith S. Brook, Martin Whiteman, and
Patricia Cohen

Introduction

Over the past two decades, substantial research has documented the interrelation of different problem behaviors (Elliott, Huizinga, & Menard, 1989; Hawkins, Jenson, Catalano, & Lishner, 1988; Jessor & Jessor, 1977; Zabin, Hardy, Smith, & Hirsch,1986). The research has shown strong linkages among characteristics such as drug use, delinquency, and aggression. For instance, Jessor and colleagues maintain that such behaviors as delinquency and drug use represent different aspects of problem behavior. Despite these advances, little evidence has been obtained with respect to the determinants of different components of problem behavior. These outcomes have been studied separately rather than simultaneously. Therefore, whether or not these outcomes share similar risk factors is not well documented. Identification of the shared and unshared patterns of different behaviors remains a central task. Such information is critical to the emerging field of developmental psychopathology in its goal to describe the etiology

Judith S. Brook • Department of Community Medicine, Mount Sinai School of Medicine, New York, New York 10029.   **Martin Whiteman** • Columbia University, New York, New York, New York 10027.   **Patricia Cohen** • New York State Psychiatric Institute and School of Public Health, Columbia University, New York, New York 10032.

Drugs, Crime, and Other Deviant Adaptations: Longitudinal Studies, edited by Howard B. Kaplan. Plenum Press, New York, 1995.

of different problem behavior outcomes, their various pathways, and eventually developmental sequelae.

In recent years, we have conducted a number of analyses of different samples and outcome variables and have documented the existence of both specific and common antecedents for a number of different components of problem behavior. In a previous analysis, we examined the shared and unshared risk factors for adolescent psychopathology and problem behavior. Problem behavior included two components—substance abuse and conduct problems. Our findings suggested that psychological distress and problem behavior share some common risks, but there is also substantial specificity in risk factors. An attempt was also made to assess the common and uncommon pathways to still another component of problem behavior—delinquency. The findings regarding certain aspects of the family, peer, and school environment were consistent with a common-cause model for both drug use and delinquency. Certain aspects of the environmental context and parent–child domains were in accord with a dissimilar-cause model. (P. Cohen & Brook, 1987).

In another study, we examined the common and uncommon pathways to drug use and delinquency in a sample of young black and Puerto Rican adolescents (Brook, unpublished paper). Although drug use and delinquency had a number of common risks, they also had a number of specific risks. The number of risk factors related to delinquency was greater than the number of risk factors associated with drug use. Building on previous research, we propose to further differentiate the components of delinquency, namely, theft/vandalism and interpersonal aggression. Thus, we propose to examine the shared and unshared risk factors for aggression, theft/vandalism, and drug use.

Although the identification of shared and unshared risk factors for aggression and theft/vandalism is in its preliminary stage, there is a considerable body of data on the risk factors for aggression, theft/vandalism, and drug use when examined separately. Theory and research suggest that personality attributes of unconventionality, such as tolerance of deviance and rebelliousness, are related to drug use, aggression, and vandalism (Jessor & Jessor, 1977; Penning & Barnes, 1982; Robins, 1980).

Operating within a family interactional framework, the authors have noted that patterns of attachment, whether based on the parent's or the child's report, are related to the child's behavior (Bowlby, 1988; Sroufe & Fleeson, 1986). A mutual parent–child attachment characterized by a nonconflictual relationship and one in which the child identifies with the parent has been found to be related to drug use. An affectionate parent–child relationship has also been associated with children who are less likely to be aggressive and less involved in theft/vandalism (Wilson & Herrnstein, 1985).

Parental modeling has been found to be related to the child's use of drugs. For example, parental alcohol use has been found to be related to the child's use of alcohol (Cloninger, Bohman, Sigvardson, & Von Knorring, 1985). In a related vein, peer models of marijuana and deviance have been found to be related to self drug use and delinquency (Brook, Whiteman, & Gordon, 1983; Brook, Brook, Gordon, Whiteman, & Cohen, 1990; Kandel, 1978; Newcomb & Bentler, 1988).

As regards the risk factors in the behavioral domain, substantial research has documented the continuity of aspects of individual development. The research has shown strong stability beginning in middle childhood, particularly for externalizing characteristics such as aggression (Eron & Huesmann, 1990; McCord, 1988; Olweus, 1980; Urban, Carlson, Egeland, & Sroufe, 1991). Substantial stability has also been shown for theft/vandalism (Wilson & Herrnstein, 1985). Considerable evidence has also been obtained with respect to the continuity of drug use (Brook & Cohen, 1992; Brook, Whiteman, & Finch, 1993; Robins & Pryzbeck, 1985). Our interest also focuses on early behaviors that predict related, but not identical, outcomes. For instance, drug use is also associated with increased violence by the user.

Of interest is the reciprocal nature of drug use, aggression, and theft/vandalism. Aggression and antisocial behavior persisting into early adolescence have also been found to predict later adolescent drug abuse or alcohol problems or both (Loeber, 1988; McCord, 1981). Involvement in delinquent behavior was a consistent predictor of substance initiation, as shown in a recent study by Wells, Morrison, Gillmore, Catalano, Iritani, and Hawkins (1992). Reciprocally, drug use has also been found to affect intrapersonal and interpersonal functioning (Newcomb & Bentler, 1988).

Finally, in the context area, neighborhood quality and school variables have been found to be related to drug use, aggression, and vandalism (Brook, Nomura, & Cohen, 1987; Robins, 1980; Simcha-Fagan & Schwartz, 1986; Wilson & Herrnstein, 1985).

The study presented in this chapter builds on our previous research but departs in a significant way. Drug use, aggression, and theft/vandalism are examined simultaneously in an attempt to identify both shared and unshared risk factors.

There is a danger in such analysis that risk factors may simply be marker variables for still earlier risk factors. Therefore, we have attempted to control for relevant variables antedating or concurrent with the risk factors in question.

Method

Sample and Procedures

These analyses are based on the Children in the Community Project, in which a longitudinal cohort of children have been assessed since early childhood. Families were originally sampled in 1975 when the children were of ages

1–10 and the families were living in one of two upstate New York counties (for a detailed description of the original sampling plan and study procedures, see Kogan, Smith & Jenkins, 1977).

The families were recontacted for interviews in 1983, again in 1985–1986, and again in 1991–1992. Over 80% were interviewed two, three, or four times. However, families with the youngest children who were living in urban poverty areas were lost to follow-up.

In order to rebalance the cohort to better represent the population, an additional sample of 54 such families was drawn, using the sampling procedures used in the original study. Of this sample, 52% were male. The resulting combined sample includes the full range of socioeconomic status and is generally representative of families with children of these ages in the northeastern United States, although somewhat more rural, Catholic, and white because of the characteristics of the sampled counties.

Follow-up interviews were conducted with mothers and youth separately but simultaneously in their homes by pairs of trained lay interviewers. Families resided predominantly in the original area, but also in 27 other states. Interviews typically took about 2 hours each and covered a range of demographic, psychiatric, personality, health, environmental, and quality-of-life issues. The current analyses are based on the 632 children for whom the data on drug use, aggression, and delinquency at the T4 interview were complete.

Measures

The scales used in this study were based on item correlation and reliabilities and were grouped in five domains: (1) personality, (2) family, (3) behavior, (4) peer, and (5) context. The scales for the most part are adaptations of existing scales with adequate psychometric properties. More detailed descriptions of the measures appear in Brook, Whiteman, Gordon, and Cohen (1986) and Brook et al. (1990). The measures and their sources are as follows:

Domain of Adolescent Personality Measures

The scales included in this domain were tolerance of deviance (Jessor and Jessor, 1977), ego integration (original), achievement (original), and rebelliousness (Smith & Fogg, 1979). Reliabilities ranged from 0.58 to 0.79, with a median of 0.59.

Domain of Family Measures

The scales used for this domain were maternal and paternal identification (original), maternal and paternal alcohol use, and maternal and paternal conflict (Schaefer, 1965). Reliabilities ranged from 0.90 to 0.93, with a median of 0.91.

Domain of Peer Measures

Peer deviance (Gold, 1966) had a Cronbach alpha of 0.78. Measures of peer marijuana use and alcohol use were also included.

Domain of Context

The scales in this domain included neighborhood quality (P. Cohen, Struening, Muhlin, Genevie, Kaplan, & Peck, 1982), school conflict (Brook et al., 1987), school rejection (Brook et al., 1987), and school negative learning environment (Brook et al., 1987). Reliabilities ranged from 0.53 to 0.83, with a median of 0.60.

The dependent variable, stage of drug use, is based on work by Kandel (1975). The questions on the use of legal drugs, marijuana, and other illicit drugs were designed to form a scale assessing increased self-involvement with drugs. A respondent who answered affirmatively to a higher stage of drug use (e.g., other illicit drugs) was expected to have passed all the proceeding stages (e.g., legal drugs, marijuana). In an earlier study, we found that the stages do form a satisfactory Guttman scale (Brook et al., 1983).

The second and third dependent variables are theft/vandalism and aggression. These two measures were adapted from Gold (1966). In addition, more extreme items were added.

Analytical Plan

The technique used in this study was developed for our earlier comparison of the predictors of drug use, externalizing problems, and internalizing problems and is called "net regression" (P. Cohen, Brook, Cohen, Velez, & Garcia, 1990). It was also used in a more recent study (Brook & Cohen, 1992). This procedure provides a statistical comparison of the partial or direct effects of risk factors on different outcome variables. Thus, the more common practice of noting that a risk is statistically significant for one outcome, but not for another, or that some estimate of magnitude of effect appears to be larger for one outcome than another, without assessment of the significance of these differences, can be avoided. In addition, net regression provides an overall test of the net differences in the partial regression coefficients, as well as a test of each risk factor. Thus the overall test may be used to control Type II errors of inference.

In this procedure, an ordinary least-squares equation is produced for each of the standardized dependent variables, Y and Z, using all risk factors of interest. (In our case, we also included as covariants age, sex, and the age–sex interaction.) The two predicted or estimated dependent variables $\hat{Y}$ and $\hat{Z}$ are then produced. Their equations are, of course, the sum of the regression-weighted risk factors plus a constant. This sum for $\hat{Y}$ is then subtracted from Z, and this new variable, $Z - \hat{Y}$, is regressed on the original set of predictors (risk factors). The overall R^2 for this equation and its associated F provides a test of the significance of the aggregate differences in risk factors, and each partial regression coefficient and its t indicates the magnitude and significance of the difference in risk for each variable. These analyses were readily accomplished by means of the SECTOR module of the SYSTAT statistical package for microcomputer (J. Cohen, 1989; Wilkinson, 1990).

Results

The intercorrelations of the three dependent variables are presented in Table 1. As shown in this table, the three outcome variables are significantly intercorrelated. Drug stage, however, is more highly related to theft/vandalism than to aggression. Theft/vandalism is equally related to drug stage and to aggression.

Pearson correlations were computed between the earlier psychosocial risk factors at T3 and the later problem behavior outcomes at T4 (drug use, theft/vandalism, and aggression).

As shown in Table 2, a number of risk factors contribute to the notion of a general problem behavior, since they correlate with each of the outcome variables. It appears that only the more general risk factors and not the more drug-related variables were related to all three outcomes. For instance, T3 variables, including rebelliousness, father conflict, peer deviance, aggression, theft/vandalism, and school rejection, were related to all three outcomes. None of the drug-related variables (e.g., parental or peer drug use) was related to all three outcome variables.

Table 3 also presents the relationships between earlier psychosocial risk variables and later problem behavior outcomes. However, in these analyses, the effects of age, sex, and the T3 independent variables in the domain were partialed out. Such control enables us to pinpoint more directly the relationship between the T3 variables and the T4 outcomes.

As shown in Table 3, four of the domains (personality, family, behavior, and context) are implicated in all three outcome variables. Furthermore, all the

Table 1.   Correlation Coefficients among the Outcome Variables at T4[a]

	Variables	
Variables	Theft/vandalism	Aggression
Drug use	0.35[b]	0.16[b]
Theft/vandalism	—	0.39[b]

[a]Age, sex, T3 aggression, theft/vandalism, and drug use are partialed out.
[b]$p < 0.001$.

Table 2.   Pearson Correlation Coefficients

T3 variables	T4 variables		
	Drug use	Theft/vandalism	Aggression
Personality			
Tolerance of deviance	0.32[c]	0.16[c]	—
Low ego integration	0.18[c]	0.15[c]	0.10[c]
Low achievement	0.09[a]	—	0.09[a]
Rebelliousness	0.30[c]	0.28[c]	0.21[c]
Family			
Low mother identification	0.13[c]	0.19[c]	0.14[c]
Low father identification	0.16[c]	0.11[b]	—
Mother alcohol use	0.20[c]	0.08[a]	—
Father alcohol use	0.16[c]	0.08[a]	—
Mother–child conflict	—	0.10[a]	0.17[c]
Father–child conflict	0.08[a]	0.10[b]	0.13[c]
Behavior			
Aggression	0.17[c]	0.21[c]	0.36[c]
Theft/vandalism	0.29[c]	0.29[c]	0.13[c]
Drug use	0.40[c]	0.11[b]	—
Peer			
Peer marijuana dse	0.26[c]	—	—
Peer alcohol use	0.19[c]	—	—
Peer deviance	0.19[c]	0.21[c]	0.11[b]
Context			
Neighborhood quality	—	—	—
School conflict	0.09[a]	—	—
School rejection	0.13[c]	0.16[c]	0.17[c]
School negative learning	0.11[b]	0.13[b]	—

[a-c]Probability: [a]$p < 0.05$; [b]$p < 0.01$; [c]$p < 0.001$.

domains are more highly related to drug use and theft/vandalism than to aggression.

Only two of the specific risk factors (rebelliousness and school rejection) were related to all three outcomes once the control variables were partialed out. Looking at the specific variables within the domains, the results indicate that the total number of earlier risk factors related to the three outcome measures was the greatest for drug use (9 predictors), next for theft/vandalism (8 predictors), and least for aggression (4 predictors).

Examination of Table 3 indicates that earlier drug use is not related to later theft/vandalism. Similarly, earlier theft/vandalism is not related to later drug use. (The significant relationships between these variables vanished with control on antecedent and concurrent variables referred to above.) Similarly, reciprocity

Table 3. Partial Relationships of Drug Use, Aggression, and Vandalism at T4 with Each Risk Factor at T3 Controlling for Variables within the T3 Domain[a]

T3 domains and variables	T4 variables					
	Drug use beta	R^2	Aggression beta	R^2	Vandalism beta	R^2
Personality		0.14^c		0.14^c		0.22^c
Tolerance of deviance	0.28^c		−0.03		0.18^c	
Low ego integration	0		0.03		0.01	
Low achievement	−0.02		0.04		−0.05	
Rebelliousness	0.15^b		0.15^b		0.16^b	
Family		0.10^c		0.15^c		0.20^c
Low mother identification	0.04		0.13^b		0.15^c	
Low father identification	0.14^b		−0.01		0.05	
Mother alcohol	0.17^c		0.03		0.06	
Father alcohol	0.07		.02		0.06	
Mother conflict	−0.03		0.09		−0.02	
Father conflict	0.07		0.04		0.06	
Behavior		0.21^c		0.20^c		0.24^c
Aggression	0.04		0.30^c		0.01	
Theft/vandalism	0.06		−0.04		0.28^c	
Drug use	0.45^c		0.08		0.08	
Peer		0.10^c		0.12^c		0.18^c
Peer marijuana use	0.23^c		0.07		0.08	
Peer alcohol use	0.10		−0.04		0.00	
Peer deviance	0.03		0.05		0.15^c	
Context		0.07^c		0.13^c		0.19^c
Neighborhood quality	0.05		0.03		0.04	
School conflict	0.16^c		−0.04		0.11^b	
School rejection	0.15^c		0.12^b		0.12^b	
School negative attitude	0.12^b		0.03		0.16^c	

[a]Betas are net of child's age, sex, age by sex, and other variables in the T3 domain. R^2 is the variance for each domain.
[b,c]Probability: [b]$p < 0.01$; [c]$p < 0.001$.

does not obtain in the case of aggression and its relation to theft/vandalism or drug use. Thus, earlier aggression is not related to later drug use or theft/ vandalism. Conversely, earlier drug use or theft/vandalism is not related to later aggression.

There was stability between earlier and later problem behaviors: drug use, theft/vandalism, and aggression. Thus, the most highly related risk factor for T4 drug use was T3 drug use. A similar pattern emerged for theft/vandalism and aggression. The most predictive risk factors for the outcomes of aggression and theft/vandalism were earlier aggression and theft/vandalism, respectively.

Net regression analysis (see Table 4) was used to examine whether a specific risk factor showed a significantly different relation with later drug use, theft/ vandalism, or aggression. For example, is the relationship between the risk factor and later aggression significantly different from the relationship between this risk factor and later drug use? The control variables described for Table 3 were also imposed on the data presented in Table 4.

Examination of the variables within the behavioral domain in Table 4 indicates that early aggression is more highly related to later aggression than to later theft/vandalism or drug use. Similarly, early theft/vandalism is more highly related to later theft/vandalism than to later aggression or drug use. Early drug use is related more highly to later drug use than to later theft/vandalism or aggression.

Of the risk factors, 13 differentiated aggression from drug use and 7 differentiated aggression from theft/vandalism. Finally, only 6 factors differentiated drug use from theft/vandalism.

Discussion

Our results lend support to the existence of the "problem behavior syndrome" identified by previous investigators (Elliott et al., 1989; Jessor & Jessor, 1977; Kaplan, Martin, & Robbins, 1984). First of all, the three outcome variables are significantly interrelated. Second, four of the domains (personality, family, peer, and context) had a significant impact on each of the later problem behaviors despite stringent controls. It appears that risk factors recruited from a variety of domains measured during middle and late adolescence (T3) have a pervasive impact on different problem behaviors. Third, looking more closely at the variables within the domains, we have isolated a number of risk factors that correlate with all three outcomes. Understandably, such variables are of a general nature and relate to attitudinal unconventionality, familial conflict, and peer deviance. However, risk factors that reflect drug use by parent or peer appear to have a more specific impact. Once we introduced stringent controls on earlier risk factors, as shown in Table 3, only rebelliousness and school rejection were related to all three outcomes. Thus, rejection of conventional roles, whether

Table 4.   Net Regression Analysis of Significantly Different Partial Relationships of Drug Use, Aggression, and Theft/Vandalism with Risks[a]

Variables	Theft/vandalism–aggression	Drug use–theft/vandalism	Drug use–aggression
Personality			
Tolerance of deviance	0.19[d]	0.08	0.27[d]
Low ego integration	−0.01	−0.01	−0.02
Low achievement	−0.10[b]	0.02	−0.08[b]
Rebelliousness	0	0	0.01
Family			
Low mother identification	0.02	−0.11[b]	−0.09[b]
Low father identification	0.06	0.09	0.15[c]
Mother alcohol	0.02	0.10[b]	0.13[c]
Father alcohol	0.04	−0.01	0.03
Low mother conflict	0.12[b]	0.02	0.14[c]
High father conflict	0.02	0	0.02
Behavior			
Aggression	−0.29[d]	0.03	−0.26[d]
Vandalism	0.31[d]	−0.19[d]	0.12[b]
Drug use	0	0.34[d]	0.34[d]
Peer			
Marijuana use	0	0.12[b]	0.12[b]
Alcohol use	0.04	0.08	0.12[b]
Deviance	0.08	−0.09[b]	−0.01
Context			
Neighborhood quality	0	0.02	0.02
Low school conflict	0.14[d]	0.05	0.19[d]
Rejection	−0.02	0.02	0
Negative school attitude	0.12[c]	−0.04	0.09[b]

[a]The differential partial relationship between theft/vandalism and aggression and drug use and theft/vandalism was significant (see Table 1). However, the betas of neighborhood quality and theft/vandalism and drug use were not significant (see Table 3). A positive beta indicates a more positive or less negative relationship for theft/vandalism than for aggression, for drug use than for theft/vandalism, and for drug use than for aggression.
[b–d]Probability: [b]$p < 0.05$; [c]$p < p.01$; [d]$p < 0.001$.

directed mainly against the family (e.g., rebellion) or against a social institution externally (school rejection), manifests itself in a diversity of antisocial acts.

As regards the two-outcome variables, drug use and theft/vandalism, 70% of the psychosocial variables related significantly to both. In contrast, fewer of these risks (45%) were shared between either of these variables (drug use and theft/vandalism) and aggression. Specific variables related to theft/vandalism and drug use, but not to aggression, included personality factors, tapping risk-taking behavior, parent–child attachment measures (e.g., less conflict with parents), peer alcohol use, and an adverse school environment. Numerous studies examining these problem behaviors in isolation have identified these psychosocial variables as correlates of either drug use or delinquency (Newcomb & Felix-Ortiz, 1992). The analysis presented in this chapter also takes earlier research a step further by demonstrating that these relationships are maintained even when one controls for earlier delinquency and drug use. Thus, it appears that these psychosocial variables predict later drug use and theft/vandalism, and the relationship does not merely reflect earlier drug use and delinquency.

However, there is also support for a degree of dissimilarity among the outcome variables. Drug use is more highly related to theft/vandalism than to aggression. The interrelationship among the outcome problem behaviors suggests that the three indicators of problem behavior reflect three different levels of aggression. Our aggression index seems to be tapping the greatest amount of physical aggression, since the items tap direct physical harm to other people (e.g., the adolescent is asked to report on the frequency with which he or she engages in a fight in which a group of his or her friends is against another group). The theft/vandalism index deals with aggression against property, but does not assess bodily harm to others. The items of drug use seem to be tapping the least amount of aggression, whether of bodily harm to others or damage to property of others. Therefore, if we array the three problem behavior indices in terms of severity of aggression, the order would be drug use, theft/vandalism, and aggression. We would expect the highest correlation between the variables more proximal in terms of seriousness of aggression (aggression and theft/vandalism; theft/vandalism and drug use). The lowest correlation would occur between the two indices least similar on our hypothetical aggression continuum, namely, aggression and drug use. The intercorrelations among the outcome variables are in accord with this pattern. (The correlation between aggression and theft/vandalism is 0.39**; between theft/vandalism and drug use, 0.35**; and between aggression and drug use, 0.16*).

Further support for the specificity of the outcomes derives from our domain analysis. All five of the domains were more highly related to stage of drug use and theft/vandalism than to aggression.

Support for the specificity of drug use and aggression is provided by an examination of the antecedents of these acts. When comparing the risk factors for aggression and drug use, the findings supported a dissimilar-cause model. Two thirds of the risk factors were differentially related to aggression and drug use. Overall, these findings provide empirical support for the growing number of researchers and clinicians who note that although there may be similarities among different aspects of problem behaviors, there are differences in the antecedents of these developmental outcomes (Loeber, 1991).

In earlier research, investigators had highlighted the pattern of covariation among drug use, aggression, and theft/vandalism, as measured by a composite index dealing with problem behavior (Jessor & Jessor, 1977; Windle, 1990). This research indicates that while these behaviors share some common antecedents, at least in young adulthood they are not causally related. There is no predictability between an earlier problem behavior and either of the other later problem behaviors. Perhaps the reason for the difference between our results and theirs is that once we introduced stringent controls in our analyses, the predictive patterns between the components of problem behavior vanished.

Also contributing to the lack of commonality of later behaviors is the relatively strong predictability of earlier behaviors on their corresponding behaviors at later periods. Thus, early drug use was more highly implicated in later drug use, and early vandalism places one at greater risk for later vandalism than for later drug use. Early aggression was more highly related to later aggression than to theft/vandalism or drug use. There is therefore a decrease in the amount of variance in an outcome behavior that can be accounted for by other antecedent behaviors. These findings support interventions aimed at early problem behaviors in order to forestall their later emergence.

In sum, the findings indicate that drug use, theft/vandalism, and aggression share a number of common antecedents that all lend credibility to the notion of problem behavior. Furthermore, drug use and theft/vandalism show particularly strong inferential attributes to shared risk factors. At the same time, there were a number of specific antecedents of the three outcome measures, particularly for aggression versus theft/vandalism, and for theft/vandalism versus drug use. Thus, the reciprocal relationship between aggression, drug use, and theft/vandalism was not found. Last, the importance of an earlier risk behavior in predicting its corresponding later problem behavior contributes to specificity among the three problem behaviors.

ACKNOWLEDGMENTS.   This investigation was supported in part by research grant DA03188 and by Research Scientist Award DA00178 to J.S.B. from the National Institute on Drug Abuse. The authors wish to thank Coryl Jones, Thomas Walker, and Pe Shein Wynn for their assistance.

References

Bowlby, J. (1988). *A secure base: Parent child attachment and healthy human development.* New York: Basic Books.
Brook, J. S., & Cohen, P. (1992). A developmental perspective on drug use and delinquency. In J. McCord (Ed.), *Advances in criminological theory,* Vol. 3, *Crime facts, fictions, and theory* (pp. 231–251). New Brunswick, NJ: Transactions Publishers.

Brook, J. S., Whiteman, M., & Gordon, A. S. (1983). Stages of drug use in adolescence: Personality, peer, and family correlates. *Developmental Psychology, 19,* 269–277.

Brook, J. S., Whiteman, M., Gordon, A. S., and Cohen, P. (1986). Some models and mechanisms for explaining the impact of maternal and adolescent characteristics on adolescent stage of drug use. *Developmental Psychology, 22*(4), 460–467.

Brook, J. S., Nomura, C., & Cohen, P. (1987). A network of influences on adolescent drug involvement: Neighborhood, school, peer, and family. *Genetic, Social, and General Psychology Monographs, 115*(1), 123–145.

Brook, J. S., Brook, D. W., Gordon, A. S., Whiteman, M., & Cohen, P. (1990). The psychosocial etiology of adolescent drug use: A family interactional approach. *Genetic, Social, and General Psychology Monographs, 116*(2), 111–267.

Brook, J. S., Whiteman, M., & Finch, S. (1993). The role of mutual attachment and adolescent drug use: A longitudinal study. *Genetic, Social, and General Psychology Monographs, 115*(1), 123–145.

Cloninger, C. R., Bohman, M., Sigvardson, S., & Von Knorring, A. L. (1985). Psychopathology in adopted-out children of alcoholics: The Stockholm adoption study. *Recent Developments in Alcoholism, 3,* 37–51.

Cohen, J. (1989). SETCOR: A supplemental module for SYSTAT and SYGRAPH. Evanston, IL: SYSTAT.

Cohen, P., & Brook, J. S. (1987). Family factors related to the persistence of psychopathology in childhood and adolescence. *Psychiatry, 50,* 332–345.

Cohen, P., Struening, E. L., Muhlin, G. L., Genevie, L. E., Kaplan, S. R., & Peck, H. B. (1982). Community stressors, mediating conditions and well-being in urban neighborhoods. *Journal of Community Psychology, 10,* 377–391.

Cohen, P., Brook, J. S., Cohen, J., Velez, C. N., & Garcia, M. (1990). Common and uncommon pathways to adolescent psychopathology and problem behavior. In L. Robins & M. Rutter (Eds.), *Straight and devious pathways from childhood to adulthood* (pp. 242–258). London: Cambridge University Press.

Elliott, D. S., Huizinga, D., & Menard, S. (1989). *Multiple problem youth: Delinquency, substance use and mental health problems.* New York: Springer-Verlag.

Eron, L. D., & Huesmann, L. R. (1990). The stability of aggressive behavior—even into the third generation. In M. Lewis & S. M. Miller (Eds.), *Handbook of developmental psychopathology* (pp. 147–156). New York: Plenum, Press.

Gold, M. (1966). Undetected delinquent behavior. *Journal of Research in Crime and Delinquency, 3,* 27–46.

Hawkins, J. D., Jenson, J. M., Catalano, R. F., & Lishner, D. M. (1988). Delinquency and drug abuse: Implications for social services. *Social Service Review, 62,* 258–284.

Jessor, R., & Jessor, S. L. (1977). *Problem behavior and psychosocial development: A longitudinal study of youth.* San Diego: Academic Press.

Kandel, D. (1975). Stages in adolescent involvement in drug use. *Science, 190,* 912–914.

Kandel, D. B. (1978). Homophily selection and socialization in adolescent friendships. *American Journal of Sociology, 84,* 427–436.

Kaplan, H. B., Martin, S. S., & Robbins, C. (1984). Pathways to adolescent drug use: Self-derogation, peer influence, weakening of social controls, and early substance use. *Journal of Health and Social Behavior, 25,* 270–89.

Kogan, L. S., Smith, J., & Jenkins, S. (1977). Ecological validity of indicator data as predictors of survey findings. *Journal of Social Service Research, 1,* 117–132.

Loeber, R. (1988). Natural histories of conduct problems, delinquency, and associated substance use: Evidence for developmental progressions. In B. B. Lahey & A. E. Kazdin (Eds.), *Advances in clinical child psychology,* Vol. 11 (pp. 73–124). New York: Plenum.

Loeber, R. (1991). Questions and advances in the study of developmental pathways. In D. Cicchetti & S. Toth (Eds.), *Proceedings of the Rochester symposium on developmental psychopathology,* Vol. 3 (pp. 97–116). Rochester, NY: University of Rochester Press.

McCord, J. (1981). Alcoholism and criminality. *Journal of Studies on Alcohol, 42,* 739–748.

McCord, (1988). Parental behavior in the cycle of aggression. *Psychiatry, 51,* 14–23.

Newcomb, M. D., & Bentler, P. M. (1988). *Consequences of adolescent drug use: Impact on the lives of young adults.* Newbury Park, CA: Sage Publications.

Newcomb, M. D., & Felix-Ortiz, M. (1992). Multiple protective and risk factors for drug use and abuse: Cross-sectional and prospective findings. *Journal of Personality and Social Psychology, 63*(2), 280–296.

Olweus, D. (1980). Bullying among school boys. In R. Barnen (Ed.), *Children and violence* (pp. 259–297). Stockholm: Academic Literature.

Penning, M., & Barnes, G. E. (1982). Adolescent marijuana use: A review. *International Journal of Addictions, 17,* 749–791.

Robins, L. N. (1980). The natural history of drug abuse. *Acta Psychiatric Scandinavica, 62*(Supplement 284), 7–20.

Robins, L. N., & Pryzbeck, T. R. (1985). Age of onset of drug use as a factor in drug and other disorders. In C. L. Jones & R. J. Battjes (Eds.), *Etiology of drug abuse: Implications for prevention* (NIDA Research Monograph No. 56, DHHS Publication No. ADM 85-1335) (pp. 178–192). Washington, DC: U.S. Government Printing Office.

Schaefer, E. S. (1965). Children's support of parental behavior: An inventory. *Child Development, 36,* 413–424.

Simcha-Fagan, O., & Schwartz, J. E. (1986). Neighborhood and delinquency: An assessment of contextual effects. *Criminology, 24,* 667–703.

Smith, G. M. & Fogg, C. P. (1979). Psychological antecedents of teenage drug use. In R. Simmons (Ed.), *Research in community and mental health: An annual compilation of research,* Vol. 1 Greenwich, CT: JAL Press.

Sroufe, L. A. & Fleeson, J. (1986). Attachment and the construction of relationships. In W. Hartup & Z. Rubin (Eds.), *Relationships and Developments* (pp. 51–71). Hillsdale, NJ: Lawrence Erlbaum.

Urban, J., Carlson, E., Egeland, B., & Sroufe, L. A. (1991). Patterns of individual adaptation across childhood. *Development and Psychopathology, 3,* 345–450.

Wells, E. A., Morrison, D. M., Gillmore, M. R., Catalano, R. F., Iritani, B., & Hawkins, J. D. (1992). Race differences in anti-social behaviors and attitudes and early initiation of substance abuse. *Journal of Drug Education, 22*(2), 115–130.

Wilkinson, L. (1990). SYSTAT: The system for statistics. Evanston, IL: SYSTAT.

Wilson, J. Q., & Herrnstein, R. J. (1985). *Crime and human nature.* New York: Simon & Schuster.

Windle, M. (1990). A longitudinal study of antisocial behaviors in early adolescence as predictors of late adolescent substance use: Gender and ethnic group differences. *Journal of Abnormal Psychology, 99*(1), 86–91.

Zabin, L. S., Hardy, J. B., Smith, E. A., & Hirsch, M. B. (1986). Substance use and its relation to sexual activity among inner-city adolescents. *Journal of Adolescent Health Care, 7,* 320–331.

III

RECIPROCAL INFLUENCES AMONG DRUG USE, CRIME, AND OTHER FORMS OF DEVIANCE

Frequently, researchers focus on the causal relationship between two patterns of deviance because of their intrinsic theoretical interest in this relationship. This interest does not extend to other patterns of deviance except possibly insofar as they represent controls that might render the relationship spurious. While any one researcher might be interested in only one causal direction in any given analysis, other researchers or the same researcher in a different analysis might hypothesize the opposite causal direction instead of, or in addition to, the original hypothesized direction.

Part III comprises two reports that are concerned with the causal relationship between particular patterns of deviance. In Chapter 4, Stacy and Newcomb estimate the longitudinal effects of adolescent drug use on criminal behavior in adulthood, controlling on a number of constructs derived from traditional theories of deviance. Using structural equation modeling procedures, the investigators observe that adolescent drug use predicts adult criminal deviance, controlling for the possible predictive effects of a number of other variables including adolescent criminal deviance, social conformity, and peer deviance.

In Chapter 5, McCord considers the relationship between alcoholism and crime over the life course by critically examining the assumption that alcohol increases the likelihood of criminality. Data for the analysis came from records, questionnaire responses, and interviews with 205 middle-aged men who were first examined as part of the Cambridge–Somerville Youth Study, during which the subjects were on average 10.5 years of age at the start of treatment and 16 when the treatment ended. Conclusions are based on the inspection of the trajectories leading from disruptive behavior in childhood through adolescent delinquency-prone life-styles to adult alcoholism or criminality. On the basis of these data, the author concludes that the concurrence of alcoholism and crime cannot be accounted for by assertions that alcoholism is merely a manifestation of delinquency-prone life-styles or that a single underlying dimension of deviance explains both alcoholism and criminality. However, two other compatible explanations may be entertained. First, the relationship between alcoholism and criminality may be explained in terms of samples overrepresenting one type of alcoholic (the antisocial alcoholic) from among a heterogeneous classification. Second, criminals, by virtue of rarely being married or legitimately employed, tend to frequent bars, drink too much, and become alcoholics.

4

Long-Term Social–Psychological Influences on Deviant Attitudes and Criminal Behavior

Alan W. Stacy and Michael D. Newcomb

Introduction

Various forms of antisocial attitudes and deviant behaviors have been addressed in traditional theoretical perspectives, such as theories of strain (Cloward, 1959; Merton, 1957), control (Hirschi, 1969), and social learning (Akers, Krohn, Lanza-Kaduce, & Radosevich, 1979). There have also been attempts to integrate some combination of strain, control, and social learning propositions in the explanation of deviance (Elliot, Huizinga, & Ageton, 1985; Jessor, Graves, Hanson, & Jessor, 1968; Kaplan, 1985). Even though substantial progress in theoretical development is apparent in this line of research, few studies have investigated differential predictions over an extended period of time using comprehensive analytical designs (for reviews, see Johnson, Wish, Schmeidler, & Huizinga, 1991; Loeber & Dishion, 1983).

The traditional theories just mentioned specify certain general factors underlying all forms of deviant behavior and, less often, specific factors that influence particular forms of deviance or conformity in a given set of circumstances

Alan W. Stacy • Institute for Prevention Research, Department of Preventive Medicine, University of Southern California, Los Angeles, California 90007; Department of Psychology, University of California, Los Angeles, Los Angeles, California 90024.   **Michael D. Newcomb** • Division of Counseling and Educational Psychology, University of Southern California, Los Angeles, California 90007.

Drugs, Crime, and Other Deviant Adaptations: Longitudinal Studies, edited by Howard B. Kaplan. Plenum Press, New York, 1995.

(e.g., Cloward, 1959; Jessor & Jessor, 1977). Overall, less theoretical attention has been devoted to explaining how one type of deviance may directly influence another class of deviant behavior. That is, possible processes through which deviance of one form may beget further deviance of a different form have been identified only rarely (Newcomb & McGee, 1991; Osgood, Johnston, O'Malley, & Bachman, 1988). It is possible that these processes can be interpreted in terms of traditional theories, because deviant behavior itself may increase strain, weaken control, or increase one's association with deviant peers, thereby increasing the likelihood, or extending the range of, further deviance. A more conservative interpretation of traditional theories would suggest that one form of deviance can be only a spurious predictor of another form of deviance, because associations among different forms of deviance arise because all forms are determined by a common cause (Donovan & Jessor, 1985; Hirschi, 1969; Newcomb & McGee, 1991). On the other hand, if spuriousness can be ruled out, and mediation by traditional constructs is not apparent, alternative viewpoints may be needed to explain the prediction of one form of deviance by another.

In the study presented in this chapter, we investigated the potential processes through which one class of deviance may influence another type, by evaluating the longitudinal effects of a specific form of deviance (drug use) in adolescence on a different form of deviance (criminal behavior) in adulthood. The prospective effects of constructs relevant to strain, control, and social learning theories were also studied. The investigation of these latter constructs helped to control for alternative explanations of associations between the two types of deviance and also provided a long-term evaluation of several key propositions from traditional theories of deviance. Effects studied in terms of traditional perspectives are described first, to provide a theoretical background helpful in our subsequent outline of alternative explanations of associations between drug use and criminal deviance.

Effects Consistent with Traditional Theoretical Perspectives

Control, Social Support, and Family Disruption

Constructs from control theories represent one of the sets of variables that should be evaluated in any study of the predictors of deviance, at least as a control of alternative explanations. Control theories have focused on internalization of traditional norms and bonding to conventional institutions/groups as determinants of conformity (e.g., Elliott et al., 1985; Hirschi, 1969; Jessor et al., 1968). One construct relevant to this perspective in our study was social support, as operationalized by measures of quality of personal relationships. In our view, low social support in adolescence is likely to imply poor bonding to socialization groups (e.g., family, parents, adults) that exert normative control over individual behavior. In control theory (e.g., Elliott et al., 1985; Hirschi, 1969), a lack of social support or bonding suggests that the costs associated with deviant behavior will be low. In other words, there is little reason or motivation to comply with normative standards under these circumstances. Without a reason for compliance, deviant behavior patterns may be chosen as an expedient method of obtaining desired goals. Thus, in this perspective, lack of social support is anticipated to predict more deviance and less socially conforming attitudes. Although it is possible that level of social support could also imply level of strain, we considered strain to be manifested primarily through social–emotional security, as outlined in the following section. Social disorganization in the adolescent's family may also reduce social integration or bonding, thereby decreasing the effect of normative sanctions and increasing the likelihood of deviance (Needle, Su, & Doherty, 1990). We used a measure of family disruption to represent this source of disorganization and as a potential predictor of later deviance and lack of social conformity.

Strain and Social–Emotional Security

As reflected in both basic sociological (Cloward, 1959; Merton, 1957) and social–psychological extensions (Jessor et al., 1968), strain theory and its variants have focused on disjunctions between aspirations and abilities to obtain desired goals as precursors to deviance. We selected one construct as a social–psychological counterpart, or reflection, of strain. This construct is social–emotional security, in terms of self-acceptance and low depression. In a social–psychological perspective, it is reasonable to assume that the common variance of these latter indicators reflects the outcomes of previous social interactions as well as the degree of discrepancy between personal goals and achievements. In other words, higher social–emotional security, as a general factor, is likely to reflect a relative absence of strain in a variety of life domains.

Another construct, academic orientation, is relevant to both strain and control theories. In a control theory perspective, adolescents with high grades and academic aspirations are relatively more bonded to conventional institutions (schools) and activities and hence are more susceptible to conventional norms. In a strain theory viewpoint, adolescents with greater academic achievement are more likely to have reached their previous academic goals and should have less strain. However, those with excessive aspirations or a disjunction between achievement and aspirations should be prone to strain and hence deviance. Although in control theory it is appropriate to consider achievement and aspirations as indicators of a more general factor, in strain theory these indicators should diverge in the direction of prediction. Our analytical approach, which is outlined below, addresses these alternative possibilities simultaneously in the prediction of deviance.

Social Learning

Sociological applications of social-learning theory have emphasized the influence of differential association with peer groups as the predominant cause of conformity or deviance (Akers et al., 1979). In our study, differential association was assessed with measures of peer deviance, which should predict deviant behavior and attitudes even after an extended period of time. To the extent that an individual associates with peers who exhibit deviant behavior, the individual should encounter greater normative pressure to engage in deviance. Although normative pressure may be ephemeral in its effects, and may depend on continued participation in the group exerting the pressure, differential association is also likely to affect long-term *informational* social influences (Deutsch & Gerard, 1955) on behavioral and attitudinal tendencies. Deviant peers provide a source of informational social influence, in which processes such as vicarious learning can affect long-term predispositions (Bandura, 1977). In one interpretation of the literature, White (1991) concluded that most studies have found peer influence to be the strongest predictor of both drug use and delinquency.

Alternative Explanations of Associations between Drug Use and Criminal Deviance

There has been an increasing interest in investigating the long-term influences of one particular type of deviant behavior (drug use) on criminal deviance (Dembo et al., 1991; Kandel, Simcha-Fagan, & Davies, 1986b), as well as the effects of drug use on a more general range of outcomes in adulthood (Kandel, Davies, Karus, & Yamaguchi, 1986a; Newcomb & Bentler, 1988a,b; Stacy, Newcomb, & Bentler, 1991a). There are several broad schools of thought regarding the association between these two forms of deviance. Some reviews of this literature suggest that correlations between drug use and criminal behavior are spurious (Fagan & Chin, 1991) and reflect a common ("third-variable") cause rather than a direct causal linkage (also see Donovan & Jessor, 1985; Hirschi, 1969, p. 165; Jessor & Jessor, 1977; Newcomb & McGee, 1991). Other researchers suggest that drug use influences criminal deviance (Dembo et al., 1991), that early antisocial behavior influences drug use (Dishion, Patterson, & Reid, 1988), or that other specific factors account for different forms of deviant behavior (Kandel et al., 1986b). Depending on what type of research is emphasized in one's review, some evidence for each of these interpretations can be found.

This study sheds light on the controversy by studying the drug use–criminal deviance association over an extended period of time, controlling for the effects of a number of variables relevant to traditional theories of deviance. However, because theories of how one form of deviance may influence another form of deviance have received relatively less attention than have traditional theories, we first describe in detail several of the diverse theoretical frameworks that can be used to argue for this relationship.

Adolescent Development

In a general perspective that focuses on adolescent development, drug use is seen as a cause of impaired social functioning. In one version of this perspective, drug use in adolescence may interfere with successful identity formation, which may hinder one's ability to function in adult social roles (Baumrind & Moselle, 1985). Alternatively, drug use may decrease social functioning because of premature involvement in adult roles (Newcomb, 1987; Newcomb & Bentler, 1988a,b). Regardless of the specific intervening processes advanced by these alternatives, a decrease in social function caused by drug use may exacerbate strain and decrease social bonding. Strain may increase, because social aspirations are impeded; strain is likely to increase deviance through the processes discussed earlier and may be reflected in lower social–emotional security. Bonding may decrease, because of ineffective social role performance; decreased bonding or attachment is expected to reduce the controlling function of normative sanctions (Hirschi, 1969) and may be reflected in lower social support as well as increased deviance.[*] However, it is also possible that impaired social development from drug use may impair functioning in ways not well represented by either strain or control propositions.

Social–Psychological Processes

A second perspective emphasizes social–psychological processes that involve differential association and attitudinal effects. Increased involvement in drug use, though probably determined in part by differential association (Akers et al., 1979), is also likely to influence differential association (Stein, Newcomb, & Bentler, 1987). That is, by transiting from a drug nonuser to a drug user, or from little involvement with drugs to greater drug involvement, one is likely to also transit to a social group that is more generally deviant or problem-prone on a variety of dimensions (Hays, Widaman, DiMatteo, & Stacy, 1987; Jessor, 1978, p. 77; Osgood et al., 1988), thereby increasing the chances that normative and informational social influences will promote a diversity of deviant acts. A similar process of broadening scope of influences toward deviance may operate attitudinally, such that once an individual uses drugs in adolescence, the latitude of acceptance (Hovland, Harvey, & Sherif, 1957) of other forms of deviance

---

*Hirschi's theory, however, emphasizes that engaging in "adult" forms of drug use is a symptom or sign of a premature claim to adult status and lack of commitment to conventional age-appropriate activities, which have more etiological significance than drug use per se.

increases. An increased latitude of acceptance of deviance implies that internal standards of acceptance of deviance have liberalized, and previously "bad" behaviors may be seen as "not so bad" or even "good" (Hays et al., 1987). In these complementary attitudinal and differential association approaches, greater involvement with drugs may be seen as a "stepping stone" not only toward use of a wider range of drugs (Kandel, 1975; Kandel & Faust, 1975), but also toward a wider range of deviance.*

Addictive Properties and Legal Status of Drug Use

A third perspective that suggests causal linkages between drug use and criminal deviance relies on the addictive properties and legal status of drugs, rather than on the social–psychological or developmental processes mentioned earlier. In one approach, it is argued that drugs that are both illegal and highly addictive are likely to be associated with more criminally deviant activities. For example, the illegality of hard drugs, coupled with the urgency with which users of some hard drugs (e.g., heroin) seek the next high and avoid withdrawal symptoms, make criminal deviance a likely consequence of hard drug use. Suggestive evidence for this interpretation is provided in a number of studies on narcotics addicts (for a review, see Deschenes, Anglin, & Speckart, 1991) and cocaine addicts (Goldstein, Belluci, Spunt, & Miller, 1991). On the other hand, use of tobacco, though also highly addictive, is legal. The potential importance of con-

---

*It is important to note that Donovan and Jessor (1983) acknowledged that a stage patterning of drug-use involvement is apparent in their data and the data of others (e.g., Kandel, 1975; Newcomb & Bentler, 1986), even though they also argue that a broad class of problem behaviors show syndromelike characteristics (Donovan & Jessor, 1985; Jessor & Jessor, 1977). In this hypothesized syndrome, problem behaviors are seen as resulting more from a common set of causal factors than from an influence of one problem behavior on another. To explain stagelike sequences, the more recent emphasis of this research group has been on increased opportunity to use different drugs as a function of increasing drug involvement (Donovan & Jessor, 1983), though other possibilities were acknowledged in earlier writings (Jessor, 1978; Jessor & Jessor, 1977). The opportunity hypothesis is not inconsistent with the common-cause, or problem-behavior syndrome, explanation. In this syndrome, a problem-prone individual is expected to be predisposed to all behaviors in the syndrome; if there is no opportunity to engage in the behavior, of course, the behavior cannot be performed (also see Cloward, 1959). The opportunity hypothesis is restricted to problem behaviors, such as drug use, in which opportunity logically covaries with increased involvement in problem behavior, but is not logically applicable to forms of deviance, such as many types of criminal behavior, in which opportunity to engage in a behavior does not necessarily vary as a function of increased deviance. Thus, Donovan and Jessor's opportunity hypothesis is consistent with their earlier views, which suggests that when one form of deviance (e.g., crime) is predicted by another (e.g., drug use), it is a spurious association explained by a common cause. However, the social influence and attitudinal approaches summarized earlier are amenable to a nonspurious predictive effect of drug use on deviance.

sidering both the addictive properties and the legality of a given drug is underscored by some findings indicating that tobacco use is not as strongly associated with crime or delinquency as is use of other drugs, such as alcohol (Hirschi, 1969). However, differential association and latitude of acceptance approaches could also account for this finding, because variables from these approaches are likely to covary with legal status.

Disinhibition

Another approach that merits consideration is the view that use of drugs that have certain psychoactive properties leads to the disinhibition of behaviors that are normally under social or self-control. The more diverse evidence for disinhibition is found in alcohol use. Experimental evidence supports the view that alcohol has acute effects on aggression (for a review, see Bushman & Cooper, 1990). Alcohol use also predicts criminal aggression longitudinally (Dembo et al., 1991). Qualitative interview data in the study by Strug, Wish, Johnson, Anderson, Miller, and Sears (1984) also suggest that alcohol is often used with other drugs and during criminal acts. In that study, some respondents reported that alcohol disinhibited their actions and was used deliberately to provide "courage" to commit crimes. In the disinhibition perspective, frequent drinking may predict deviant, aggressive behavior even over an extended period of time, because frequent drinking implies frequent disinhibition, increasing the chances that aggression will be displayed.

General vs. Specific Effects

One final point is relevant to the conceptualization and analysis of alternative theories of deviance. This point concerns the distinction between generality and specificity in social phenomena (Osgood et al., 1988), which has implications for each of the approaches to the drug use–deviance association. In the disinhibition and legality/addiction approaches, for example, only certain (specific) drugs should influence deviance (e.g., drugs that disinhibit behavior or that are illegal and highly addictive). In these approaches, then, specificity in drug use is more important than generality in the prediction of deviance. The differential association and latitude of acceptance frameworks, on the other hand, suggest that any form of (general) drug use in adolescence may increase the likelihood of increased deviance, but that the increase in deviance may be ordered in a stagelike sequence (Hays et al., 1987). That is, the more illicit (and usually counternormative) the drug of choice, the more antisocial deviance may be promoted through the social and attitudinal processes mentioned earlier. However, use of illicit and hard drugs is usually accompanied by use of licit drugs as well, and the extent of polydrug (general) involvement may imply the greatest level of involvement in deviance-prone social groups. As a greater number of different types of drugs are used, not only may one be exposed to a wider range of deviance in peers, but also one's latitude of acceptance toward a variety of deviant acts may broaden. Overall, the differential association and latitude of acceptance viewpoints suggest that a general factor of polydrug use may lead to greater deviance than use of any particular drug; that is, generality in drug use is more important that specificity in predicting deviance. The developmental approach makes a similar general prediction, in that greater polydrug involvement in adolescence should lead to greater impairment of adequate socialization, leading to an increased risk of a range of deviant tendencies in adulthood.

Both Osgood et al. (1988) and Newcomb and Bentler (Newcomb & Bentler, 1988a,b; Newcomb, 1990) have illustrated useful analytical frameworks for differentiating between generality and specificity. In the study presented herein, we apply a similar framework to investigate the predictive effects of both a general factor of drug use and indicators of specific types of drugs on subsequent deviant behavior and attitudes. In this manner, we are able to differentiate among some of the alternative explanations of the links between drug use and deviance summarized earlier. This approach is also applied to the more traditional explanations of deviance, wherein the differentiation between generality and specificity is just as appropriate. The theoretical alternatives were investigated in an 8-year longitudinal study from adolescence to adulthood.

Method

Subjects and Procedure

Respondents were 536 participants (28% men, 72% women) in an ongoing longitudinal study (Newcomb, 1991; Newcomb & Bentler, 1988a,b). This chapter examines two waves of data within the larger study that provided assessments of the constructs of interest over an 8-year interval of time, from late adolescence to adulthood. Subjects were recruited several years earlier for participation in the study from junior high schools sampled to be representative of schools in Los Angeles County (Newcomb & Bentler, 1988a). The mean age of the subjects at the first time of measurement used in this study was 18.9, and was 26.9 (S.D. = 0.92) at the second time of measurement. The sample was predominantly white and middle class; additional descriptive information about the sample was provided in earlier articles (Newcomb & Bentler, 1988a; Stacy, Newcomb, & Bentler, 1991b; Stein et al., 1987), including comparisons with national probability samples (Newcomb & Bentler, 1988a).

The greater percentage of women than men in the study has been an unfortunate feature since initial data collection and obtains because more females than males volunteered to participate. Although this study does not run separate models for males and females, because of the need to maximize the sample size used in our large multivariate models, the linear effects of gender were partialed from the data to help control for possible gender effects.

Newcomb (1992) reported extensive attrition analyses on the most recent wave of measurement, revealing that loss of subjects over the entire length of the study was about 60%. Although this degree of attrition would be considered large in short-term prospective studies, it is not excessive considering the length of time spanned in this study. Furthermore, subject loss was only slightly systematic (Newcomb, 1992). For example, the percentage of variance in attrition in the final wave of measurement, as accounted for by a set of 38 adolescent drug use and personality predictors, was less than 4%. Threats to internal and external validity from attrition (for a discussion, see Dent, 1988) can be considered very small, because attrition was mostly random. In addition, the sample was quite similar, on a variety of measures, to national samples of young adults (Newcomb & Bentler, 1988a). On the basis of these findings and the lack of systematic attrition biases, the results from this sample are likely to be applicable to a population more general than the southern California population from which the sample was recruited.

Measures

Measures were obtained from a self-administered questionnaire mailed to subjects at both times of measurement. Subjects were informed that their responses would be kept secret and private and were protected by a Federal certificate of confidentiality. Athough the validity of self-report measures of drug use is sometimes questioned, previous research indicated that drug-use frequency measures, similar to those used in this study, exhibited a reasonable degree of convergent and discriminant validity (Stacy, Widaman, Hays, & DiMatteo, 1985; Stacy, Flay, Sussman, Brown, Santi, & Best, 1990).

Whenever a sufficient number of items was available, several measures of each construct were summed to form different indicators (subscales) of the constructs. These indicators were then used to reflect latent variable factors (e.g., Bentler, 1989) of their respective constructs, as described below. Descriptive statistics for the indicators are provided in Table 1.

Drug Use

A general factor of drug use during adolescence was represented with five indicators of a latent variable. Each of the indicators was a sum of frequency items, which assessed how often subjects used particular drugs in the last 6 months on 7-point scales ranging from "Never" to "More than once a day."

Table 1.   Summary of Indicator Characteristics

Construct/indicator	Number of items in scale	Frequency			Skew	Kurtosis
		Mean	Range	S.D.		
Adolescence						
Social conformity						
Law abidance	4	13.14	4–20	3.90	−0.20	−0.67
Liberalism	4	10.00	4–19	2.55	0.23	0.10
Religiosity	4	15.41	4–20	3.96	−0.69	−0.28
Criminal deviance						
Confrontations	4	0.38	0–9	1.04	4.19	22.46
Theft	3	1.15	0–18	2.56	3.40	13.57
Property crime	4	0.41	0–12	1.24	4.60	27.39
Peer deviance						
Friends' theft	4	5.27	4–14	1.59	1.57	2.90
Friends' dishonesty	3	7.73	4–20	2.70	0.99	1.26
Friends' violence	2	2.79	2–10	1.07	2.49	11.19
Friends' driving while intoxicated	1	2.10	1–5	1.15	0.83	−0.34
Social–emotional security						
Depression	4	7.62	4–18	3.22	0.89	0.15
Self-acceptance	4	15.97	4–20	3.10	−0.72	0.12
Social support						
Parental support	4	15.93	6–20	3.39	−0.73	−0.19
Family support	4	14.50	4–20	4.11	−0.54	−0.43
Other adult support	4	17.11	7–20	2.28	−0.71	0.37
Peer support	4	16.75	6–20	2.80	−1.12	1.24
Drug use						
Cigarettes	1	2.43	1–7	2.22	1.31	0.04
Alcohol	3	7.51	3–18	3.68	0.41	−1.00
Marijuana	2	3.96	2–13	2.73	1.31	0.56
Hard drugs	14	15.27	14–55	3.79	5.46	39.05
Cocaine	1	1.39	1–6	0.92	2.48	5.52
Academic orientation						
Grade point average	1	2.75	1–4	0.73	0.04	−0.50
Educational aspirations	1	3.91	1–6	1.14	−0.22	−0.31
Family disruption (single-indicator construct)						
Family disruption	1	1.24	1–2	0.42	1.25	−0.45

Table 1. Summary of Indicator Characteristics (*cont.*)

Construct/indicator	Number of items in scale	Frequency			Skew	Kurtosis
		Mean	Range	S.D.		
		Adulthood				
Social conformity						
Law abidance	4	15.02	4–20	3.24	−0.61	0.00
Liberalism	4	9.49	4–18	2.37	0.82	1.32
Religiosity	4	15.39	4–20	4.12	−0.78	−0.16
Criminal deviance						
Confrontations	4	0.12	0–4	0.46	4.68	25.26
Theft	3	0.46	0–15	1.39	4.76	30.98
Property crime	4	0.10	0–6	0.49	7.37	66.80

The five frequency indicators were: cigarette frequency (1 item), alcohol frequency (sum of beer, wine, and liquor), marijuana frequency (sum of marijuana and hashish), hard drug frequency (sum of 14 items, including heroin, barbiturates, amphetamines, and other drugs), and cocaine frequency (1 item).

Peer Deviance

Peer deviance in adolescence was represented by a latent construct with four indicators: friends' theft, friends' violence, friends' dishonesty, and friends' driving while intoxicated (DWI). Each indicator was the sum of multiple items inquiring about the deviant behavior of friends in the last 6 months. Friends' theft was composed of the sum of 4 items measuring how many friends have (1) stolen money from parents, (2) stolen things from kids at school, (3) been arrested for burglary or robbery, and (4) shoplifted. Friends' violence was the sum of 2 items measuring how many friends have (1) carried a deadly weapon and (2) gotten into fights. Friends' dishonesty was the sum of 4 items measuring how many friends have (1) regularly lied to parents, (2) cheated on exams, (3) been suspended from school, and (4) cut class. Friends' DWI was measured with 1 item asking how many friends have driven a car while high on drugs or alcohol. Each of the items was assessed on 5-point scales coded fom "No friends" (1) to "All friends" (5).

Social–Emotional Security

Social–emotional security in adolescence was represented by a latent variable of two indicators: depression and self-acceptance. Depression was measured with the 4-item, bipolar scale of depression from the Bentler Medical–Psychological Inventory (Newcomb, Huba, & Bentler, 1986). Self-acceptance was measured with the 4-item, bipolar scale of self-acceptance from the Bentler Psychological Inventory (Stein, Newcomb, & Bentler, 1986).

Social Support

Social support in adolescence was represented by a latent variable of four 5-item bipolar scales assessing the degree of support experienced from different social reference groups, including support from peers, parents, family, and other adults (Newcomb & Bentler, 1988b). A thorough investigation of the factor structure of this construct has been provided in earlier research (Newcomb & Bentler, 1986). Low social support has been found to predict longitudinally a variety of life problems (Newcomb & Bentler, 1988b).

Academic Orientation and Family Disruption

Academic orientation in adolescence was represented by a latent variable of two indicators: grade-point average (GPA) and educational aspirations. GPA was assessed with 1 item asking respondents to indicate what their approximate GPA was in the last year, on a 4-point scale from D (1) to A (4). Educational aspirations were assessed with one 6-point item asking what level of education the respondent expected to obtain, from some high school (1) to doctor's degree (6). Family disruption in adolescence was assessed with a single, dichotomous item, asking respondents to indicate whether they lived with both parents at home (1) or with only one parent (0). Although only one item was available to measure this latter construct, we included it in our analysis because of its social relevance.

Social Conformity

In both adolescence and adulthood, social conformity represented a latent variable for conforming/deviant attitudes, as in previous research using this construct (Newcomb & Bentler, 1988a,b). The three indicators of this construct were law abidance, (low) liberalism, and religiosity. Each of the three indicators was composed of the sum of four bipolar, 5-point items used in earlier research (Stein et al., 1986). Evidence for the general predictive utility of this latent variable and its indicators can be found in several earlier reports (e.g., Newcomb & Bentler, 1988a,b; Stein et al., 1987).

Criminal Deviance

In both adolescence and adulthood, criminal deviance was represented by a latent variable with three indicators: confrontations, theft, and property crime.

The theft indicator was the sum of 3 items assessing the number of times the respondent had engaged in different types of theft (shoplifting, minor theft, major theft) in the past 6 months. The property crimes indicator was the sum of 4 items assessing the number of times the respondent had engaged in various types of property offenses (trespass, vandalism of workplace or school, arson) in the past 6 months. The confrontations indicator was the sum of 4 items measuring the number of times the respondent had engaged in violent offenses (serious fighting, gang violence, serious harm to other person, and use of deadly weapon) in the past 6 months. Further details about these indicators were provided in earlier research (Huba & Bentler, 1984).

Analytical Procedure

Alternative latent variable path models were analyzed using structural equation modeling (SEM) procedures (e.g., Bentler, 1989; Bentler & Bonett, 1980; MacCallum, 1986). The advantages of using these procedures for the analysis of large path models have been outlined previously (Bentler, 1990; Newcomb, 1990). Use of the SEM procedures of Newcomb and Bentler (e.g., Newcomb, 1990; Newcomb & Bentler, 1988a,b) provides for the evaluation of both general and specific effects. In this approach, specific effects include, for example, prediction of a latent construct from the residual, or unique, component of a measured variable. Consistent with common factor measurement theory (Rummel, 1970), such residual variables are not composed of error variance alone, but include specific variance that is often of theoretical importance. To the extent that specific effects are demonstrated longitudinally, and if they have no reasonable interpretation as method effects (e.g., Stacy et al., 1985), they are more likely to represent effects that have substantive meaning and theoretical relevance. The simultaneous evaluation of both general (factor-to-factor) and specific (indicator-to-factor, factor-to-indicator, and indicator-to-indicator) types of effects is beneficial when indicators and their general factors may diverge in patterns of association with other constructs, and the investigation of such divergence is essential to the approach in this chapter to studying generality vs. specificity.

The EQS program (Bentler, 1989) was used for all SEM procedures, using maximum likelihood estimation. Two indices of model fit from this program, the nonnormed fit index (NNFI) (Bentler & Bonett, 1980) and the comparative fit index (CFI) (Bentler, 1989, 1990), were used to evaluate the fit of the final models. Both of these fit indices are relatively robust to sample size biases compared to alternative fit indices (see Bentler, 1990; Marsh, Balla, & McDonald, 1988). In addition, the χ^2/df ratio is provided. Because of the large size of the models, our primary analyses were conducted on the total sample of subjects. However, we controlled for the possible linear effects of gender in this sample by partialing gender from the data prior to conducting our primary analysis. This was accomplished using traditional regression procedures for obtaining partialed data.

Results

Confirmatory Factor Analysis Models

Before alternative structural models were examined, initial confirmatory factor analysis (CFA) measurement models were estimated to evaluate the latent constructs, their intercorrelations, and hypothesized factor loadings. CFA of the initial measurement model yielded fit values of 0.84 for the NNFI, 0.87 for the CFI, and 2.9 for the χ^2/df ratio. This model did not reach statistical nonsignificance [$\chi^2(355, N = 536) = 1012.02, p \leq 0.001$). Correlations between pairs of measured-variable residuals (unique variances) were added to these models based on Lagrange multiplier modification indices (Chou & Bentler, 1990). This resulted in 22 correlated residuals added to the model. The fit indices for this final CFA model showed that the model fit reasonably well (NNFI $= 0.95$, CFI $= 0.96$, $\chi^2/df = 1.6$). The factor loadings, measured variables, and constructs in this final CFA model are shown in Fig. 1. Correlations among the constructs in these models are provided in Table 2.

Each of the hypothesized factor loadings was significant in the final CFA model (see Fig. 1). The pattern of factor intercorrelations was very similar across the initial and final CFA models (see Table 2), indicating that the addition of correlated residuals did not perturb or alter the basic correlational structure among constructs. The mean absolute difference between correlations in these two models was 0.02, further documenting the close similarity between the two factor correlation matrices.

Of most interest to our concerns here are the longitudinal correlations among constructs from adolescence to adulthood. Many of these longitudinal correlations were significant. In order of decreasing magnitude of the absolute size of correlations, the significant longitudinal correlates of adult social conformity were adolescent social conformity, criminal deviance, peer deviance, drug use, social support, emotional distress, and academic orientation. In order of decreasing magnitude of the absolute size of correlations, the significant longitudinal correlates of adult criminal deviance were adolescent drug use, criminal deviance, peer deviance, and social conformity.

Structural Equation Models

To evaluate the alternative viewpoints outlined in the Introduction, the predictive effects of constructs in adolescence (drug use, social conformity, criminal

Adolescence

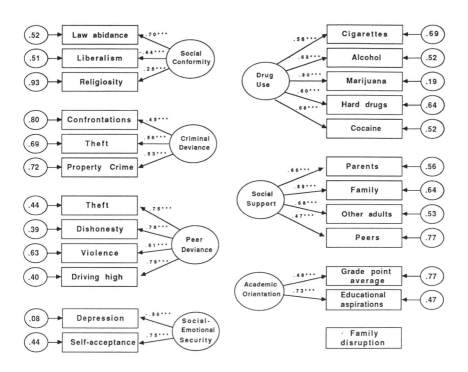

Adulthood

Figure 1. Final CFA model. The large ovals represent latent constructs, the rectangles represent measured variables, and the small ovals represent residual variables, with residual variances shown. Estimates of factor correlations, not shown in the figure, are provided in Table 2. Significance levels are based on critical ratios on unstandardized estimates. ***$p < 0.001$.

deviance, social support, peer deviance, academic orientation, social–emotional security, and family disruption) on the target constructs in adulthood (social conformity and criminal deviance) were estimated. To evaluate the alternative models and their accompanying parameter estimates, the final CFA model was first transformed into an initial SEM, in which directional paths were specified

Table 2. Factor Intercorrelations for the Initial and Final Confirmatory Factor Analysis Measurement Model[a]

	1	2	3	4	5	6	7	8	9	10
					Adolescence					
1. Social conformity	—	-0.80^d	-0.77^d	0.38^d	-0.76^d	0.48^d	0.39^d	-0.17^c	0.67^d	-0.20^b
2. Criminal deviance	-0.73^d	—	0.76^d	-0.20^c	0.52^d	-0.28^d	-0.22^c	0.13^b	-0.41^d	0.24^b
3. Peer deviance	-0.79^d	0.71^d	—	-0.25^d	0.74^d	-0.31^d	-0.38^d	0.14^c	-0.37^d	0.26^d
4. Social–emotional security	0.40^d	-0.20^d	-0.24^d	—	-0.19^d	0.62^d	0.32^d	-0.03	0.20^d	-0.05
5. Drug use	-0.78^d	0.57^d	$.73^d$	-0.20^d	—	-0.26^d	-0.36^d	0.16^d	-0.39^d	0.34^d
6. Social support	0.56^d	-0.27^d	-0.33^d	0.76^d	-0.32^d	—	0.34^d	-0.11^b	0.23^d	-0.13
7. Academic orientation	0.42^d	-0.22^c	-0.39^d	0.32^d	-0.38^d	0.46^d	—	-0.05	0.12	-0.13
8. Family disruption	-0.17^c	0.13^b	0.14^c	-0.04	0.15^b	-0.11^b	-0.05	—	-0.06	0.11
9. Social conformity	0.68^d	-0.42^d	-0.38^d	0.21^d	-0.39^d	0.26^d	0.14	-0.06	—	-0.67^d
10. Criminal deviance	-0.23^b	0.25^b	0.27^d	-0.05	0.35^d	-0.13	-0.13	0.11	-0.67^d	—

[a]Factor intercorrelations from the initial CFA model are above the diagonal; factor intercorrelations from the final CFA model are below the diagonal.
[b-d]Probability: [b]$p < 0.05$; [c]$p < 0.01$; [d]$p < 0.001$.

114

from all adolescent constructs to both adulthood constructs. The statistical significance of paths in this model was evaluated using hierarchical model testing strategies and critical ratios (Bentler & Bonett, 1980). Following the recommendations of MacCallum (1986), the SEM model was first somewhat overfit by adding parameter estimates prior to the removal of nonsignificant estimates. That is, a relatively "saturated" model was first estimated, before it was trimmed to derive the final, best-supported model. Both general and specific effects were estimated in this model.

The first step in deriving the relatively saturated SEM model was the maximum likelihood estimation of paths from constructs assessed in adolescence to constructs assessed in adulthood. Also during this step, correlations among all constructs assessed in adolescence and the correlation between the two construct residuals in adulthood were allowed. According to our previous classification of types of effects (see the Method section), these effects were general effects. The second major step in deriving the saturated model added parameter estimates that we classified earlier as specific effects (i.e., effects other than construct-to-construct). These estimates were longitudinal paths added in hierarchical steps (Newcomb & Bentler, 1988a) on the basis of Lagrange multiplier (LM) tests (Chou & Bentler, 1990). The three types of specific effects outlined in the Method section were evaluated for possible entry into the saturated model. This procedure followed the analytical strategy outlined in previous work on specific effects in SEM models (Stacy et al., 1991a,b).

After deriving the saturated model, we conducted the final stage of model evaluation, in which the Wald test (Chou & Bentler, 1990) was used to delete sets of nonsignificant parameter estimates in "constrained steps" (Stacy et al., 1991b). This procedure deletes small sets of nonsignificant parameters one at a time to avoid the inappropriate removal of parameter estimates that may have been suppressed. Nonsignificant parameter estimates were deleted until no nonsignificant effects remained in this trimmed, final model. The final model derived with these procedures adequately reproduced the sample covariance matrix, according to the practical indices of fit (NNFI = 0.97; CFI = 0.07; χ^2/df = 1.4). The general-effect paths from this model are shown in Fig. 2; specific-effect paths are summarized in Table 3.

Supplementary Model

Although goodness-of-fit indices and parameter estimates with maximum likelihood are reasonably robust to violations of distributional assumptions under a variety of conditions (e.g., Huba & Harlow, 1987; Muthen & Kaplan, 1985), there are some conditions under which violation of the normality assumption may lead to biased χ^2 values and standard errors (Browne, 1984; Hu, Bentler, & Kano, 1991). Because of this concern, we ran several model evaluations, in

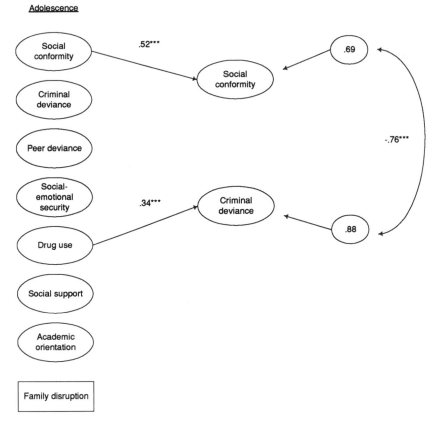

Figure 2. Final SEM and standardized estimates. The large ovals represent latent constructs, the single rectangle represents a measured variable used as a single-indicator construct, and the small ovals represent construct residuals. Path coefficients are depicted with single-headed arrows, and the double-headed arrow represents a correlation between construct residuals. Significance levels are based on critical ratios on unstandardized estimates. ***$p < 0.001$. Several additional regression effects, not depicted in the figure, are given in Table 3.

addition to the aforementioned evaluations, to obtain robust estimates of model fit and significance of parameters. The robust χ^2 estimate was that of Satorra and Bentler (1988), which has recently been found to be more robust than the major alternatives in the analysis of nonnormal data in covariance structure models (Hu et al., 1992). The robust χ^2 was used to compute both NNFI and the χ^2/df ratio. In addition, robust estimates of standard errors (Bentler & Dijkstra, 1985) were used to compute z-tests of the significance of parameter estimates.

The final model derived with robust procedures differed only slightly in overall model fit and in the pattern of significant parameter estimates, when

Table 3. Specific Effects: Across-Time Predictive Paths Not Depicted in Figure 2

Adolescent predictor variable		Adulthood dependent variable		Standardized parameter estimate[b]
Observed (R)[a]	Latent	Observed	Latent	
Specific effects on latent variables				
Alcohol use			Social conformity	-0.21[c]
Effects of latent variables on specific variables				
	Social support	Confrontations		-0.09[c]
Specific effects on specific variables				
Support from adults		Law abidance		0.10[d]
Theft		Law abidance		-0.18[c]
Liberalism		Law abidance		-0.10[d]
GPA		Religiosity		-0.09[c]
Support from peers		Religiosity		-0.07[c]
Theft		Property crime		0.12[d]

[a](R) Variable residual.
[b]Two-tailed tests of significance of parameter estimates are based on critical ratios on unstandardized maximum likelihood estimates.
[c-e]Probability: [c]$p < 0.05$; [d]$p < 0.01$; [e]$p < 0.001$.

compared with the maximum likelihood (ML) results. The robust model fit the data slightly better, with respect to the fit indexes that could be readily computed (NNFI = 0.98; χ^2/df = 1.2). The robust procedures led to slightly fewer significant parameter estimates than did the standard ML procedures. The differences in models involved only specific-effect paths and not general-effect (factor-to-factor) paths. The two paths that dropped to nonsignificance in two-tailed tests were the path from the adolescent social support factor to the confrontations indicator in adulthood and the path from the residual of adolescent theft to property crime in adulthood. The former path, but not the latter path, was still significant ($p < 0.05$) in a one-tailed test.

Paths Most Relevant to Control Theory

Several longitudinal paths from adolescence to adulthood were significant. These paths were specific paths, rather than general paths from factor-to-factor. Paths from the social support factor and its indicators are relevant to control theory, and three of these potential paths were significant. First, the support from adults indicator residual in adolescence positively predicted the law abidance indicator in adulthood. Also, the support from peers indicator residual negatively predicted the religiosity indicator in adulthood; as with all significant paths, we ensured that the sign of this association was not due to suppression effects. Third, the social support factor in adolescence negatively predicted the confrontations indicator in adulthood, in both ML (two-tailed) and robust (one-tailed only) tests. Other paths relevant to control theory were paths from adolescent family disruption and academic orientation, but only one of these potential paths was significant. This path was from one of the indicator residuals of academic orientation (grade-point average) to religiosity in adulthood. The predictors just summarized were each significant at $p < 0.05$ or less using both ML and robust procedures.

Paths Most Relevant to Strain Theory

Paths from academic orientation and its indicators are relevant to strain theory, as well as to control theory, but only one of these potential paths was significant, as described in the preceding paragraph. The only other potential predictors relevant to strain theory were the factor of adolescent social–emotional security and its indicator residuals. None of these predictors was significant using either ML or robust procedures.

Paths Most Relevant to Social Learning/Differential Association Theory

No path directly relevant to differential association postulates of social learning theory was significant using either ML or robust procedures.

Paths Most Relevant to Theories of Deviance–Drug Use Associations

The general-effect path from the adolescent drug use factor to the criminal deviance factor in adulthood was significant according to both ML ($p < 0.001$) and robust ($p < 0.01$) procedures. It is important to note that this was the *only* significant general-effect path predicting criminal deviance in adulthood. To further verify this finding, we ensured that the significance of this path, and the lack of significance of other paths, was not due to suppression effects. Suppression could have occurred, for example, because drug use and criminal deviance in adolescence are highly correlated, and the regression estimates of the effects of these constructs on adulthood criminal deviance could therefore be suppressed and inaccurate (see Cohen & Cohen, 1983). However, classic symptoms of suppression (e.g., Cohen & Cohen, 1983) did not occur when such potentially strong adolescent effects as peer deviance, criminal deviance, and drug use were estimated simultaneously as predictors of adult criminal deviance. The only specific-effect path relevant to drug use–deviance associations was the negative prediction of the adulthood social conformity factor by the alcohol use indicator residual of adolescent drug use ($p < 0.001$ for both procedures).

Other Paths

Only one of the two possible autoregressive paths between the same factor measured over time was significant. This path was between the two assessments of social conformity (see Fig. 2). Three additional significant paths were between indicator residuals of adolescent criminal deviance or social conformity and indicators of adulthood criminal deviance or social conformity (see Table 3). Although we had no a priori justification for these three paths, their significance suggested that it was necessary to include them in the model to avoid the biased estimation of paths of more theoretical relevance.

Discussion

In the Introduction, we summarized a number of diverse perspectives that are available to explain how adolescent social–psychological characteristics may lead to later deviant behavior and attitudes in adulthood. These perspectives include several frameworks that suggest that one form of deviance may influence another form, as well as the traditional theories of strain, control, and differential association. Although our study assessed only a subset of the variables that are relevant to each of these perspectives, the pattern of predictive effects found in this research is consistent with certain theoretical interpretations and inconsistent with others. However, we make no claim to having provided an exhaustive "test" of alternative theories. Instead, the patterns of prediction and lack of prediction provide insight into several perspectives that have not received empirical scrutiny in previous longitudinal research.

Longitudinal Regression Paths

The strongest predictors relevant to alternative theories of deviant behavior and attitudes were the drug use factor and the alcohol use indicator in adolescence. The adolescent drug use factor significantly predicted criminal deviance in adulthood, controlling for the possible predictive effects of each of the other adolescent factors and indicator residuals. The alcohol use indicator residual significantly predicted (less) social conformity in adulthood, also independently from the other predictive effects. The significance tests of these parameter estimates did not vary substantially as a function of type of statistical test used (ML vs. robust).

Although there are several theoretical approaches that could explain these significant predictive effects, it it perhaps best to first point out why these effects do not seem to be spurious. First and foremost, these effects were significant despite the control of the earlier, adolescent effects of criminal deviance and social conformity. Second, these effects remained intact, even though many other potentially important influences on deviance (e.g., peer deviance) were analyzed in the model. Though it is always possible that an unmeasured "third variable" may account for the effects of adolescent drug use, many of the stronger correlates of drug use and criminal deviance were examined in the model.

Because the effects of drug use that we obtained may not be spurious, it is reasonable to consider the processes that may account for, or mediate, these effects. Without an explicit evaluation of intervening (or mediating) variables that elaborate the association between adolescent drug use and adult deviance, we must consider a range of plausible explanations of this association. Nevertheless, the existence of the associations in the absence of other effects does limit this range in ways that have important implications. For example, the absence of predictive effects of adolescent peer deviance on adult deviance is inconsistent not only with differential association effects over this time period but also with the view that effects of adolescent drug use would operate only indirectly through peer deviance; in this hypothesis, based on earlier reasoning outlined in the Introduction and elsewhere (e.g., Hays et al., 1987), more extensive drug users may associate with more deviant peers, but deviant peers may constitute the only direct influence on deviant behavior. No support for this hypothesis was obtained in this study, because peer deviance should have remained significant as a predictor in the SEM analysis, whereas adolescent drug use should have dropped to nonsignificance to maintain consistency with the hypothesis.

A similar line of reasoning can be applied to the latitude-of-acceptance hypothesis. This perspective suggests that drug use, and especially a wide range of drug use as reflected by a general factor of polydrug use, may lead to an attitudinal "stepping stone" toward an increased range of deviance. This attitudinal effect does not necessarily depend on an increased association with deviant peers. Instead, the effect depends on a more lenient attitude and increased tolerance of a wide range of deviant behavior. However, the social conformity factor in adolescence, which reflects attitudes toward a range of socially conforming and deviant behaviors, did not directly predict the criminal deviance factor in adulthood. If adolescent drug use influenced criminal deviance in adulthood through deviant attitudes, then the path from adolescent social conformity to criminal deviance in adulthood should have been significant, while the drug use–criminal deviance path should have dropped to nonsignificance. Although it is possible that social conformity does not fully or adequately reflect the latitude-of-acceptance construct as traditionally defined (Hovland et al., 1957), the absence of the social conformity path is still not consistent with attitudinal approaches.

Another set of hypotheses that do not find general support from our results includes notions that rely on use of specific drugs to predict deviance. These approaches rely on the disinhibiting, addictive, and illegal properties of some drugs as mediators of drug effects on deviance. Although there is evidence for acute disinhibiting effects of some specific drugs on behavior (e.g., Bushman & Cooper, 1990), chronic or long-term effects of specific drugs on criminal deviance were not apparent in the data of this study. However, one specific effect of a particular drug on deviant attitudes was found, in the prediction of (lower) social conformity by the alcohol use indicator residual.

Theories that predict effects of a general factor of polydrug use on deviance, unmediated by differential association, specific drug effects, or attitude, are most consistent with the pattern of findings obtained. One set of these theories could not be ruled out by the presence of contradictory associations. Theories of delayed development (Baumrind & Moselle, 1985) or truncated development (Newcomb & Bentler, 1988a,b) suggest that a greater degree of polydrug involvement would predict later life problems, which may include the exhibition of deviant behavior. This effect could occur through increased strain or decreased bonding in adolescence, or both, or it could occur through a more general ineffectiveness in social relationships (e.g., Newcomb & Bentler, 1988a). However, it is likely that increased strain would have been mediated through less social–emotional security and that decreased bonding would have been mediated through less social support or lower academic orientation. Because drug use predicted criminal deviance despite the control of the predictive effects just mentioned, a strain or control theory interpretation of impaired development does not find support in these data. Other types of potential developmental effects in adolescence were not assessed in this study, but may mediate the drug use–criminal deviance association. These effects include negative effects of drug use on the development of social skills, coping abilities, and other qualities that lead to effective social role functioning in adulthood (Baumrind & Moselle, 1985; Newcomb & Bentler, 1988a).

In addition to the plausible, but unsupported, mediation of strain through social–emotional security, strain could have had an effect through higher academic orientation or through a disjunction between educational aspirations and achievement (GPA). The former possibility was not supported in the SEM analysis. To evaluate the later (disjunction) hypothesis, we performed a series of supplementary multiple regression analyses, in which the aspiration–achievement interaction was tested for statistical significance. In these analyses, the hierarchical regression procedures of Aiken and West (1991) were followed to evaluate the interaction. Even when only the two "main effects" (deviation scores for educational aspiration and GPA) were entered into the hierarchical regression before the interaction effect (the product of deviation scores of educational aspirations and GPA), the interaction was not significant.

One effect highly relevant to control theory was found to be significant, though it was of only marginal significance when robust estimation procedures were used. This effect was the negative prediction of the confrontations indicator of criminal deviance in adulthood by the social support factor in adolescence. This effect is consistent with the notion that less attachment to important social groups indicates a relative absence of countervailing influences on deviant behavior (e.g., Hirschi, 1969). It is particularly relevant that the general factor of social support, rather than any particular indicator of social support, predicted confrontations. In alternative viewpoints, as in some interpretations of peer group theory (e.g., Hirschi, 1969), higher peer social support would be indicative of a greater risk for deviance. Because this specific effect was not found, and because the effect of social support was negative rather than positive, the control theory viewpoint is more consistent with the data. It should be underscored, however, that only a particular form of deviance was predicted by social support: confrontations. It may be noteworthy that a particularly "antisocial" behavior involving physical harm to the victim, rather than harm to property, was predicted by lower levels of social support. This pattern of findings further documents the importance of differentiating between generality and specificity in social–psychological and sociological processes (Osgood et al., 1988).

Bivariate Associations

Because of the extensive time interval between waves of measures used in this study, it is possible that some theoretically important associations were not detected. More specifically, some social–psychological processes may operate within a much shorter time interval than the one examined herein. Among the more likely associations that may have been detectable in a shorter time span are the ones that were significant in the confirmatory factor analysis (CFA) model, which provided estimates before controlling for the predictive effects of other constructs in the structural equation modeling (SEM) model. Indeed, several longitudinal associations among constructs were significant in the CFA model, but were nonsignificant in the SEM model. These longitudinal correlates of adulthood criminal deviance included adolescent levels of criminal deviance, peer deviance, and (less) social conformity. Longitudinal correlates of adulthood social conformity that were not significant in the SEM model included lower adolescent levels of criminal deviance, social support, and academic orientation, as well as higher levels of adolescent emotional distress. It may be fruitful for future research to examine whether these associations can be detected in SEM prospective models using shorter intervals of time between waves of measurement.

The cross-sectional correlates of deviance and conformity in adolescence should also be mentioned briefly. Each of the estimated correlations of criminal deviance and social conformity with other constructs in adolescence was statistically significant in the CFA model. Peer deviance and drug use were the strongest cross-sectional correlates of criminal deviance and (less) social conformity, followed by lower social support, lower academic orientation, higher emotional distress, and higher family disruption. The existence of several very strong correlations, especially involving peer deviance, suggests further that some prospective associations might have been detectable in a shorter-term longitudinal study. However, it is also possible that the selection of deviant peers as friends and the influence by deviant peers are so intertwined during short intervals of time that questions about the predictive precedence of selection vs. peer influence cannot be answered unequivocally.

Limitations

The first limitation we address follows directly from the preceding discussion. This limitation concerns the two-wave design and the time interval used in our study. Each of the interpretations based on our regression effects assumed that if the constructs assessed in adolescence had causal effects, they would have shown significant predictive effects in the models analyzed. However, it is possible that some of these constructs had effects that were not captured by the time interval evaluated in this study. For example, it is possible that although constructs assessed in adolescence relevant to strain or differential association theory were not predictive, these same constructs might have shown effects if they had been measured in an intervening time period between our two waves of measures. This possibility suggests that effects of drug use on deviance could have been mediated through some of the processes mentioned earlier, though these processes found no support from the data obtained in adolescence. Because the statistical significance of predictive effects often depends on the time interval between assessments, it is likely that no single interval of time will be generalizable to all possible intervals of time. This issue may be particularly relevant to this study, because respondents were first assessed during a typical "peak" period of deviance (late adolescence), followed by an assessment in adulthood, a period known for significant levels of "maturing out" (see Hirschi & Gottfredson, 1983). The pattern of means in our study across adolescent and adult assessments of deviance and conformity mostly conforms to these age trends.

Another potential limitation is the sampling design of this study. It is possible that the sample is not representative of a large, general population, because the respondents did not constitute a national probability sample. Earlier in this chapter, however, we cited evidence that our sample of respondents was similar in important dimensions to national probability samples obtained in other research. Finally, for some of the theoretical perspectives addressed, we had available only a few of the relevant variables. Nevertheless, a number of plausible hypotheses of associations between drug use and deviance were shown to be unlikely, whereas several alternative hypotheses were found to be deserving of more theoretical and empirical attention.

ACKNOWLEDGMENT.   Support for this research was provided by research grant DA01070 from the National Institute on Drug Abuse.

References

Aiken, L. S., & West, S. G. (1991). *Multiple regression: Testing and interpreting interactions.* Newbury Park, CA: Sage Publications.

Akers, R. L., Krohn, M. D., Lanza-Kaduce, L., & Radosevich, M. (1979). Social learning and deviant behavior: A specific test of a general theory. *American Sociological Review, 44,* 636–655.

Bandura, A. (1977). *Social learning theory.* Englewood Cliffs, NJ: Prentice-Hall.

Baumrind, D., & Moselle, K. A. (1985). A developmental perspective on adolescent drug use. *Advances in Alcohol and Substance Use, 5,* 41–67.

Bentler, P. M. (1989). *EQS structural equations program manual.* Los Angeles: BMDP Statistical Software.

Bentler, P. M. (1990). Comparative fit indexes in structural models. *Psychological Bulletin, 107,* 238–246.

Bentler, P. M., & Bonett, D. G. (1980). Significance tests and goodness of fit in the analysis of covariance structures. *Psychological Bulletin, 88,* 588–606.

Bentler, P. M., & Dijkstra, T. (1985). Efficient estimation via linearization in structural models. In P. R. Krishnaiah (Ed.), *Multivariate analysis VI* (pp. 9–42). Amsterdam: North-Holland.

Browne, M. W. (1984). Asymptotically distribution-free methods for the analysis of covariance structures. *British Journal of Mathematical and Statistical Psychology, 37,* 62–83.

Bushman, B. J., & Cooper, H. M. (1990). Effects of alcohol on human aggression: An integrative research review. *Psychological Bulletin, 107,* 341–354.

Chou, C. P., & Bentler, P. M. (1990). Model modification in covariance structure modeling: A comparison among likelihood ratio, Lagrange multiplier, and Wald tests. *Multivariate Behavioral Research, 25,* 115–136.

Cloward, R. A. (1959). Illegitimate means, anomie, and deviant behavior. *American Sociology Review, 24,* 164–176.

Cohen, J., & Cohen, P. (1983). *Applied multiple regression/correlation analysis for the behavioral sciences,* 2nd ed. Hillsdale, NJ: Lawrence Erlbaum.

Dembo, R., Williams, L., Getreu, A., Genung, L., Schmeidler, J., Berry, E., Wish, E. D., & La Voie, L. (1991). A longitudinal study of the relationships among marijuana/hashish use, cocaine use and delinquency in a cohort of high risk youths. *Journal of Drug Issues, 21,* 271–312.

Dent, C. W. (1988). Using SAS linear models to assess and correct for attrition bias. *SAS User's Group International Proceedings of the 13th Annual Conference, 13,* 54–659.

Deschenes, E. P., Anglin, M. D., & Speckart, G. (1991). Narcotics addiction: Related criminal careers, social and economic costs. *Journal of Drug Issues, 21,* 383–411.

Deutsch, M., & Gerard, H. B. (1955). A study of normative and informational social influences upon individual judgment. *Journal of Abnormal and Social Psychology, 51,* 629–636.

Dishion, T. J., Patterson, G. R., & Reid, J. R. (1988). Parent and peer factors associated with drug sampling in early adolescence: Implications for treatment. In National Institute on Drug Abuse (Ed.), *Adolescent drug abuse: Analysis of treatment research* (pp. 64–93). Washington, DC: National Institute on Drug Abuse.

Donovan, J. E., & Jessor, R. (1983). Problem drinking and the dimensions of involvement with drugs: A Guttman scalogram analysis of adolescent drug use. *American Journal of Public Health, 73,* 543–552.

Donovan, J. E., & Jessor, R. (1985). Structure of problem behavior in adolescence and young adulthood. *Journal of Consulting and Clinical Psychology, 53,* 890–904.

Elliott, D. S., Huizinga, D., & Ageton, S. S. (1985). *Explaining delinquency and drug use.* Newbury Park, CA: Sage Publications.

Fagan, J., & Chin, K. (1991). Social processes of initiation into crack. *Journal of Drug Issues, 21,* 313–343.

Goldstein, P. J., Bellucci, P. A., Spunt, B. J., & Miller, T. (1991). Volume of cocaine use and violence: A comparison between men and women. *Journal of Drug Issue, 21,* 345–367.

Hays, R. D., Widaman, K. F., DiMatteo, M. R., & Stacy, A. W. (1987). Structural equation models of current drug use: Are appropriate models so simple(x)? *Journal of Personality and Social Psychology, 52,* 134–144.

Hirschi, T. (1969). *Causes of delinquency.* Los Angeles: University of California Press.

Hirschi, T., & Gottfredson, M. (1983). Age and the explanation of crime. *American Journal of Sociology, 89,* 552–584.

Hovland, C. I., Harvey, O. J., & Sherif, M. (1957). Assimilation and contrast effects in reactions to communication and attitude change. *Jornal of Abnormal and Social Psychology, 55,* 244–252.

Hu, L., Bentler, P. M., & Kano, Y. (1992). Can test statistics in covariance structure analysis be trusted? *Psychosocial Bulletin, 112,* 351–362.

Huba, G. J., & Bentler, P. M. (1984). Causal models of personality, peer culture characteristics, drug use and criminal behaviors over a five year span. In D. W. Goodwin, K. T. Van Dusen, & S. A. Mednick (Eds.), *Longitudinal research in alcoholism* (pp. 73–94). Boston: Kluwer-Nijhoff.

Huba, G. J., & Harlow, L. L. (1987). Robust structural equation models: Implications for developmental psychology. *Child Development, 58,* 147–166.

Jessor, R. (1978). Psychosocial factors in the patterning of drinking behavior. In J. Fishman (Ed.), *The bases of addiction* (pp. 67–80). Berlin: Dahlem Konferenzen.

Jessor, R., & Jessor, S. L. (1977). *Problem behavior and psychosocial development: A longitudinal study of youth.* New York: Academic Press.

Jessor, R., Graves, T. D., Hanson, R. C., & Jessor, S. L. (1968). *Society, personality, and deviant behavior: A study of a tri-ethnic community.* New York: Holt, Rinehart, & Winston.

Johnson, B., Wish, E. D., Schmeidler, J., & Huizinga, D. (1991). Concentration of delinquent offending: Serious drug involvement and high delinquency rates. *Journal of Drug Issues, 21,* 205–229.

Kandel, D. (1975). Stages in adolescent involvement in drug use. *Science, 190*, 912–914.

Kandel, D. B., & Faust, R. (1975). Sequence and stages in patterns of adolescent drug use. *Archives of General Psychiatry, 32*, 923–932.

Kandel, D. B., Davies, M., Karus, D., & Yamaguchi, K. (1986a). The consequences in young adulthood of adolescent drug involvement. *Archives of General Psychiatry, 43*, 746–754.

Kandel, D., Simcha-Fagan, O., & Davies, M. (1986b). Risk factors for delinquency and illicit drug use from adolescence to young adulthood. *Journal of Drug Issues, 16*, 67–90.

Kaplan, H. B. (1985). Testing a general theory of drug abuse and other deviant adaptations. *Journal of Drug Issues, 15*, 477–492.

Loeber, R., & Dishion, T. (1983). Early predictors of male delinquency: A review. *Psychological Bulletin, 94*, 68–99.

MacCallum, R. (1986). Specification searches in covariance structure modeling. *Psychological Bulletin, 100*, 107–120.

Marsh, H. W., Balla, J. R., & McDonald, R. P. 1988. Goodness-of-fit indices in confirmatory factor analysis: The effect of sample size. *Psychological Bulletin, 103*, 391–410.

Merton, R. K. (1957). *Social theory and social structure*. Glencoe, NY: Free Press.

Muthén, B., & Kaplan, D. (1985). A comparison of some methodologies for the factor analysis of non-normal Likert variables. *British Journal of Mathematical and Statistical Psychology, 38*, 171–189.

Needle, R. H., Su, S. S., & Doherty, W. J. (1990). Divorce, remarriage, and adolescent substance use: A prospective longitudinal study. *Journal of Marriage and the Family, 52*, 157–169.

Newcomb, M. D. (1987). Consequences of teenage drug use: The transition from adolescence to young adulthood. *Drugs and Society, 1*, 25–60.

Newcomb, M. D. (1990). What structural equation modeling can tell us about social support. In B. R. Sarason, I. G. Sarason, & G. R. Pierce (Eds.), *Social support: An interactional view* (pp. 26–63). New York: John Wiley.

Newcomb, M. D. (1992). Understanding the multidimensional nature of drug use and abuse: The role of consumption, risk factors, and protective factors. In M. D. Glantz & R. Pickens (Eds.), *Vulnerability to drug abuse* (pp. 255–297). Washington, DC: American Psychological Association.

Newcomb, M. D., & Bentler, P. M. (1986). Frequency and sequence of drug use: A longitudinal study from early adolescence to young adulthood. *Journal of Drug Education, 16*, 101–120.

Newcomb, M. D., & Bentler, P. M. (1988a). *Consequences of adolescent drug use: Impact on the lives of young adults*. Beverly Hills: Sage Publications.

Newcomb, M. D., & Bentler, P. M. (1988b). Impact of adolescent drug use and social support on problems of young adults: A longitudinal study. *Journal of Abnormal Psychology, 97*, 64–75.

Newcomb, M. D., & McGee, L. (1991). The influence of sensation seeking on general and specific problem behaviors from adolescence to young adulthood. *Journal of Personality and Social Psychology, 61*, 614–628.

Newcomb, M. D., Huba, G. J., & Bentler, P. M. (1986). Life change events among adolescents: An empirical consideration of some methodological issues. *Journal of Nervous and Mental Disease, 174*, 280–289.

Osgood, D. W., Johnston, L. D., O'Malley, P. M., & Bachman, J. G. (1988). The generality of deviance in late adolescence and early adulthood. *American Sociological Review, 53*, 81–93.

Rummel, R. J. (1970). *Applied factor analysis*. Evanston, IL: Northwestern University Press.

Satorra, A., & Bentler, P. M. (1988). Scaling corrections for chi-square statistics in covariance structure analysis. *Proceedings of the Business and Economic Statistics Section of the American Statistical Association*, pp. 308–313.

Stacy, A. W., Widaman, K. F., Hays, R., & DiMatteo, M. R. (1985). Validity of self-reports of alcohol and other drug use: A multitrait–multimethod assessment. *Journal of Personality and Social Psychology, 49,* 219–232.

Stacy, A. W., Flay, B. R., Sussman, S., Brown, K. S., Santi, S., & Best, J. A. (1990). Validity of alternative self-report indices of smoking among adolescents. *Psychological Assessment: A Journal of Consulting and Clinical Psychology, 2,* 442–446.

Stacy, A. W., Newcomb, M. D., & Bentler, P. M. (1991a). Cognitive motivation and problem drug use: A nine-year longitudinal study. *Journal of Abnormal Psychology, 100,* 502–515.

Stacy, A. W., Newcomb, M. D., & Bentler, P. M. (1991b). Personality, problem drinking, and drunk driving: Mediating, moderating, and direct effect models. *Journal of Personality and Social Psychology, 60,* 795–811.

Stein, J. A., Newcomb, M. D., & Bentler, P. M. (1986). Stability and change in personality: A longitudinal study from early adolescence to young adulthood. *Journal of Research in Personality, 20,* 276–291.

Stein, J. A., Newcomb, M. D., & Bentler, P. M. (1987). An 8-year study of multiple influences on drug use and drug use consequences. *Journal of Personality and Social Psychology, 53,* 1094–1105.

Strug, D., Wish, E., Johnson, B. D., Anderson, K., Miller, T., & Sears, A. (1984). The role of alcohol in the crimes of heroin users. *Crime and Delinquency, 30,* 551–567.

White, H. R. (1991). Marijuana use and delinquency: A test of the "independent cause" hypothesis. *Journal of Drug Issues, 21,* 231–256.

5

Relationship between Alcoholism and Crime over the Life Course

Joan McCord

Introduction

Two facts have colored perceptions of the role alcohol plays in producing crimes. First, the rise of modern criminology accompanied movement toward the prohibition of drinking alcoholic beverages. Second, drinking often accompanies criminal incidents either because crimes occur where victims are drinking or because criminals had been drinking at the time they committed crimes.

Criminology as a field of research developed in the midst of claims regarding the putative causal potency of intoxicating beverages in relation to most forms of social ills. The received opinion about the role of alcohol has seldom been questioned, and research has focused on examining conditions under which alcohol increases aggression (Fagan, 1990; Pernanen, 1981, 1991). Of course, not all drinking leads to alcoholism, but because alcoholism is widely seen to be a potential consequence of the use of alcohol, a study of relations between alcoholism and criminality over the life course can enlighten the debate. The study presented in this chapter inspects the assumption that alcohol increases the probability of criminality by considering alcoholism from a longitudinal perspective.

Joan McCord • Department of Criminal Justice, Temple University, Philadelphia, Pennsylvania 19122.

Drugs, Crime, and Other Deviant Adaptations: Longitudinal Studies, edited by Howard B. Kaplan. Plenum Press, New York, 1995.

The Rise of Prohibition and Criminology

Evidence about the relation between drinking alcohol and aggressive criminality is colored by the concurrent birth of criminology as a discipline and the Prohibition movement. Problems believed to be related to public drinking gave rise to a variety of regulations for its control during the first half of the 19th century (Dunford, 1945). By 1874, the Supreme Court had made the manufacture and sale of liquor a privilege rather than a right, and in 1887 the Court ruled that it was unnecessary to compensate owners for confiscated liquor or equipment to manufacture liquor. Between 1900 and passage of the Hobson Resolution, which restricted sale, manufacture for sale, and transportation for sale of intoxicating liquor in December 1914, a series of restrictive laws were passed by Congress. By 1917, when legislators introduced the resolution that became the 18th Amendment, which prohibited "manufacture, sale, or transportation of intoxicating liquors within, the importation thereof into, or the exportation thereof from the United States and all territory subject to the jurisdiction thereof for beverage purposes," 26 states had outlawed the sale of liquor.

Although local elections revealed resistance to the temperance movement, those favoring Prohibition claimed that alcohol was at least indirectly responsible for "degeneracy, pauperism, poverty, disease, and crime." The sociologist George Elliott Howard (1918) asserted (pp. 61–62) that scientists had proven that alcohol "impairs the judgment, clouds the reason, and enfeebles the will; while at the same time it arouses the appetites, inflames the passions, releases the primitive beast from the artificial restraint of social discipline."

Howard relied partly on figures showing that in Germany, Italy, France, and the United States, crimes of violence rose sharply during holidays when liquor flowed most freely. Using similar reasoning, the criminologist Enrico Ferri (1897) tracked wine consumption and crime in France between 1829 and 1887. He summarized the results (p. 117): "Despite a certain inevitable variation from year to year, there is a manifest correspondence of increase and decrease between the number of homicides, assaults, and malicious wounding, and the more or less abundant vintage." Cesare Lombroso (1912/1968), considered by many to be the father of modern criminology, estimated that alcoholism was a contributing cause in about three quarters of the crimes in England. Charles Goring (1913), who compared Cambridge students with British prisoners, reported a correlation of 0.39 between alcoholism and criminality.

More recent studies parallel such claims, relying on similarly coincidental patterns. Wolfgang and Strohm (1956) and Wolfgang (1958), for example, noted that alcohol was more likely to be a factor in homicides committed Friday through Sunday than in those committed Monday through Thursday (70% vs. 50%). Goodman, Mercy, Loya, Rosenberg, Smith, Allen, Vargas, and Kolts (1986) reported figures for Los Angeles: Over the decade 1970–1979, 51% of male victims and 26% of female victims were found to have alcohol in their blood. As in Philadelphia, alcohol was more likely to be present in victims during the weekend, and victims killed in bars or restaurants were likely to have been drinking. Those killed by friends or acquaintances and those killed with knives or other cutting weapons, the report continued, were most likely to have alcohol in their blood. Although the researchers themselves recognize that without information about drinking among relevant general populations, the data do not support causal hypotheses, their work has contributed to a view that alcohol causes crime.

A display of drinking rates among offenders or during criminal events characterizes modern discussions of the relationship between alcohol and crime. For example, Shupe (1954) analyzed reports of the urine alcohol concentrations of 882 suspects in Columbus, Ohio. The proportion whose urine exceeded 0.10% blood alcohol ranged from 43% for felonious assault to 88% for knifing. Wolfgang and Strohm (1956) and Wolfgang (1958), discussing homicides committed between 1948 and 1952 in Philadelphia, reported that alcohol was involved in 64% of the situations. Alcohol was present in victims only in 9% of cases, in offenders only in 11%, and in both victims and offenders in 44%.

The Bureau of Justice Statistics surveys of jails provide estimates of the proportion of inmates who were under the influence of either drugs or alcohol at the time an offense was committed. In 1989, among those convicted for violent offenses, 47% reported being under the influence of alcohol; among those convicted for property offenses, 31% so reported (Flanagan & Maguire, 1992). Slightly over half the 1986 inmates in state corrections facilities who had been incarcerated for violent crimes were under the influence of either alcohol or drugs when committing crimes (Innes & Greenfeld, 1990). Among the 245,562 inmates in the study, only 36% of the convicts reported that neither they nor their victims had been using drugs or alcohol at the time of the violent crimes that put them in prison.

There is little reason to doubt that many habitual criminals have problems with drinking. In one study, 43% of 223 consecutive releases from prisons and reformatories were diagnosed as alcoholics (Guze, 1976). Comparing violent with nonviolent recidivists, violent criminals have been found more likely to be alcoholics, younger, and less intelligent than nonviolent ones (Nicol, Gunn, Griswood, Foggitt, & Watson, 1973).

Nor does there seem to be reason to doubt that a sizeable number of criminals were drinking at the time they committed crimes. The proportion varies by type of crime, with crimes of violence more likely than crimes against property to involve alcohol (Amir, 1971; Banay, 1942, 1945; Bohman, Cloninger, Sigvardsson, & von Knorring, 1982, 1983; Collins, 1981; Flanagan & Maguire, 1992; Gerson & Preston, 1979; Murdoch, Pihl, & Ross, 1990; Nicol et al., 1973; Virkkunen, 1974; Wikström, 1985). Questions regarding whether the co-occurrence of drinking and crime ought to be interpreted as showing that alcohol contributes to criminality, however, deserve more careful consideration.

A study by Bard and Zacker (1974) raises doubts that alcohol is a contributing factor in violence. They examined police reports of calls for family crises. These calls involved 1358 occasions among 962 families. Disputes that did *not* involve assault were about twice as likely to have included alcohol as those that did.

In sum, the debate over Prohibition left as its legacy a style of displaying rates of alcohol-related crime in isolation from contextual information valuable to its interpretation. The rates leave an impression that alcohol contributes to crime, although they do not show that drinking is more common among criminals than among noncriminals who share their neighborhoods and social backgrounds.

Alcoholism and Delinquent Life-styles

An alternative to the view that alcohol increases violence has been suggested in theories that postulate a general underlying tendency toward deviant activities (Donovan & Jessor, 1985; Gottfredson & Hirschi, 1990; Jessor & Jessor, 1984; Kaplan, 1980; Kaplan, Johnson, & Bailey, 1986, 1987; Robins, 1978; Smith & Newman, 1990). Support comes from studies showing that heavy drinking and aggressive behavior are parts of a life-style for many delinquents (Farrington, 1979; Pulkkinen & Hurme, 1984). Jones (1968) traced a community sample of white, American-born, urban, predominantly middle-class subjects from age 10 to their mid-40s. He found that those who became problem drinkers had been undercontrolled, rebellious, assertive, aggressive, and sometimes sadistic in their school years. Others have found relatively high rates of subsequent alcoholism among juvenile delinquents, and many alcoholics report histories of juvenile delinquency (Collins, 1981; Lindelius & Salum, 1973; J. McCord, 1980; W. McCord & J. McCord, 1960; Zucker & Gomberg, 1986).

Several studies provide evidence that alcoholics can often be found among serious recidivist criminals. Some of these studies show that alcoholics with a high degree of familial alcoholism also tend to meet criteria for DSM-III antisocial personality disorder (Alterman, Gerstley, Strohmetz, & McKay, 1991; Lewis, Rice, & Helzer, 1983; Yates, Petty, & Brown, 1988). Hesselbrock, Stabenau, Hesselbrock, Roger, and Babor (1982) found that with bilineal family histories of alcoholism, probands were more likely to be arrested, have accidents, and show loss of control with drinking. Similarly, McKenna and Pickens (1981, 1983) found that among chronic alcoholic patients in a rehabilitation center, those who had two alcoholic parents were most likely to become alcoholics at earlier ages, to have been suspended from school, and to have been arrested.

Schuckit (1984) analyzed family histories among 99 consecutive admissions of primary alcoholics to an alcohol treatment program. He found that those having two alcoholic parents were youngest and were most likely to have been convicted as incorrigible. Similar results were obtained in a study of 137 men convicted of driving while intoxicated (Harwood & Leonard, 1989).

Early onset, for both alcoholism and criminality, presages particularly severe problems (Blumstein, Cohen, Roth, & Visher, 1986; Farrington, 1983, 1986; Foulds & Hassall, 1969; J. McCord, 1981a; Schuckit, 1973; Schuckit, Rimmer, & Winokur, 1970; Stabenau, 1984; Wolfgang, Figlio, & Sellin, 1972). Recent longitudinal evidence also suggests that early delinquency is linked with the early use of alcohol (van Kammen, Loeber, & Stouthamer-Loeber, 1991). Plausibly, then, one could argue that alcoholism and criminality are symptoms of a single underlying dimension.

Yet doubts about the sufficiency of explaining alcoholism and criminality in terms of an underlying single dimension arise from at least two sources. In one study, adolescents aged 11–17 in 1976 were restudied periodically through 1983 (Elliott, Huizinga, & Menard, 1989). The results showed that teenagers who used drugs typically also committed minor delinquencies, although there was little overlap between drug use and serious criminal activity. In another study, high school seniors were retraced to age 21 or 22 (Osgood, Johnston, O'Malley, & Bachman, 1988). The authors were able to identify a relatively stable general factor of deviance, accounting for most of the association among criminal behavior, heavy drinking, marijuana use, use of other illicit drugs, and dangerous driving. That general tendency toward deviance, however, became less significant over time.

In order to increase understanding of relations between alcoholism and criminality, this study considers life histories of 205 subjects reared in Cambridge and Somerville, Massachusetts.

Methods

Designed to assist families living in pockets of poverty in the greater Boston area, the Cambridge–Somerville Youth Study included both "difficult" and "average" boys (Powers & Witmer, 1951). The boys were born between 1926 and 1934, with the mean and mode in 1928. A selection committee identified pairs of children they considered similar in terms of conditions thought to cause delinquency. Selection included teachers' reports collected between 1933 and 1938. A toss of a coin determined which member of each pair would receive treatment.

The larger study included 253 pairs of boys. The boys in the treatment group were visited, on average, twice a month over a period of 5.5 years. Shortly after each visit, counselors reported details about their interaction with the boys and with members of the family. Because records for the control group had been based largely on interviews with the mothers and the boys, evidence about the boys' behavior lacked the detail present in records for the treatment group.

Between 1978 and 1982, the boys—by then middle-aged men—were re-traced. Records, questionnaire responses, and interviews provide data for this study.

The boys were between the ages of 4 and 9 years (mean = 7.5) when their teachers described them by checking descriptive phrases on a "Trait Record Card." Boys were considered to have been disruptive in childhood if their teachers checked "fights" as part of the description or if their teachers checked more than three of the following: blames others for his difficulties; secretive, crafty, sly; rude, saucy, impudent; disobeys; refuses to cooperate; cruel; cheats; lies; steals; destroys property.

A measure of adolescent behavior was coded from the records describing what went on over a period of approximately 5.5 years between 1939 and 1945, when social workers visited the homes in order to provide a variety of types of assistance to the boys and their families. On average, the boys were 10.5 at the start of treatment and 16 when it ended. These records were coded in 1957.

Adolescents were considered to have delinquency-prone lifestyles if they had been convicted for any crime prior to reaching the age of 18 years or had been heavy smokers or had a delinquent reference group. Both smoking and reference groups had been coded in 1957. In the 10% random sample of cases coded independently to assess reliability, there was no disagreement for coding whether or not a boy smoked "more than occasionally." Coders agreed whether or not a youth had a delinquent reference group in 84% of the cases read to assess reliability.

A judgment of criminality as an adult was based on criminal records collected between 1978 and 1982. Men were considered criminals if they had been convicted for an index crime (e.g., automobile theft, burglary, assault, rape, breaking and entering, attempted murder, murder) after reaching the age of 18.

Men were considered to be alcoholics if, in either the questionnaire or the interview, they had responded affirmatively to three of the four questions in the CAGE test for alcoholism (Ewing & Rouse, 1970; Mayfield, McLeod, & Hall, 1974). In this test, respondents are asked if they have ever felt the need to cut down on drinking, felt annoyed by criticism of their drinking, felt guilty about drinking, or taken a morning eye-opener. Men were also considered alcoholics if they had received treatment for alcoholism or had been arrested at least three times for public drunkenness or driving while intoxicated. Additionally, anyone who described himself as an alcoholic or had been arrested twice for alcoholism and answered affirmatively to two of the CAGE questions was considered an alcoholic.

After elimination of siblings (in order to justify treating cases as independent) and men who had died, 205 cases remained. These cases provided data to inspect trajectories leading from disruptive childhood behavior through delinquency-prone life-styles in adolescence to alcoholism or criminality as adults.

Results

Children who had been disruptive in school had a relatively high probability of adopting delinquency-prone life-styles as adolescents ($\chi^2_{(1)}$ = 8.76, p = 0.003). Over half the disruptive boys, compared with less than a third of the nondisruptive boys, had seemed to accept delinquency-prone life-styles during adolescence. Less than half, however, had been convicted for serious crimes as adults: Among those who had adopted delinquency-prone life-styles (N = 33), 36.4% had become criminals, as had 21.9% of those who had not adopted delinquency-prone lifestyles (N = 32). Among those who had not been disruptive in childhood, those who exhibited a delinquency-prone life-style during adolescence were more likely to have been convicted for serious crimes as adults ($\chi^2_{(1)}$ = 5.41, p = 0.02).

As can be seen in Figure 1, adult criminals were more likely than noncriminals to be alcoholic. Only through the relationship to crime, however, did prior disruptive behavior or delinquency-prone life-style seem to influence whether alcoholism developed.

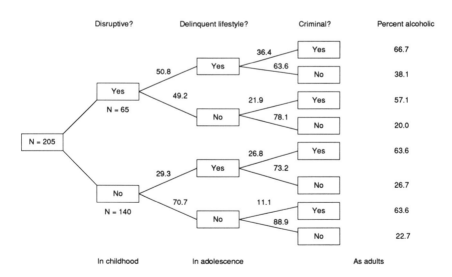

Figure 1. Crime and alcoholism.

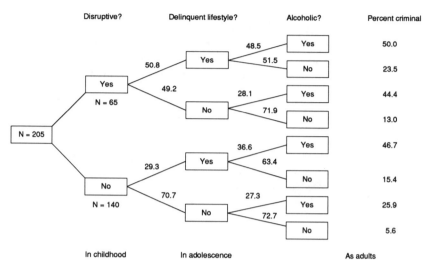

Figure 2. Alcoholism and crime.

The probability of alcoholism among criminals differed little between those criminals who had been disruptive children and exhibited delinquency-prone life-styles as adolescents (among whom 66.7% became alcoholics) and those criminals who had neither been disruptive nor exhibited delinquency-prone life-styles as adolescents (among whom 63.6% became alcoholics). Nor was there much difference in the probabilities for alcoholism among noncriminals in relation to their adolescent life-styles or childhood disruptive behavior.

Neither disruptive behavior in childhood nor delinquency-prone lifestyle had much independent impact on adult alcoholism. Small differences in the probability of becoming alcoholic in relation to deliquency-prone lifestyle appear to be chance fluctuations when early disruptive behavior is taken into account. As shown in Figure 2, however, having a history of either disruptive childhood behavior or adolescent delinquency-prone life-style seemed to increase the probability that nonalcoholics would be criminal ($\chi^2_{(1)} = 4.388$, $p = 0.036$).

The probability that an alcoholic would be convicted of a serious crime as an adult was more than 3 times as great as the probability that a nonalcoholic would be so convicted ($\chi^2_{(1)} = 21.999$, $p = 0.0001$). The 15 nonalcoholic criminals (among 138 nonalcoholics) had been convicted of a mean of 3.9 crimes. The 26 alcoholic criminals (among 67 alcoholics) had been convicted of a mean of 3.5 crimes. Therefore, it seems unlikely that the high proportion of alcoholics who were convicted for serious crimes were convicted because their drinking made them easier to detect.

Summary

Disruptive behavior during childhood tends to forecast delinquency-prone life-style during adolescence, and although only a minority became adult criminals, the combination of disruptive behavior in childhood and delinquency-prone life-style during adolescence contributed to the likelihood of further criminal behavior.

On the other hand, antisocial behavior during childhood or adolescence seemed not to influence whether criminals became alcoholics. Although alcoholism and criminality tended to co-occur, there was no evidence that alcoholic criminals tended to commit more crimes of a serious nature than did nonalcoholic criminals.

Discussion

The compilation of evidence showing proportions of crimes with which alcohol can be associated has led to little knowledge. People are not equally at risk for being in public drinking places. We do not yet know enough about who attends public bars or their proclivity for fighting. Therefore, the studies based on what might be called a "Prohibition model" have not demonstrated that alcohol causes crimes.

The fact that a noticeable proportion of alcoholics commit crimes does not, of course, imply that alcohol contributes to the causes of criminal behavior. Analyzing material drawn from interviews, biographies, and case studies of men convicted for crimes against property, Cordilia (1985) found that although most professional thieves drank heavily, they rarely drank immediately prior to committing a crime. Had they been drinking, several reported, they would have been unreliable partners. Nevertheless, because they rarely were married or legitimately employed and often frequented places where drinking provided the entertainment, these men led the types of lives likely to promote drinking.

Laboratory studies show that alcohol can increase the amount of pain one person will inflict on another (Gantner & Taylor, 1982; Gustafson, 1992; Murdoch & Pihl, 1985; Zeichner & Pihl, 1979, 1980). This effect may partially be reflecting an influence of alcohol to make otherwise impermissible behavior excusable. The pain-inflicting experiments set levels of pain that were not devastating, however, and liquor may reduce inhibition at such levels without necessarily having any disinhibiting effects against fundamental moral principles.

This study points to a group of alcoholic criminals, many of whom had been disruptive children and displayed delinquency-prone life-styles as adolescents. Because it is longitudinal, the study is able to show that prior histories of antisocial behavior precede a good deal of alcoholic–criminal behavior. It also shows that apart from delinquency-prone lifestyle and regardless of whether or not the subjects were disruptive as children, alcoholism is related to being criminal. In addition, because of differences in their relationship to delinquency-prone life-styles, the study suggests that the etiology of alcoholism and of criminality are not the same.

The evidence of this study indicates that two "solutions" to the puzzle about relationships between alcoholism and crime should be rejected. Alcoholism does not appear to be merely a manifestation of delinquency-prone life-styles, nor does a single underlying dimension of deviance appear to explain both alcoholism and criminality.

At least two plausible and compatible explanations remain. The first, as has been suggested by many researchers, considers alcoholism to be a heterogeneous classification. If one type of alcoholic is antisocial, samples overrepresenting this type could account both for the obtained relationships of alcoholism to criminality and for the differences in etiology between alcoholism and criminality. There is some evidence that patterns of criminal behavior distinguish between alcoholic and nonalcoholic criminals (J. McCord, 1981b). As juveniles, those who later became alcoholic criminals were more likely to have been seen by the Crime Prevention Bureau. They were more likely to have begun their criminal careers with convictions for larceny. And they were more likely to have committed a subsequent crime more serious than that for which they were first convicted. The alcoholic criminals differed from noncriminal alcoholics in terms of childhood characteristics and family interactions.

The second explanation builds on the study reported by Cordilia (1985). Rarely married or legitimately employed, criminals tend to hang out in bars. Many will drink too much, and eventually, some will become alcoholics. By this explanation, criminality could be considered a cause of one form of alcoholism.

References

Alterman, A. I., Gerstley, L. J., Strohmetz, D. B., & McKay, J. R. (1991). Psychiatric heterogeneity in antisocial alcoholics: Relation to familial alcoholism. *Comprehensive Psychiatry, 32* (5), 423–431.

Amir, M. (1971). *Patterns in forcible rape.* Chicago: University of Chicago Press.

Banay, R. S. (1942). Alcoholism and crime. *Quarterly Journal of Studies on Alcohol, 2,* 686–716.

Banay, R. S. (1945). Alcohol and aggression. In E. M. Jellinek (Ed.), *Alcohol, science, and society* (pp. 143–152). New Haven, CT: *Quarterly Journal of Studies on Alcohol.*

Bard, M., & Zacker, J. (1974). Assaultiveness and alcohol use in family disputes: Police perceptions. *Criminology, 12* [3 (November)], 281–292.

Blumstein, A., Cohen, J., Roth, J. A., & Visher, C. A. (Eds.), (1986). *Criminal careers and "career criminals."* Washington, DC: National Academy Press.

Bohman, M., Cloninger, C. R., Sigvardsson, S., & von Knorring, A. (1982). Predisposition to petty criminality in Swedish adoptees. *Archives of General Psychiatry, 39*, 1233–1241.

Bohman, M., Cloninger, C. R., Sigvardsson, S., & von Knorring, A. (1983). Gene–environment interaction in the psychopathology of Swedish adoptees: Studies of the origins of alcoholism and criminality. In S. B. Guze, F. J. Earls, & J. E. Barrett (Eds.), *Childhood psychopathology and development* (pp. 265–278). New York: Raven Press.

Collins, J. J., Jr. (1981). Alcohol careers and criminal careers. In J. J. Collins (Ed.), *Drinking and crime* (pp. 152–206). New York: Guilford Press.

Cordilia, A. (1985). Alcohol and property crime: Exploring the causal nexus. *Journal of Studies on Alcohol, 46*(2), 161–171.

Donovan, J. E., & Jessor, R. (1985). Structure of problem behavior in adolescence and young adulthood. *Journal of Consulting and Clinical Psychology, 53*(6), 890–904.

Dunford, E. (1945). Legal aspects of prohibition. In E. M. Jellinek (Ed.), *Alcohol, science and society* (pp. 321–353). New Haven, CT: *Quarterly Journal of Studies on Alcohol.*

Elliott, D. S., Huizinga, D., & Menard, S. (1989). *Multiple problem youth.* New York: Springer-Verlag.

Ewing J., & Rouse, B. A. (1970). Identifying the hidden alcoholic. Paper presented at the 29th International Congress on Alcohol and Drug Dependence, Sydney, NSW Australia.

Fagan, J. (1990). Intoxication and aggression. In M. Tonry & J. Q. Wilson (Eds.), *Drugs and crime* (pp. 241–320). Chicago: University of Chicago Press.

Farrington, D. P. (1979). Environmental stress, delinquent behavior, and convictions. In I. G. Sarason & C. D. Spielberger (Eds.), *Stress and anxiety,* Vol. 6 (pp. 93–106). New York: John Wiley.

Farrington, D. P. (1983). Offending from 10 to 25 years of age. In K. T. Van Dusen & S. A. Mednick (Eds.), *Prospective studies of crime and delinquency* (pp. 73–97). Boston: Kluwer-Nijhoff.

Farrington, D. P. (1986). Stepping stones to adult criminal careers. In D. Olweus, J. Block, & M. Radke-Yarrow (Eds.), *Development of antisocial and prosocial behavior* (pp. 359–384). New York: Academic Press.

Ferri, E. (1897). *Criminal sociology.* New York: D. Appleton.

Flanagan, T. J., & Maguire, K. (1992). *Sourcebook of criminal justice statistics 1991.* Washington, DC: U.S. Government Printing Office.

Foulds, G. A., & Hassall, C. (1969). The significance of age of onset of excessive drinking in male alcoholics. *British Journal of Psychiatry, 115*, 1027–1032.

Gantner, A. B., & Taylor, S. P. (1982). Human physical aggression as a function of alcohol and threat of harm. *Aggressive Behavior, 18* (1), 29–36.

Gerson, L. W., & Preston, D. Q. (1979). Alcohol consumption and the incidence of violent crime. *Journal of Studies on Alcohol, 40*(3), 307–312.

Goodman, R. A., Mercy, J. A., Loya, F., Rosenberg, M. L., Smith, J. C., Allen, N. H., Vargas, L., & Kolts, R. (1986). Alcohol use and interpersonal violence: Alcohol detected in homicide victims. *American Journal of Public Health, 76*(2), 144–149.

Goring, C. (1913). *The English convict: A statistical study.* London: Stationary Office (available from Montclair, NJ: Paterson Smith).

Gottfredson, M. R., & Hirschi, T. (1990). *A general theory of crime.* Stanford: Stanford University Press.

Gustafson, R. (1992). Alcohol and aggression—a replication study controlling for potential confounding variables. *Aggressive Behavior, 18*(1), 21–28.

Guze, S. B. (1976). *Criminality and psychiatric disorders.* New York: Oxford University Press.

Harwood, M. K., & Leonard, K. E. (1989). Family history of alcoholism, youthful antisocial behavior and problem drinking among DWI offenders. *Journal of Studies on Alcohol, 50*(3), 210–216.

Hesselbrock, V. M., Stabenau, J. R., Hesselbrock, M. N., Roger, E., & Babor, T. F. (1982). The nature of alcoholism in patients with different family histories for alcoholism. *Progress in Neuro-psychopharmacological & Biological Psychiatry, 6,* 607–614.

Howard, G. E. (1918). Alcohol and crime: A study in social causation. *American Journal of Sociology, 24,* 61–80.

Innes, C. A., & Greenfeld, L. A. (1990). *Violent state prisoners and their victims.* BJS Special Report. Washington, DC: U.S. Department of Justice.

Jessor, R., & Jessor, S. L. (1984). Adolescence to young adulthood: A twelve-year prospective study of problem behavior and psychosocial development. In S. A. Mednick, M. Harway, and K. M. Finello (Eds.), *Handbook of longitudinal research* (pp. 34–61). New York: Praeger.

Jones, M. C. (1968). Personality correlates and antecedents of drinking patterns in adult males. *Journal of Consulting and Clinical Psychology, 32,* 2–12.

Kaplan, H. B. (1980). *Deviant behavior in defense of self.* New York: Academic Press.

Kaplan, H. B., Johnson, R. J., & Bailey, C. A. (1986). Self-rejection and the explanation of deviance: Refinement and elaboration of a latent structure. *Social Psychology Quarterly, 49,* 110–128.

Kaplan, H. B., Johnson, R. J., & Bailey, C. A. (1987). Deviant peers and deviant behavior: Further elaboration of a model. *Social Psychology Quarterly, 50*(3), 277–284.

Lewis, C. E., Rice, J., & Helzer, J. E. (1983). Diagnostic interactions: Alcoholism and antisocial personality. *Journal of Nervous and Mental Disease, 171*(2), 105–113.

Lindelius, R., & Salum, I. (1973). Alcoholism and criminality. *Acta Psychiatrica Scandinavica, 49,* 306–314.

Lombroso, C. (1912/1968). *Crime: Its causes and remedies.* Montclair, NJ: Patterson Smith.

Mayfield, D., McLeod, G., & Hall, P. (1974). The CAGE questionnaire: Validation of a new alcoholism screening instrument. *American Journal of Psychiatry, 131,* 1121–1123.

McCord, J. (1980). Patterns of deviance. In S. B. Sells, R. Crandall, M. Roff, J. Strauss, & W. Pollin (Eds.), *Human functioning in longitudinal perspective: Studies of normal and psychopathological populations* (pp. 157–162). Baltimore: Williams & Wilkins.

McCord, J. (1981a). A longitudinal perspective on patterns of crime. *Criminology, 19*(2), 211–218.

McCord, J. (1981b). Alcoholism and criminality: Confounding and differentiating factors. *Journal of Studies on Alcohol, 42*(9), 739–748.

McCord, W., & McCord, J. (1960). *Origins of alcoholism.* Stanford: Stanford University Press.

McKenna, T., & Pickens, R. (1981). Alcoholic children of alcoholics. *Journal of Studies on Alcohol, 42,* 1021–1029.

McKenna, T., & Pickens, R. (1983). Personality characteristics of alcoholic children of alcoholics. *Journal of Studies on Alcohol, 44,* 688–700.

Murdoch, D., & Pihl, R. O. (1985). Alcohol and aggression in a group interaction. *Addictive Behaviors, 10,* 97–101.

Murdoch, D., Pihl, R. O., & Ross, D. (1990). Alcohol and crimes of violence: Present issues. *International Journal of the Addictions, 25*(9), 1065–1081.

Nicol, A. R., Gunn, J. C., Gristwood, J., Foggitt, R. H., & Watson, J. P. (1973). The relationship of alcoholism to violent behavior resulting in long-term imprisonment. *British Journal of Psychiatry, 123,* 47–51.

Osgood, D. W., Johnston, L. D., O'Malley, P. M., & Bachman, J. G. (1988). The generality of deviance in late adolescence and early adulthood. *American Sociological Review, 53*(1), 81–93.

Pernanen, K. (1981). Theoretical aspects of the relationship between alcohol use and crime. In J. J. Collins, Jr. (Ed.), *Drinking and crime* (pp. 1–69). New York: Guilford Press.

Pernanen, K. (1991). *Alcohol in human violence.* New York: Guilford Press.

Powers, E., & Witmer, H. (1951). *An experiment in the prevention of delinquency: The Cambridge–Somerville youth study.* New York: Columbia University Press.

Pulkkinen, L., & Hurme, H. (1984). Aggression as a predictor of weak self-control. In L. Pulkkinen & P. Lyytinen (Eds.), *Human action and personality.* Jyvaskyla, Finland: University of Jyvaskyla Press.

Robins, L. N. (1978). Sturdy childhood predictors of adult antisocial behavior: Replications from longitudinal studies. *Psychological Medicine, 8,* 611–622.

Schuckit, M. A. (1973). Alcoholism and sociopathy—Diagnostic confusion. *Quarterly Journal of Studies on Alcohol, 34,* 157–164.

Schuckit, M. A. (1984). Relationship between the course of primary alcoholism in men and family history. *Journal of Studies on Alcohol, 45,* 334–338.

Schuckit, M. A., Rimmer, J. R., & Winokur, G. (1970). Alcoholism: Antisocial traits in male alcoholics. *British Journal of Psychiatry, 117,* 575–576.

Shupe, L. M. (1954). Alcohol and crime: A study of the urine alcohol concentration found in 882 persons arrested during or immediately after the commission of a felony. *Journal of Criminal Law, Criminology, and Police Science, 44*(5), 661–664.

Smith, S. S., & Newman, J. P. (1990). Alcohol and drug abuse/dependence disorders in psychopathic and nonpsychopathic criminal offenders. *Journal of Abnormal Psychology, 94*(4), 430–439.

Stabenau, J. R. (1984). Implications of family history of alcoholism, antisocial personality, and sex differences in alcohol dependence. *American Journal of Psychiatry, 141*[10 (October)], 1178–1182.

van Kammen, W. B., Loeber, R., & Stouthamer-Loeber, M. (1991). Substance use and its relationship to conduct problems and delinquency in young boys. *Journal of Youth and Adolescence, 20*(4), 399–415.

Virkkunen, M. (1974). Alcohol as a factor precipitating aggression and conflict behavior leading to homicide. *British Journal of Addictions, 69,* 149–154.

Wikström, P. H. (1985). *Everyday violence in contemporary Sweden: Situational and ecological aspects.* Stockholm: National Council for Crime Prevention Sweden.

Wolfgang, M. E. (1958). *Patterns in criminal homicide.* New York: John Wiley.

Wolfgang, M. E., & Strohm, M. A. (1956). The relationship between alcohol and criminal homicide. *Quarterly Journal of Studies on Alcohol, 17*[3 (September)], 411–425.

Wolfgang, M. E., Figlio, R. M., & Sellin, T. (1972). *Delinquency in a birth cohort.* Chicago: University of Chicago Press.

Yates, W. R., Petty, F., & Brown, K. (1988). Alcoholism in males with antisocial personality disorder. *International Journal of the Addictions, 23*(10), 999–1010.

Zeichner, A., & Pihl, R. O. (1979). Effects of alcohol and behavior contingencies on human aggression. *Journal of Abnormal Psychology, 88*(2), 153–160.

Zeichner, A., & Pihl, R. O. (1980). Effects of alcohol and instigator intent on human aggression. *Journal of Studies on Alcohol, 41*(3), 265–276.

Zucker, R. A., & Gomberg, E. S. L. (1986). Etiology of alcoholism reconsidered: The case for a biopsychosocial process. *American Psychologist, 41,* 783–793.

IV

INTERVENING VARIABLES IN CAUSAL RELATIONSHIPS AMONG DRUG USE, CRIME, AND OTHER FORMS OF DEVIANCE

As Stacy and Newcomb observed in Chapter 4, the relationship over time between two patterns of deviance may be informed in terms of any of a number of theoretical premises. In order to test the tenability of different theoretical premises, it is necessary to specify the intervening variables that reflect the theoretical processes that are hypothesized to mediate the relationship between two patterns of deviance.

The two studies that constitute Part IV illustrate different ways of testing for the existence of theoretically informed intervening mechanisms. One study estimates a structural model in which some variables are specified as mediating the effects of earlier measured variables on later measured variables. The other study estimates two models in which a particular variable is a dependent variable in one model and an independent variable in another. The two models together permit inferences regarding the mediating role of the variable in the relationship between the independent variable in the first model and the dependent variable in the second model. As it happens, the mediating role of the hypothesized intervening variables in the two studies is problematic.

In Chapter 6, Martin and Robbins examine the potential mediating role of attachment to conventional adults and affiliation with deviant peers in the relationship between sensation-seeking and drug use for a cohort of 9th-grade public-school students who were first surveyed in the 6th grade. The structural model did not confirm the theoretical expectations. While sensation-seeking is negatively associated with attachment to parents and schools as expected, neither attachment to parents nor deviant peers is associated with drug use in the 9th grade. Further, attachment to school is positively related to drug use, also contrary to expectations. This study is also noteworthy because it anticipates the appropriate use of moderating variables that characterize the studies to be considered in Part V. The use of moderating variables appears to be warranted in light of the frequent failure to confirm hypotheses in the two studies. This suggests the need to further specify the conditions under which the theoretical expectations will be supported.

In Chapter 7, Krohn, Thornberry, Collins-Hall, and Lizotte estimate two models dealing with the relationship between dropping out of school and delinquency and drug use. The first model specifies prior delinquency and drug use as predictors of dropping out, while the second model specifies dropping out as influencing subsequent changes in delinquency and drug use, controlling for family and school variables in both models. The data are drawn from a multiwave panel study of a high-risk urban study in which youths and their primary caretakers are interviewed every 6 months. The results indicate that drug use, but not serious delinquency, contributes to the prediction of dropping out. Further, dropping out does not influence subsequent drug use (when school-related variables are included in the analyses) or serious delinquency (whether or not school-related variables are included in the analysis). However, the authors speculate that the failure to confirm certain of the hypotheses might be the result of the short time span considered and the nature of the consequences of drug use and delinquency.

6

Personality, Social Control, and Drug Use in Early Adolescence

Steven S. Martin and Cynthia A. Robbins

Introduction

Sociological theories of crime and delinquency have been criticized for failing to take into account biological and personality factors that may predispose people to antisocial behavior (Gottfredson & Hirschi, 1989; Wilson & Herrnstein, 1985). According to these critics, dispositional differences produced by heredity, environmental conditions (e.g., nutrition and lead exposure), and parental behavior emerge and are identifiable in early childhood. It is charged that criminologists who fail to take these dispositional characteristics into account may exaggerate the importance of later social experiences in their explanations of delinquency and crime. Differential association and bonding theories, in particular, have been criticized in this regard.

In the analyses reported in this chapter, we attempt to reconcile dispositional and traditional sociological theories of delinquency by simultaneously considering personality, social bonding, and social learning risk factors for delinquency. Specifically, we examine drug use in a cohort of 9th-grade public-school students who were first surveyed in the 6th grade. Since baseline measures were obtained when most respondents were only 11 years old and had little experience with alcohol or drugs, this sample provides a good opportunity to explore the notion that personality differences formed early in life can influence

Steven S. Martin and **Cynthia A. Robbins** • Center for Drug and Alcohol Studies, Department of Sociology and Criminal Justice, University of Delaware, Newark, Delaware 19716.

Drugs, Crime, and Other Deviant Adaptations: Longitudinal Studies, edited by Howard B. Kaplan. Plenum Press, New York, 1995.

subsequent delinquency. In addition to examining the independent effects of personality, social bonding, and peer delinquency as predictors of drug use, we build on previous explanations in two respects. First, we examine the interrelationship of personality, social bonding, and differential association variables to see whether attachment to conventional adults or affiliation with deviant peers mediates the effects of personality on drug use. Second, we test the hypothesis that personal dispositions may moderate youths' susceptibility to influence by adults or peers.

Sensation-Seeking as a Personal Disposition

The dispositional factor considered in this analysis is sensation-seeking. Sensation-seeking, as considered by Marvin Zuckerman (1979, p. 10), is a trait "defined by the need for varied, novel, and complex sensations and experiences and the willingness to take physical and social risks for the sake of such experience." He posits that individuals with a high need for sensations get a positive feeling that results from a physical cortical arousal; that is, high sensations provide a drug-like experience. The traditional measure of the sensation-seeking scale (SSS) was developed by Zuckerman to measure this trait. Four subscales within the SSS measure are posited to tap: boredom susceptibility (BS), disinhibition (DIS), experience-seeking (ES), and thrill- and adventure-seeking (TAS). Not surprisingly, alcohol and drug use, which produce a chemical effect that mimics such sensations, have been shown in numerous studies to be related to the measure(s) of sensation-seeking (Andrucci, Archer, Pancoast, & Gordon, 1989; Ratliff and Burkhart, 1984; Segal & Singer, 1976; Segal, Huba, & Singer, 1980).

The explanation offered by these researchers for the positive relationship between sensation-seeking and substance abuse is twofold. First, high sensation-seekers (HSS) obtain a direct neurological stimulation from the substance itself that transcends the stimulation afforded to low sensation-seekers (LSS). Variations in levels of need for physiological arousal form the basis for study of this individual trait. The particular effect of the drug (e.g., stimulant, depressant) does not seem to be of great importance; rather, it is simply the drug's ability to alter states of consciousness (Carrol, Zuckerman, & Vogel, 1982). Second, the illegality or surreptitiousness associated with substance use provides a secondary source of stimulation (Segal et al., 1980).

Many studies have demonstrated the relationship between sensation-seeking and alcohol and other drug use in various adult populations. These include college students (Galizio, Rosenthal, & Stein, 1983; Jaffe & Archer, 1987; Kohn & Coulas, 1985; Segal & Singer, 1976; Segal et al., 1980; Zuckerman, 1972, 1979), substance abusers (Kilpatrick, Sutker, & Smith, 1976; Sutker, Archer, &

Allain, 1978), psychiatric patients (McGlothlin & Arnold, 1971), medical students (Carrol et al., 1982), and inmates (Kern, Kenkel, Templer, & Newell, 1986). Many of these studies start from a given of substance use and then measure levels of sensation-seeking. Most also make use only of cross-sectional data.

Until recently, however, few studies assessed the influence of sensation-seeking on adolescent drug use. This omission was somewhat surprising, because sensation-seeking is theorized to be biologically based, to manifest itself in childhood, and to be exacerbated by the physical and hormonal changes that accompany puberty. This paucity of study has changed dramatically, however, in the last five years.

The study by Bates, Labouvie, and White (1986) of sensation-seeking and alcohol and marijuana use found the DIS subscale to be a strong predictor of drug use. In their study, 584 subjects aged 15 and 18 at Time 1 (T1) and 18 and 21 at Time 2 (T2) reported the frequency and quantity of their alcohol and marijuana use and completed the DIS subscale. Results showed a positive relationship between each of the four use measures and DIS at T1. In addition, use at T2 was predicted not only by use at T1, but also by DIS at T1, and by changes in DIS from T1 to T2 (increases in DIS from T1 to T2 predicted increased levels of use at T2; decreases in DIS from T1 to T2 predicted lower levels of use at T2).

As part of an ongoing investigation of the influence of sensation-seeking on alcohol and other drug use and the effects of anti-drug abuse messages, Donohew (1988) and associates found highly significant differences in drug use between HSS and LSS at both the junior high and senior high school age levels. Junior high HSS ($N = 565$) were significantly more likely to have used marijuana, cocaine, liquor, beer, uppers, and downers in the previous 30 days than were junior high LSS ($N = 658$). In addition, senior high HSS ($N = 420$) were also significantly more likely to have used marijuana, cocaine, liquor, beer, uppers, and downers in the previous month than were senior high LSS ($N = 450$).

Andrucci et al. (1989) investigated the relationship of the Minnesota Multiphasic Personality Inventory and sensation-seeking to adolescent drug use in a sample of 123 subjects aged 14–18. Using Zuckerman's SSS measure, they found the extent and duration of drug use across several categories—including alcohol, amphetamines, barbiturates, caffeine, cocaine, hallucinogens, and marijuana—to have significant positive relationships with the total SSS measure. In a series of discriminant analyses, SSS was selected consistently as the first variable to enter the stepwise equations to predict levels of drug use and was selected as the only variable for the equation to predict single vs. polydrug use. In a study of 1900 Israeli adolescents aged 14–19, Teichman, Barnea, and Rahav (1989) found sensation-seeking to be significantly related to lifetime and current (past 30 days) drug use. In general, higher levels of sensation-seeking had a direct effect on "readiness to use substances" as well as on actual experimentation (see also, Teichman, Rahav, & Barnea, 1988).

From an analysis of the final 2 years of data collected during a 5-year longitudinal study of 847 California high school students, Newcomb and McGee (1989) concluded that HSS needs predict increased alcohol use for women, but not for men. They explain this in terms of the hypothesis of Zuckerman (1979) that the more prevalent and socially acceptable the use of a substance in a particular population, the less likely there is to be a relationship between sensation-seeking and drug use. Newcomb and McGee conclude that drinking is normal for high school males, but not for females.

Social Bonding and Peer Influence

The other major underpinning to our analyses is to consider the effect of sensation-seeking in relation to social influences central to sociological theories of delinquency—parents, schools, and peers. Such an approach has been suggested by Zuckerman (1983), who seemed to modify his view of sensation-seeking to deemphasize the primary role of arousal. In this later writing, he sees sensation-seeking as a general sensitivity to reinforcement from other circumstances, including social circumstances.

Three social influences central to traditional sociological theories of delinquency are parents, schools, and peers. According to the social bonding theory of Hirschi (1969), youths who feel emotionally attached or close to parents, teachers, and peers are less likely to commit deviant acts. Several mechanisms may operate to reduce delinquency among highly attached youths. Hirschi likens attachment to the Freudian concept of superego; that is, highly attached youths are likely to have internalized conventional norms and values against antisocial behavior. Even if they have not internalized nondelinquent norms and values, however, highly attached youth may resist opportunities to engage in delinquent acts if they consider the potential consequences of their actions for loved ones or valued relationships. For example, a youth who does not believe marijuana use is intrinsically wrong may nevertheless forgo a chance to try it in the belief that parents or teachers would be disappointed or embarrassed if he or she were caught or reported.

Though research has generally supported the attachment hypothesis regarding conventional *adults,* most studies find attachment to peers to be either unrelated or *positively* related to delinquency, in general, and to drug use in particular. Instead, most analyses support the social learning theory prediction that it is the behavior of peers rather than closeness to them that is critical for predicting delinquency. Substance abuse by peers is consistently found to be one of the strongest predictors of adolescent alcohol and drug use.

Work by Donovan and Jessor (1985) on social conformity and by Kandel and colleagues (Kandel, 1980; Kandel & Logan, 1984; Kandel, Kessler, & Margulies, 1978; Yamaguchi & Kandel, 1984, 1985) and Bentler and colleagues (Maddahian, Newcomb, & Bentler, 1986, 1988) Robbins on peer and parental influences has clearly documented the strong associations of these primary networks with adolescent drug use. The meaning of these correlations, however, is debated.

The extreme position is that the association of the social bond and peer behavior with delinquency is spurious. Dispositional characteristics such as intelligence or impulsivity form in early childhood and influence subsequent attachment to conventional adults, selection of deviant friends, and delinquency. Wilson and Herrnstein (1985), for instance, minimize the role of school experiences as a cause of delinquency by suggesting that low intelligence and impulsivity cause some youths to dislike school and engage in problem behavior in the primary school grades before tracking or other negative school experiences could influence their propensity for delinquency.

A second possibility acknowledged by Wilson and Herrnstein and by Gottfredson and Hirschi (1989) is that personality may influence delinquency indirectly by route of the social processes featured in control and learning theories. This position allows for mediating effects of parental and school attachment and deviant peers. For instance, the impulsivity and disinhibition of HSS youth could result in early and frequent misbehavior (and consequent punishment) that erodes their attachment to parents, teachers, and conventional peers and encourages them to seek out delinquent companions.

A third possibility implicit in Zuckerman's later formulation of sensation-seeking and reduced responsiveness to distant reinforcers is that dispositional factors may *interact* with bonding and social learning variables. A highly impulsive youth attracted to novel experiences may act on delinquent opportunities without thinking through the possibility of angering or disappointing significant adults. Therefore, HSS may be more influenced by the immediate positive reinforcement of joining delinquent peers, but less influenced by the more remote and uncertain negative reinforcements of conventional adults.

Hypotheses to Be Tested

These questions and arguments led us to test the following hypotheses:

H1: HS Seekers will be more likely than LSS to use tobacco, alcohol, and illicit drugs.
H2: HSS will report lower school and parental attachment than LSS.
H3: Compared to LSS, HSS will report more drug use by friends.

H4: Sixth graders who report less attachment to school and parents will be more likely to use tobacco, alcohol, and illicit drugs by the 9th grade.

H5: Sixth graders who report more drug use by friends will report more tobacco, alcohol, and illicit drug use by the 9th grade.

H6: Parental and school attachment will have weaker effects on subsequent drug use among HSS than among LSS.

H7: HSS will be more influenced than LSS by drug-using friends.

Methods

Sample and Data Collection

The data presented here come from a study that began as an evaluation of the effectiveness of project DARE (Drug Abuse Resistance Education) in the Lexington, Kentucky, school system. DARE is a school-based, primary prevention program that is taught by police officers and is targeted for children of elementary-school age in either the fifth or sixth grade. In September 1987, with support from a National Institute on Drug Abuse grant, interviews began with the 6th-grade cohort of the academic year 1987–1988. The 6th graders who participated in the first year of the study were resurveyed in the 7th, 8th, 9th, and 10th grades.

This study analyzes data collected during the 1st and 4th years of the study (academic years 1987–1988 and 1990–1991) for the cohort who were in the 6th grade in 1987–1988. In each year, students completed a questionnaire in class. Confidentiality was emphasized verbally by data collectors who were independent of the school system and dramatized by having the students tear off the first page of their questionnaires, which contained identifying information. For this cohort, 2091 baseline interviews were obtained. In the 9th grade, 1381 (66%) of these subjects again completed a confidential questionnaire in class. Sample attrition was large, but analyses do not reveal any major systematic biases in cases lost. The main reasons for sample attrition, in decreasing order of importance, were: students changing schools (two thirds of the attrition came between the 6th and 7th grades when students changed schools and school records did not allow for adequate tracing); students moving out of the country; unreturned questionnaires that were left at the school to be completed at a later date, and returned; and incorrect or unentered matching ID numbers.

Of the 944 students from whom complete information was obtained,[*] 51% are female and 49% male. The majority (77%) are white, with black (18%) being

---

[*]In the latent structure model, complete cases are necessary. This requirement accounts for the smaller case base for the analyses we report ($N = 944$) than for the total subjects interviewed in the ninth grade ($N = 1381$).

the next largest racial group. Other race and ethnic groups make up about 5% of the sample. Most of the sixth-graders were either 11 or 12 years old; about 9% were older. In terms of lifetime substance use among the sixth-graders, alcohol had the highest prevalence rate; 30% of the students had used alcohol at least once or twice. Cigarettes were the next most widely used, with 28% of the students having at least tried them. Slightly over 4% of the sample had tried marijuana.

Variables Used in Analyses

Except for the drug use outcome measure, all the indicators come from the 6th-grade questionnaires. Female is a dichotomy scored 1 for females and 0 for males. Black is a dichotomy scored 1 for blacks and 0 for other.

A single indicator of poor school performance, self-reported, asks, "How well are you doing in school this year?" Sensation-seeking is a latent construct composed of 4 mean indices of items derived from three of the four Zuckerman subscales. Items for boredom susceptibility are not available in the data. Of the 18 sensation-seeking items available in the data, 15 are used; 2 items that referred to alcohol and drugs were excluded, as was 1 item about liking love scenes, which did not load with any of the other items. All the sensation-seeking items are scored on a 5-point scale; scoring is adjusted so that all are measured toward increasing sensation or risk-taking, and the items are shown in the Appendix. Attachment to parents is a latent construct composed of 7 items scored on a 5-point scale, with higher scores indicating increasing attachment to parents and home; the items used are shown in the Appendix. Attachment to school is a latent construct of 6 items scored on a 5-point scale, as shown in the Appendix. Deviant peers influence is composed of 3 items, listed in the Appendix, that ask the respondent how many friends use cigarettes, alcohol, and marijuana.

For lifetime drug use, questions were asked about lifetime use of cigarettes, chewing tobacco, alcohol, and marijuana in each of the 6th-grade and 9th-grade questionnaires. In addition, in the 9th grade, a question was asked about lifetime use of cocaine. Seven answer categories were provided for each question, with use of cigarettes ranging from "none" to "31 or more cigarettes" and use of chewing tobacco, alcohol, marijuana, and cocaine ranging from "0 times" to "40 or more." Three of the drug use questions from the sixth grade and the 9th grade refer to use of substances that for adults would be legal: cigarettes, chewing tobacco, and alcohol. These three items are combined in an index. In the 6th grade marijuana use is the only illegal drug measure, but in the 9th grade, the measure of marijuana use and of cocaine use are combined into a mean index for illegal use.

Descriptive information (means, standard deviations, and ranges) on the specific indicators used in the analysis is presented in Table 1.

Table 1. Descriptive Information on Study Indicators[a]

Indicators	Mean	S.D.	Range
Gender (1 = female, 0 = male)	0.51	0.50	0.00–1.00
Race (1 = black, 0 = other)	0.18	0.38	0.00–1.00
Poor school performance scale	1.75	0.60	1.00–4.00
Sensation-seeking: Sixth grade			
Thrill and adventure 1	3.41	1.02	1.00–5.00
Thrill and adventure 2	2.54	1.24	1.00–5.00
Experience-seeking	2.50	0.86	1.00–5.00
Disinhibition	3.15	0.85	1.00–5.00
Lifetime drug use: Sixth grade			
"Legal" drug scale	1.40	0.82	1.00–7.00
Used marijuana	1.03	0.26	1.00–7.00
Attachment to parents: Sixth grade			
Get along with mother	4.69	0.73	1.00–5.00
Get along with father	4.55	0.89	1.00–5.00
Have fun with parents	4.29	1.10	1.00–5.00
Happy at home	4.52	0.92	1.00–5.00
Get attention at home	4.04	1.17	1.00–5.00
Parents understand you	4.16	1.16	1.00–5.00
Feel close to family	4.58	0.82	1.00–5.00
Attachment to school: Sixth grade			
Look forward to school	3.11	1.45	1.00–5.00
Feel good when at school	3.44	1.27	1.00–5.00
Like to stay home from school (not)	3.16	1.39	1.00–5.00
Like school better than friends do	2.90	1.21	1.00–5.00
Like teachers' questions	2.87	1.32	1.00–5.00
Change schools if could (not)	3.40	1.52	1.00–5.00
Deviant peers: Sixth grade			
Friends smoke cigarettes	1.47	0.77	1.00–5.00
Friends use alcohol	1.14	0.46	1.00–5.00
Friends use marijuana	1.11	0.43	1.00–5.00
Lifetime drug use: Ninth grade			
"Legal" drug scale	2.47	1.58	1.00–7.00
Illegal drug scale	1.31	0.90	1.00–7.00

[a]There were 944 complete cases on all variables.

Analyses and Results

The indicators for the constructs of sensation-seeking, attachment to parents, attachment to school, and deviant peers all come from established series of items that have been used in the past by other researchers. We did a factor analysis to examine unidimensionality in the purported item groupings, however, because (1) these questions are self-administered, (2) the sixth-graders are younger than those for whom the indices were developed, and (3) we wanted to ensure that each group of indicators measured a distinct concept. An unconstrained factor analysis of the items revealed that they loaded primarily on the indicated factor without appreciable cross-loadings. The one difference we found was that two of the sensation-seeking items thought to indicate TAS did not load with the other thrill items (or with any other of the indicators, for that matter). These two items were indexed together and then included as a separate indicator in the sensation-seeking latent construct.

The structural model we test is operationalized as a path model with latent variables in LISREL. The variables are ordered in the structural model on the basis of the putative causal linkages and the temporal measurement of the variables. The two demographic variables, gender and race, are treated as exogenous measures. Three endogenous measures—poor school performance, sensation-seeking, and drug use—are treated as preceding the other constructs: School performance and lifetime drug use can be thought of as reporting on behavior prior to the questionnaire; sensation-seeking is posited as an underlying personality trait (with an arguably more or less biological basis). The two attachment measures, parents and school, and deviant peers, are posited to be subsequent variables. The causal order for the ultimate dependent variable, ninth-grade drug use, is straightforward. The ordering of the sixth-grade constructs is theoretically based. Nevertheless, we investigated alternate specifications among the constructs. The only empirically based alternative was including a two-way path between sixth-grade drug use and deviant peers, where the fit was as good as that with a recursive path from use to peers. We report the model including this two-way path.

Estimating the model from a covariance matrix requires certain constraints. In the cases of the exogenous variables and of poor school performance, for which there is only a single indicator of each variable, the unstandardized loading is fixed at 1.0 and the error variance constrained to 0. For the exogenous variables, the values of the Φ matrix are fixed to the observed variance/covariance. In the latent constructs, one indicator in each construct has been set at 1.0 in the unstandardized loadings to set the metric for the factor in the covariance solution. Table 2 reports the measurement model characteristics for the constructs and indicators. The first column reports the standardized loadings for the indicators on the latent variables, the second column the unstandardized loadings. All the loadings are highly significant. Besides the loadings shown, there are a few significant correlated error terms that have been included to improve model fit, based on question wording and item similarities. The inclusion of the correlated errors did not affect the loadings of the indicators on the individual latent constructs.

The fit of the model is good, with an adjusted goodness of fit (AGFI) of 0.94. An examination of the modification indices and the first-order derivatives supports no major model misspecification, but some "noise" across factors. This noise may be a function of the large number of individual indicators included in the latent constructs. The results in Table 2 suggest that there are some weaker items in attachment to school and some differences between the combination of "legal" and illegal drugs in the drug use constructs. For example, cigarette use, at least in Kentucky, may not be a majority practice, but it is not a very deviant one. In future analyses, it may be instructive to separate legal and illegal drugs and perhaps have legal drugs predict to illegal drugs, making use of the data available for seventh- and eighth-graders to model more intervening paths.

Figure 1 presents the significant structural paths in the model. All paths are significant at $p < 0.05$ (two-tailed test). The model was trimmed in both reverse and forward stepwise procedures before the nonsignificant paths were set to zero and the final model was estimated. The squared multiple correlation predicting to 9th-grade drug use is 0.38.

The exogenous variables show a number of significant effects in the path model. As other studies have found, being female, or being black, is associated with lower levels of sensation-seeking and lower levels of drug use, in both the sixth and ninth grades. However, females are also less attached to parents and more likely to have drug-using friends. Being black, as well, displays the same pattern of effects—negatively related to attachment to parents, and positively related to having drug-using friends.

Turning to the endogenous variables, as would be expected, the sixth-grade measure of lifetime use of drugs is by far the most powerful predictor of ninth-grade use. Poor school performance and sensation-seeking also positively predict to ninth-grade drug use, and each is negatively associated with attachment to parents and attachment to school. These results were expected, as outlined in hypotheses 1 and 2.

What was not expected was the lack of significant relationships between the social bonding and social learning constructs and subsequent drug use. Neither attachment to parents nor deviant peers is significantly related to ninth-grade drug use, net of sixth-grade use, while attachment to school is modestly but *positively* related to 9th-grade use.

Since several of the hypotheses imply that differences between HSS and LSS may be a function of sensation-seeking acting as an interactive or moderating variable, rather than simply additive effects, we carried the analyses one stage further. To investigate these distinctions, we looked at a two-group LISREL model, with the two groups being low and high sensation seekers. Although it does not make the best use of the ordinality of sensation-seeking, this approach is a graphic way of demonstrating alternative path structures. We estimated the two-group model with two divisions: first, simply dividing the sample on the basis of a median split on an index of all 15 of the sensation-seeking items; then an upper third and lower third, excluding the middle.

With both divisions, the basic measurement model fit quite well for each of the HSS and LSS groups. Using the median split did not reveal any major dif-

Table 2. Standardized and Unstandardized Measurement Model Loadings[a]

Variables		Loadings	
Construct	Indicator	Standardized	Unstandardized
Female	Gender	1.0	1.00
Black	Race	1.0	1.00
Poor school performance	Poor school performance scale	1.0	1.00
Sensation-seeking: Sixth grade	Thrill and adventure 1	0.45	1.00
	Thrill and adventure 2	0.40	1.07
	Experience-seeking	0.50	1.08
	Disinhibition	0.49	0.91
Lifetime drug use: Sixth grade	"Legal" drug scale	0.80	1.00
	Used marijuana	0.40	0.16
Attachment to parents: Sixth grade	Get along with mother	0.68	1.00
	Get along with father	0.54	0.97
	Have fun with parents	0.62	1.37
	Happy at home	0.73	1.34
	Get attention at home	0.67	1.56
	Parents understand you	0.67	1.57
	Feel close to family	0.79	1.30
Attachment to school: Sixth grade	Look forward to school	0.85	1.00
	Feel good when at school	0.81	0.83
	Like to stay home from school (not)	0.51	0.58
	Like school better than friends do	0.54	0.54
	Like teachers' questions	0.45	0.48
	Change schools if could (not)	0.35	0.42
Deviant peers: Sixth grade	Friends smoke cigarettes	0.78	1.00
	Friends use alcohol	0.63	0.48
	Friends use marijuana	0.62	0.45
Lifetime drug use: Ninth grade	"Legal" drug scale	0.99	1.00
	Illegal drug scale	0.53	0.30

[a]Number of cases: 944; χ^2 = 673.2; df = 293; AGFI = 0.94.

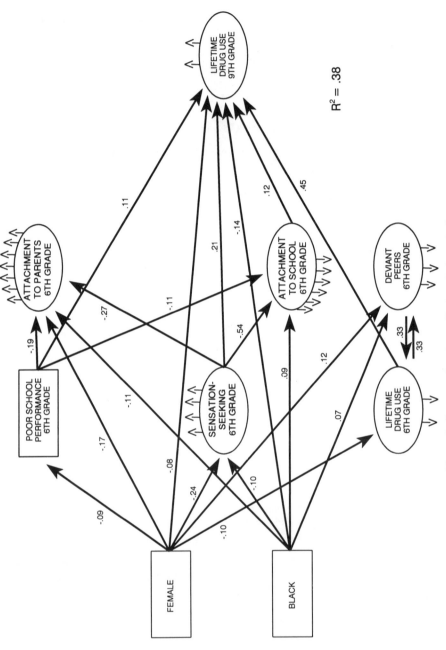

$R^2 = .38$

Figure 1. Structured paths predicting ninth-grade drug use.

ferences in the pattern of structural effects; most would even support equality constraints. The division using only the upper third and lower third on sensation-seeking did produce one noteworthy structural difference: There is a positive path between deviant peers and 9th-grade drug use for the *low* third on sensation-seeking and a negative path between peers and drug use for the *high* third on sensation-seeking. The difference is significant.

Discussion

These results are obviously preliminary. Still, both the pattern of results and the approach to the analyses are suggestive and need to be pursued.

First, a plausible explanation for the findings in the total group model is that sensation-seeking, as posited by Zuckerman, is a relatively stable trait, showing consequently robust effects over the span of several years from the 6th to the 9th grade. The social bonding variables and peer delinquency variable, however, may be more volatile over time and more responsive to situational changes, such as entering a new school and establishing a new peer group. Virtually all the students in the study changed schools in the 7th grade, so the 6th-grade measures may not adequately reflect situational changes. It is therefore unwarranted to reject the influence of social bonding and social learning without a thorough examination of measures more proximate to the measure of delinquency.

Second, looking at the two-group model, in which sensation-seeking is posited to moderate the effects of the attachment variables, we find a result opposite to what we hypothesized: HSS are negatively influenced by deviant peers, while LSS are positively influenced in subsequent drug use. This may suggest that the social learning perspective of influence from deviant peers is more appropriate for LSS while HSS not already using drugs will not be influenced to initiate by peers. As reflected in our hypotheses and analysis, we are not yet clear on how best to conceptualize the effects of the dispositional factor, sensation-seeking, in a causal model predicting drug use or delinquency. The importance of sensation-seeking as a predictor of drug use may come more from its interaction with such sociological influences as social networks, social attachments, and situational factors than from its direct additive impact; we are not sure whether this is what Zuckerman means by "sensitivity to reinforcement," but it seems plausible.

In terms of approach, latent structure models offer the ability to test alternate path orderings in longitudinal data, if not definitively, at least in terms of relative fits to the observed data. Also, the multiple-group technique can test for interactions on a variety of relevant dimensions such as sex, race, and school dropout status, as well as divisions on psychosocial measures such as sensation-seeking. In these cases, both the pattern of the structural model in each group and the significance of differences in specific structural paths can be explicitly tested. In the specific analyses reported here we have taken, and in subsequent analyses using these data we will take, advantage of the fact that we have indicators for each of the theoretical constructs in each of grade six through nine. The fact that each measure is available at each year in the data set allows us to examine reciprocal effects and alternate causal orderings among the latent variables.

There are potential implications from this line of analysis in informing prevention efforts directed at adolescents. If we can improve our ability to assess the relative importance of intrapersonal traits and interpersonal influences in predicting drug use in early adolescence, it may be possible to use such information to design prevention strategies specific to identifiable subgroups. For example, it may be possible to substitute other behaviors for drug use among high sensation-seekers and to elicit positive antidrug peer influences for low sensation-seekers.

ACKNOWLEDGMENTS.   This work was supported in part by the University of Kentucky Prevention Research Center and by research grants DA05312, DA04887, DA06124, and DA06948 from the National Institute on Drug Abuse.

Appendix: Items Used in the Latent Constructs

Sensation-seeking: sixth grade (all individual items on a 5-point scale: "agree strongly" to "disagree strongly"):
1. Thrill 1 (mean index of 4 items):
    a. I like to jump off high diving boards. (REVERSED)
    b. Someday I would like to try sky-diving or parachute jumping. (REVERSED)
    c. I would like to learn how to scuba dive. (REVERSED)
    d. I would not like to try to water ski.
2. Thrill 2 (mean index of 2 items):
    a. Climbing a steep mountain would be too scary for me.
    b. I do not like to do dangerous things.
3. Experience-seeking (mean index of 4 items):
    a. I like to try all kinds of new things, even if they scare me or I know it's something I shouldn't do. (REVERSED)
    b. I would like to take a trip without having to make any plans ahead of time. (REVERSED)
    c. I would like to visit a strange city all by myself, even if I might get lost doing it. (REVERSED)
    d. I have—or would like to have—some unusual or different people for friends. (REVERSED)

4. Disinhibition (mean index of 5 items):
   a. I like loud music. (REVERSED)
   b. I like quiet parties.
   c. I don't like to be with people who party a lot.
   d. People should not dye their hair purple, even if they want to. (RE-VERSED)
   e. People should dress neatly and follow the rules for good style.

Lifetime drug use: sixth grade (all individual items scored 1–4 for increasing frequency of lifetime use):
   1. "Legal" drugs (mean index of lifetime use of):
      a. cigarettes
      b. chewing tobacco or snuff
      c. alcohol
   2. Lifetime marijuana use

Attachment to parents: sixth grade (all items on a 5-point scale: "most of the time" to "never"):
   1. Do you get along well with your mother or guardian?
   2. Do you get along well with your father or guardian?
   3. Do you and your parents have fun together?
   4. Are you happy at home?
   5. Do you get a lot of attention at home?
   6. Do your parents understand you?
   7. Do you feel close to your family?

Attachment to school: sixth grade (all items on a 5-point scale: "agree strongly" to "disagree strongly"):
   1. Each morning I look forward to coming to school. (REVERSED)
   2. I feel good when I'm at school. (REVERSED)
   3. I like to stay home from school.
   4. I like school better than my friends do. (REVERSED)
   5. I like to have my teachers ask me questions. (REVERSED)
   6. I would change schools if I could.

Deviant peers: sixth grade (all items on a 4-point scale: "none" to "all"):
   1. About how many of your friends smoke cigarettes?
   2. About how many of your friends get drunk at least once a week?
   3. About how many of your friends smoke marijuana?

Lifetime drug use: ninth grade (all individual items scored 1–4 for increasing frequency of lifetime use):
   1. "Legal" drugs (mean index of lifetime use of):
      a. cigarettes
      b. chewing tobacco or snuff
      c. alcohol

2. Illegal drugs (mean index of lifetime use of):
   a. marijuana
   b. cocaine

References

Andrucci, G. L., Archer, R. P., Pancoast, D. L., & Gordon, R. A. (1989). The relationship of MMPI and sensation seeking scales to adolescent drug use. *Journal of Personality Assessment, 53*(2), 253–266.

Bates, M. E., Labouvie, E. W., & White, H. R. (1986). The effect of sensation seeking needs on alcohol and marijuana use in adolescence. *Bulletin of the Society of Psychologists in Addictive Behaviors, 5*(1), 29–36.

Carrol, E. N., Zuckerman, M., & Vogel, W. H. (1982). The test of the optimal level of arousal theory of sensation seeking. *Journal of Personality and Social Psychology, 42*, 572–575.

Donohew, L. (1988). Effects of drug abuse message styles: Final report. A report of a study conducted under a grant from the National Institute on Drug Abuse. Lexington, KY: University of Kentucky Department of Communication.

Donovan, L. E., & Jessor, R. (1985). Structure of problem behavior in adolescence and young adulthood. *Journal of Consulting and Clinical Psychology, 54*, 890–904.

Galizio, M., Rosenthal, D., & Stein, F. S. (1983). Sensation seeking, reinforcement, and student drug use. *Addictive Behaviors, 8*, 242–252.

Gottfredson, M., & Hirschi, T. (1989). A propensity–event theory of crime. In W. S. Lanfer & F. Adler (Eds)., *Advances in criminological theory*, Vol. 1 (pp. 57–68). New Brunswick, NJ: Transaction Publishers.

Hirschi, T. (1969). *Causes of delinquency*. Los Angeles: University of California Press.

Jaffe, L. T., & Archer, R. P. (1987). The prediction of drug use among college students from MMPI, MCMI, and Sensation Seeking Scales. *Journal of Personality Assessment, 51*, 243–253.

Kandel, D. B. (1980). Drug and drinking behavior among youth. *Annual Review of Sociology, 6*, 912–914.

Kandel, D. B., & Logan, J. A. (1984). Patterns of drug use from adolescence to young adulthood. I. Periods of risk for initiation, stabilization and decline in use. *American Journal of Public Health, 74*, 660–672.

Kandel, D. B., Kessler, R. C., & Margulies, R. S. (1978). Antecedents of adolescent initiation into stages of drug use: A developmental analysis. *Journal of Youth and Adolescence, 7*, 13–40.

Kaplan, H. B. (1980). *Deviant behavior in defense of self*. New York: Academic Press.

Kaplan, H. B., Martin, S. S., & Robbins, C. (1984). Pathways to adolescent drug use: Self-derogation, peer influence, weakening of social controls, and early substance use. *Journal of Health and Social Behavior, 25*(4), 270–289.

Kern, M. F., Kenkel, M. B., Templer, D. I., & Newell, T. G. (1986). Drug preference as a function of arousal and stimulus screening. *International Journal of the Addictions, 21*, 255–265.

Kilpatrick, D. G., Sutker, P. D., & Smith, A. D. (1976). Deviant drug and alcohol use. In M. Zuckerman & C. D. Speilberger (Eds.), *Emotions and anxieties: New concepts, new methods, and applications* (pp. 247–278). Hillsdale, NJ: Lawrence Erlbaum.

Kohn, P. M., & Coulas, J. T. (1985). Sensation seeking, augmenting–reducing, and the perceived and preferred effects of drugs. *Journal of Personality and Social Psychology, 48*, 99–106.

Maddahian, E., Newcomb, M. D., & Bentler, P. M. (1988). Adolescent drug use and intention to use drugs: Concurrent and longitudinal analyses of four ethnic groups. *Addictive Behaviors, 13,* 191–195.

Maddahian, E., Newcomb, M. D., & Bentler, P. M. (1986). Adolescents' substance use: Impact of ethnicity, income, and availability. *Advances in alcohol and substance abuse, 5,* 63–78.

McGlothlin, W. H., and Arnold, D. O. (1971). LSD revisited: A ten year followup of medical LSD use. *Archives of General Psychiatry, 24,* 35–49.

Newcomb, M. D., & McGee, L. (1989). Adolescent alcohol use and other delinquent behaviors: A one year longitudinal analysis controlling for sensation seeking. *Criminal Justice and Behavior, 16*(3), 345–369.

Ratliff, K. G., & Burkhart, B. R. (1984). Sex differences in motivations for and effects of drinking among college students. *Journal of Studies on Alcohol, 45,* 26–32.

Segal, B., & Singer, J. L. (1976). Daydreaming, drug and alcohol use in college students: A factor analytic study. *Addictive Behaviors, 1,* 227–235.

Segal, B., Huba, G. J., & Singer, J. L. (1980). Drugs, daydreaming and personality: A study of college youth. Hillsdale, NJ: Lawrence Erlbaum.

Sutker, P. B., Archer, R. P., & Allain, A. N. (1978). Drug abuse patterns, personality characteristics, and relationships with sex, race, and sensation seeking. *Journal of Consulting and Clinical Psychology, 46,* 1374–1378.

Teichman, M., Rahav, G., & Barnea, Z. (1988). A comprehensive substance prevention program: An Israeli experiment. *Journal of Alcohol and Drug Education, 33*(3), 1–10.

Teichman, M., Barnea, Z., & Rahav, G. (1989). Sensation seeking, state and trait anxiety, and depressive mood in adolescent substance users. *International Journal of the Addictions, 24*(2), 87–99.

Wilson, J. Q., & Herrnstein, R. J. (1985). *Crime and human nature.* New York: Simon & Schuster.

Yamaguchi, K., & Kandel, D. B. (1984). Patterns of drug use from adolescence to young adulthood. II. Sequences of progression. *American Journal of Public Health, 74*(7), 668–672.

Yamaguchi, K., & Kandel, D. B. (1985). On the resolution of role incompatibility: A life event history analysis of family roles and marijuana use. *American Journal of Sociology, 90*(6), 1284–1325.

Zuckerman, M. (1972). Drug use as one manifestation of a sensation seeking trait. In W. Keup (Ed.), *Drug abuse: Current concepts in research* (pp. 154–163). Springfield, IL: Charles C. Thomas.

Zuckerman, M. (1979). *Sensation seeking: Beyond the optimum level of arousal.* Hillsdale, NJ: Lawrence Erlbaum.

Zuckerman, M. (1983). *Biological basis of sensation seeking, impulsivity, and anxiety.* Hillsdale, NJ: Lawrence Erlbaum.

7

School Dropout, Delinquent Behavior, and Drug Use

An Examination of the Causes and Consequences of Dropping Out of School

Marvin D. Krohn, Terence P. Thornberry, Lori Collins-Hall, and Alan J. Lizotte

Introduction

The importance of acquiring at least a high school education in our society is well established. Those who do not complete high school experience more social disadvantages later in life, particularly in terms of employment and economic well-being. Yet an increasing number of youngsters drop out of school prior to graduating, especially youngsters who live in relatively poor areas of the inner city. Because of the negative social and economic consequences of dropping out of school, it is important that we (1) identify factors that increase the risk of dropping out of school and (2) understand better the consequences of dropping out. Only by doing so can we develop effective policies to combat this problem.

One issue that is frequently raised in examining the dynamics of dropping out is the relationship of dropping out to other problem behaviors, in particular drug use, delinquency, and crime. A number of studies have consistently found

Marvin D. Krohn and **Lori Collins-Hall** • Department of Sociology, State University of New York at Albany, Hindelang Criminal Justice Research Center, Albany, New York 12222. **Terence P. Thornberry** and **Alan J. Lizotte** • School of Criminal Justice, State University of New York at Albany, Hindelang Criminal Justice Research Center, Albany, New York 12222.

Drugs, Crime, and Other Deviant Adaptations: Longitudinal Studies, edited by Howard B. Kaplan. Plenum Press, New York, 1995.

strong relationships among dropping out and delinquency and drug use (Bachman, O'Malley, & Johnson, 1978; Elliott, Huizinga, & Ageton, 1985; Fagan, Piper, & Moore, 1986; Jessor & Jessor, 1977). While there is little question that these problem behaviors are interrelated, there is substantial ambiguity over whether delinquency or drug use plays a causal role in explaining dropping out of school and whether dropping out of school leads to an increase in the probability of delinquency and drug use.

This ambiguity is due in part to the relatively few studies that treat dropping out as both a consequence and a cause of delinquency and drug use. The study presented in this chapter addresses this deficiency by analyzing two models. The first model explains dropping out of school and incorporates prior delinquency and drug use as predictor variables. The second model examines the effect of dropping out of school on subsequent changes in delinquency and drug use. It is important to note that the analysis is done with data collected from a sample of inner-city youngsters who overrepresent youth at high risk for these problem behaviors.

Explanatory Models

Strain theory and social control theory have been used to explain both dropping out of school and involvement in delinquency and drug use (Thornberry, Moore, & Christenson, 1985). While the two models identify similar factors as being associated with dropping out of school, they provide different explanations for how these factors affect the outcome. The theories also offer opposing predictions about the consequences of dropping out with regard to subsequent delinquency and drug use. The remainder of this section first summarizes the claims of these theories concerning both dropping out and delinquency and then reviews the empirical literature in each of these areas. The discussion begins with efforts to explain dropping out of school.

Explaining School Dropout

From a strain theory perspective, failure in school is a source of frustration. This frustration causes alienation, and youngsters may turn to alternative, deviant behaviors to acquire status while they are still attending school. However, once they are able to withdraw from the aversive situation existing in school, they are more likely to drop out than are their more successful peers (Agnew, 1985). Thus, from a strain perspective, evidence of school failure and dissatisfaction with school are likely to be related to dropping out of school.

The social control perspective identifies some of the same correlates of dropping out of school, but provides a different explanation for why they might be related to dropping out. Failure in school, along with lack of involvement in or commitment to school, is interpreted as evidence of a weak bond to conventional society. Individuals who are not strongly bonded to conventional society are more likely to deviate from normative expectations and are therefore more likely to fail to complete school (Fagan & Pabon, 1990).

In addition to these school-related variables, social control theory also identifies family variables as important mechanisms by which youngsters are bonded to conventional society. Youngsters who have warm relationships with their parents are less likely to deviate from parental expectations and norms because they do not want to jeopardize those relationships. Parents also can play a more direct role in controlling the behavior of their children through diligent supervision and involvement in their activities. Hence, adolescents who have warm relationships with their parents, whose behavior is well supervised by their parents, and whose parents are involved in their activities (especially those related to school) should be more likely to graduate from high school than adolescents whose family relationships are not as close (Fagan & Pabon, 1990).

Empirically, the variables identified by both strain and control theories are predictive of dropping out of school. Low achievement in school, as measured either by standardized tests or by grade-point average (GPA), has consistently been found to be related to dropping out of school (Barrington & Hendricks, 1989; Cairns, Cairns, & Neckerman, 1989; Ekstrom, Goertz, Pollack, & Rock, 1986; Elliott & Voss, 1974; Fagan & Pabon, 1990; Mensch & Kandel, 1988; Rumberger, 1983). Not surprisingly, adolescents who perform poorly in school are also more likely to be dissatisfied with their school experience and to be less involved in and committed to school and, in turn, to be more likely to drop out before they graduate (Ekstrom et al., 1986; Elliott & Voss, 1974; Fagan & Pabon, 1990). Their poor performance in school and dissatisfaction with school is also related to lower expectations for achievement in school. Lower expectations for school achievement have also been found to be related to dropping out (Ekstrom et al., 1986; Fagan & Pabon, 1990; Rumberger, 1983).

Family background and the quality of family relationships have also been investigated as factors involved in dropping out of school. Disrupted family structure, poor attachment to parents, and parents' low expectations for their children's education have most often been found to be related to school dropout (Aston & McLanahan, 1991; Dunham & Alpert, 1987; Ekstrom et al., 1986; Mensch & Kandel, 1988; Rumberger, 1983).

In addition to the variables identified in strain and social control theories, the impact of prior delinquency and drug use on dropping out of school has also been examined. Prior drug use (Friedman, Glickman, & Utada, 1985; Mensch & Kandel, 1988) and prior delinquency (Elliott & Voss, 1974; Fagan & Jones, 1984; Hawkins & Lam, 1987; Kelly & Pink, 1971; Thornberry et al., 1985) have both been found to be related to subsequent school dropout.

Fagan and Pabon (1990), while recognizing the interrelationships among these three forms of problem behavior, caution that the relationship between prior delinquency and drug use and subsequent dropping out may be spurious. That is, because the three behaviors share similar correlates such as school and family factors, once these factors are introduced, the impact of delinquency and drug use on dropping out may be significantly reduced or disappear. It is therefore important to incorporate school and family factors, along with delinquency and drug use, in examining the causal influence of these variables on dropping out of school.

Explaining Drug Use and Delinquency

Although the strain and social control models are similar in the variables that they identify as predictive of dropping out of school, they differ significantly in how they perceive the impact of dropping out on subsequent involvement in delinquency and drug use. For strain theory, school represents for a particular youngster an aversive context that can generate a sense of strain that leads to delinquency and drug use (Cohen, 1955; Elliott & Voss, 1974). However, if school is indeed the source of frustration, dissatisfaction, and, ultimately, deviant behavior, then it follows that if those adolescents can disengage from that situation, the rate of their misbehavior will be reduced (Elliott & Voss, 1974; Thornberry, et al., 1985). Dropping out should reduce the level of frustration and strain brought about by school failure; in turn, the lowered level of strain should lead to reduced involvement in delinquency and drug use.

Social control theory, on the other hand, views the school as a conventional institution that should bond the individual to society and decrease the risk of deviant behavior (Hirschi, 1969). Although failure in and frustration with school would be evidence of a weakening of the social bond and therefore should be related to higher rates of deviant behavior, disengaging entirely from school would sever that source of social control entirely. Hence, dropping out of school should increase, not decrease, the rate of future delinquency and drug use (Thornberry et al., 1985).

Two important studies have investigated the effect of dropping out of school on delinquent behavior. Elliott and Voss (1974) followed adolescents from the 9th grade until the expected date of graduation. They compared the rate of official delinquency for high school graduates and dropouts and found that the rate of delinquency declined sharply after they dropped out. Elliott and Voss interpret this as support for strain theory.

Thornberry et al. (1985) investigated the relationship between dropping out of school and subsequent delinquency using data from the Philadelphia birth cohort study. They distinguish between the short-term and long-term effects of dropping out of school. They find that there is no evidence of a short-term re-duction in delinquent behavior following dropping out and that the long-term effect of dropping out is to increase, not decrease, the probability of criminal behavior.

Fagan and Pabon (1990) raise a third possibility concerning the relationship between dropping out and subsequent delinquency and drug use. Rather than viewing these variables as causally related, they argue that the relationship may be spurious, with all three variables caused by common antecedents. If so, then these three behaviors may "occur as part of a common set of adolescent problem behaviors" (Fagan & Pabon, 1990, p. 313). This view is consistent with the more general perspective offered by Jessor and Jessor (1977) and Donovan and Jessor (1985).

The study presented in this chapter evaluates the strain, social control, and problem behavior arguments about the relationships among delinquency, drug use, and dropping out of school. It does so by first examining the effect of prior delinquency and drug use on the probability of dropping out, while controlling for school and family variables. Then, dropping out is used to predict subsequent delinquency and drug use, also controlling for family and school variables.

Methods

The data for this analysis are drawn from the Rochester Youth Development Study (RYDS). This study is designed to track the development of drug use and delinquent behavior in a high-risk urban sample. The RYDS is a multiwave panel study in which youths and their primary caretakers (in 95% of the cases the mother or stepmother) are interviewed every 6 months. In addition, data are collected from the Rochester public schools, police department, Department of Social Services, and other agencies that have contact with youth. This analysis makes use of interview data collected in waves 2–7 and of school data covering the years immediately prior to the beginning of the study. At wave 2, the subjects were in the fall semester of their 8th or 9th grade, and at wave 7 they were in the spring semester of their 10th or 11th grade.

Sample

In order to obtain a sufficient number of youth at high risk for serious de-linquency and drug use, the following sampling strategy was implemented: The overall sample was stratified, with males being overrepresented because they are more likely than females to engage in serious delinquency. Also, students were selected proportionate to the resident arrest rate of the census tract in which they lived at the time that the study began. This strategy allowed for the overrepresentation of those individuals assumed to be most at risk of engaging in serious delinquency and drug use.

Of the 4103 students in the 7th and 8th grades in the spring of 1988, 3372 (84%) were eligible for the sample. To generate a final panel of 1000 students, all eligible students were assigned to their census tract of residence, and 1334 were selected on the basis of an estimated nonparticipation rate of 25% (Capaldi & Patterson, 1987; Elliott, Ageton, Huizinga, Knowles, & Canter, 1983). All students in the census tracts with the highest resident arrest rates (approximately the top one third) were asked to participate, whereas students in the remaining census tracts were selected at a rate proportionate to the tract's contribution to the overall resident arrest rate. Once the number of students to be selected from each tract was determined, the student population was stratified by sex and grade in school, and students were selected from those strata at random. A final panel of 987 students and their families was selected for the study.

Because the probability that a youth will live in a particular census tract is known, this sampling strategy provides a means of weighting the cases to represent all 7th and 8th graders in the Rochester public schools. The sample is weighted in the analysis to follow.

The current analysis is based on 867 adolescents and their primary caretakers for whom waves 2–7 interviews were completed. This number represents 89% of the original sample, and there is no evidence of differential attrition. Males are overrepresented by approximately 3:1 (74% to 26%); African-Americans comprise the majority of the sample (68%), with 15% of the sample being white and 17% Hispanic.

RYDS adolescent interviews were typically conducted in a private room provided by the schools. Students who had dropped out of school, moved to a different school district, been institutionalized in a juvenile detention facility, or placed in foster care were followed and interviewed in appropriate settings. Caretakers were interviewed in their homes. Adolescents and caretakers were not present at each other's interviews.

Measurement of Variables

On the basis of the literature review presented above, variables relating to school and family dimensions, as well as measures of dropout status, drug use, and serious delinquent behavior, are included in the analysis. Demographic indicators are used as control variables. Table 1 provides the coding of the variables used in this analysis and univariate statistics describing each variable.

Table 1. Coding of Variables

Variable	Coding	Mean	S.D.
Gender			
Male	Dummy coded. Female is	0.74	0.44
Female	the omitted category	0.26	0.44
	(0 = no, 1 = yes).		
Race			
White	Dummy coded. White is	0.15	0.35
Hispanic	the omitted category	0.68	0.47
African-American	(0 = no, 1 = yes).	0.17	0.38
Underclass	Dummy coded. Index combining socioeconomic status and the Hollingshead Index (0 = no, 1 = yes).	0.50	0.50
Family structure			
Biological parents	Dummy variables	0.31	0.46
Single parent	calculated from answers	0.52	0.50
Stepparent	to "Who do you live	0.09	0.28
Other	with?" Both biological parents is omitted category (0 = no, 1 = yes).	0.09	0.28
Family			
Attachment to parents	Scale of 11 items measuring subject's attachment to primary caretaker. If more than one caretaker is identified, then the female raising subject is used (items in scale include asking if subject gets along wih the caretaker, trusts the caretaker, feels proud of the caretaker, etc.) (alpha = 0.87).	3.05	0.34
Supervision	Scale of 4 items asking subject if primary caretaker usually knows and feels it important to know where subject is, who subject is with, and who subject's friends are (alpha = 0.56).	3.61	0.39
School			
Average GPA 1986–1989	Calculated from official school data, average of the subject's GPA over the years 1986–1989.	1.95	0.86

(cont.)

Table 1.   Coding of Variables (*cont.*)

Variable	Coding	Mean	S.D.
CAT score for reading 1986–1989	Calculated from official data, average score for years 1986–1989, for reading portion of California Achievement Test.	45.51	22.15
Commitment to school	Scale of 10 items asking subject to indicate extent of agreement with a number of statements, such as: I like school a lot, homework is a waste of time, getting good grades is important (alpha = 0.81).	2.80	0.31
Student's expectations	Student indicates whether he or she expects to go to college.	2.60	0.67
Parent's expectations	Parent is asked if he or she expects the subject to go to college.	2.35	0.79
Involvement in school	Index of 3 items asking if subject participates in school clubs, sports, or musical groups.	1.77	0.80
Parent's involvement in school	Index of 5 items asking parent if he or she is involved in school activities with child, e.g., as coach or driver. Also asks if parent checks if homework gets done and is done correctly.	2.01	0.59
Dropout	Cumulative count of students who dropped out permanently during waves 4–6 ($N = 86$).	0.10	0.30
Delinquency	Not logged	1.66	6.19
	Logged	0.39	0.81
	Cumulative count of subject's incidence of serious delinquent acts (e.g., theft over $50, carrying a weapon, attack with a weapon, rape) across waves 2 and 3.		

Table 1.   Coding of Variables (*cont.*)

Variable	Coding	Mean	S.D.
	Not logged	0.28	1.68
	Logged	0.10	0.37
	Incidence of serious delinquent offenses in wave 7.		
Drug use	Not logged	4.10	21.60
	Logged	.37	.98
	Cumulative count of subject's incidence of drug use (not including alcohol) across waves 2 and 3.		
	Not logged	3.39	18.97
	Logged	0.27	0.87
	Incidence of drug use in wave 7.		

Family Variables

Both the structure and the quality of family relationships have been identified as possible correlates of dropping out of school, delinquent behavior, and drug use. Family structure is measured with three dummy variables; the reference category is comprised of adolescents who live with both biological parents and is contrasted with adolescents who have a single parent (in the vast majority of the cases, this is the mother), adolescents who have a stepparent, and those who have a family structure other than the first three (e.g., adolescents who indicate that they live in foster care or with a relative).

Two measures of the quality of family relationships are included in the analysis. Attachment to parents is measured by an 11-item scale derived from Hudson's Index of Parental Attitudes and the Child's Attitude Toward Mother (Father) Scale (Hudson, 1982). If a youth identified more than one person as being responsible for raising him or her—for example, both biological parents—attachment was calculated for the female caretaker. Chronbach's alpha measure of reliability for this scale is 0.87.

The other measure of the quality of family relationships is the level of supervision that the parent exercises over the youth. Adolescents were asked whether their parents usually knew where they were, who they were with, and who their friends are. These items are combined into a scale (alpha $= 0.56$).

School Variables

Variables relating to the experience and performance that adolescents have in school are taken from official school records, the adolescent interview, and the parent interview. The student's GPA is derived from the official records of the Rochester public schools and is calculated from all the courses the student took from 1986 through 1989.

A second measure of achievement used is the student's average reading score on the California Achievement Test (CAT). The scores on this test were averaged for 1986–1989. If there was missing information on either the GPA or the CAT, scores for those years on which data were available were averaged.

Commitment to school is measured by a 10-item scale asking students to indicate their level of agreement or disagreement with statements concerning how they feel about school. Items include statements such as "I like school a lot," "School is boring to me," "Getting good grades is important," and "Homework is a waste of time" (alpha = 0.81). The data on these items are taken from wave 3 interviews.

An alternative way of measuring commitment is to ask both students and their parents what expectations they have for the student's future education. If a student expects to go to college, it might be assumed that he or she is more committed to getting an education. If a parent expects the child to go to college, more emphasis is probably placed on education in the home. These variables are also measured at wave 3.

Involvement in school activities is measured in two ways. A 3-item index is used to determine the degree to which students report being involved in school sports, clubs, or musical groups. In addition, a 5-item index from the parent interview is used to determine how much parents report being involved in the school activities in which their children participate (e.g., attending their children's activities or driving them to those activities). In addition to the activity-related involvement, an item measuring the degree to which parents check on their child's homework is included in the index.

Dropping Out of School

Information from official records on dropping out of school is ambiguous at this stage of the students' academic careers, since it is difficult to distinguish between chronic absenteeism and full-fledged dropping out. In addition, there is the problem of the lag time between the time a student in fact stops attending school and the time it is officially determined that the student has dropped out. Therefore, we use a self-report measure from the student interview that indicates whether a student reports having dropped out any time during waves 4–6 and having not returned to school by wave 6. In this sample, 10% (N = 86) are considered to be dropouts by this definition. Others who dropped out for some period of time but returned to school are not considered dropouts in this analysis.

Delinquency and Drug Use

The delinquency and drug use measures are derived from a 44-item self-report index that asks respondents if they have engaged in any of these acts during the past 6 months. These items are taken from the National Youth Survey (Elliott et al., 1985) as modified by the Denver Youth Survey (Huizinga, Esbensen, & Weiher, 1991). Follow-up questions to the reporting of a delinquent act allowed for the responses to be screened to determine whether the behavior reported fits the type of delinquency measured and represents an actionable offense. The latter criterion is intended to screen out trivial offenses (e.g., reports of siblings' squabbles with one another in response to a question about serious assault) that law enforcement officials would, in all probability, ignore. If the response meets these two criteria, the total frequency for each offense is counted to construct each summated index.

In this analysis, delinquency is measured by the serious delinquency index that includes the following 9 items: (1) breaking and entering, (2) theft between \$50 and \$100, (3) theft over \$100, (4) motor vehicle theft, (5) carrying a weapon, (6) attacking with a weapon, (7) gang fights, (8) robbery, and (9) rape. Drug use is measured by a 10-item index: (1) use of marijuana, (2) inhalants, (3) hallucinogens, (4) cocaine, (5) crack, (6) heroin, (7) PCP, (8) tranquilizers, (9) barbiturates, and (10) amphetamines. Measures of both serious delinquency and drug use are taken at two points in time. To predict future dropout (measured from waves 4 to 6), cumulative measures of waves 2 and 3 delinquency and drug use are used. When delinquency and drug use are dependent variables (predicted by dropout), they are measured at wave 7. In all cases, the measure refers to the frequency of each subject's involvement in these behaviors.

Results

The two questions that frame this analysis are (1) what are the effects of prior delinquency and drug use on the probability of dropping out of school and (2) what is the effect of dropping out of school on subsequent delinquency and drug use? To address these questions, the analysis is divided into two sections. First, equations including prior drug use and delinquency are computed to predict whether an adolescent has dropped out of school. Then, dropping out is included in regression equations designed to predict subsequent delinquency and drug use.

Explaining Dropout Status

Since dropout status is a dichotomous variable, logistic regression analysis is used in this part of the analysis. Logistic regression coefficients are reported in Table 2 along with the probability changes in the dependent variable associated with them. These changes in the probabilities are not constant over the full range of values of the dependent variable. Therefore, they must be evaluated at specific probabilities of dropping out. In this analysis, they are evaluated at the mean of dropping out. In other words, the probabilities listed in Table 2 indicate the effect of one unit change in an independent variable on the average probability of dropping out (for more information, see Peterson, 1985). In this sample, the mean is about 0.10, since 86 students, or about 10% of the sample, reported that they had remained dropouts from waves 4 through 6. The model χ^2 statistic shows that these equations are significantly improved compared to equations with zeros for parameter estimates.

Because of the relatively high correlation between delinquency and drug

Table 2. Logistic Regression of School Dropout on Demographic, Family, School, and Prior Drug Use Variables

Independent variables	Probability	b	S.E.M.
Demographic			
Male	-0.05	-0.98^a	0.38
African-American	0.01	0.12	0.71
Hispanic	0.21	1.46^a	0.71
Underclass	0.07	0.66^a	0.39
Family			
Structure:			
Single	0.03	0.31	0.47
Stepparent	0.08	0.77	0.71
Other	0.03	0.25	0.70
Attachment	-0.03	-0.46	0.51
Supervision	-0.03	-0.44	0.41
School			
GPA	-0.06	-1.33^a	0.28
CAT	0.00	0.00	0.01
Commitment	-0.07	-1.51^a	0.66
Subject college expectations	-0.02	-0.40^a	0.23
Parent college expectations	0.00	-0.01	0.24
Subject school involvement	-0.01	-0.10	0.25
Parent school involvement	0.03	0.26	0.34
Prior drug use	0.0014	0.02^a	0.01
(Constant)		6.63	2.32

$^a p < 0.05$ (one-tailed test). $\chi^2 = 118.286$; $df = 17$; $p < 0.001$.

use, they are not included in the same equations that predict dropout. Rather, the effect of drug use on dropping out is examined first; then, in a separate equation, the effect of serious delinquency on dropping out is examined.

The equations reported in Table 2 examine the effects of family-related variables, school-related variables, demographic variables, and prior drug use on the probability of dropping out. Among the family-related variables, it is evident that family structure does not significantly affect the probability of dropping out of school. Having a single parent, having a stepparent, or being a member of a family with some other structure is indistinguishable from being part of a family that still includes both natural parents. Moreover, neither attachment to parents nor parental supervision significantly affects dropping out of school. This result is somewhat surprising, since it is often assumed that the family will have a major impact on such problem behaviors as dropping out of school.

As expected, though, the variables related to school fare better as predictors of subsequent dropping out. At the average level of dropping out, adolescents with higher GPAs are 6% less likely to drop out, while those who are more committed to school are 7% less likely to drop out. Not surprisingly, those adolescents who do not expect to go to college are 2% more likely to drop out.

Turning to the demographic variables, we see that Hispanics are 21% more likely to drop out of school than are whites, and being a member of the underclass increases one's probability of dropping out by 7%. Surprisingly, at these ages, males are 5% less likely to drop out of school than are females.

Having considered the impact of these control variables, we now turn our attention to the variable that is of particular interest in this analysis, the frequency of prior drug use. Adolescents who have used drugs are significantly more likely to subsequently drop out of school. One additional use of drugs in a 1-year period increases the probability of dropping out by 0.14%, a seemingly small effect. However, to determine the impact of regular drug use (once a week), the change in the probability of dropping out was also calculated for a 52-unit change in drug use. In other words, at the average probability of dropping out (10%), how much increase in the probability of dropping out would we expect when an adolescent uses drugs once a week as opposed to never using drugs? In this scenario, we would expect a 5% increase in the probability of dropping out. Furthermore, for the child who has a higher than average risk of dropping out, the effect of weekly drug use is even greater. For example, if it is assumed that children have a 30% probability of dropping out rather than a 10% chance, then those who use drugs weekly increase their probability of dropping out by 18%. That is, at this initial probability, weekly drug use moves the individual from a 30% probability of dropping out to a 48% probability.

The equation substituting serious delinquency for drug use produces similar results, with one important exception (Table 3). The same school-related and demographic variables are significant in this equation as in the prior equation. The one important difference in the findings is that serious delinquency does not contribute significantly to the prediction of the probability of dropping out. This finding is surprising, given the correlations typically found between these variables and given the current results concerning drug use.

In sum, the results from equations that predict dropout status indicate that family-related variables do not have a significant effect on dropping out, but that some school-related variables do. Specifically, GPA, commitment to school, and expectations about going to college are significantly related to dropping out. Hispanic adolescents, the underclass, and females are more likely to drop out of school than are whites, adolescents who are not underclass status, and males. Finally, prior drug use is significantly and strongly related to subsequent dropping out, but serious delinquency is not.

Table 3. Logistic Regression of School Dropout on Demographic, Family, School, and Prior Serious Delinquency Variables

Independent variables	Probability	b	S.E.M.
Demographic			
Male	−0.05	−0.96[a]	0.38
African-American	0.02	0.21	0.71
Hispanic	0.15	1.54[a]	0.71
Underclass	0.07	0.65[a]	0.39
Family			
Structure:			
Single	0.03	0.32	0.47
Stepparent	0.08	0.77	0.71
Other	0.04	0.40	0.69
Attachment	−0.03	−0.51	0.51
Supervision	−0.03	−0.46	0.41
School			
GPA	−0.06	−1.33[a]	0.28
CAT	0.00	0.00	0.01
Commitment	−0.07	−1.51[a]	0.66
Subject college expectations	−0.05	−0.39[a]	0.23
Parent college expectations	0.00	−0.02	0.23
Subject school involvement	−0.01	−0.07	0.24
Parent school involvement	0.03	0.27	0.34
Prior serious delinquency	0.00	0.03	0.02
(Constant)		6.69	2.32

[a]$p \leq 0.05$ (one-tailed test). $\chi^2 = 116.469$; $df = 17$; $p < 0.001$.

Explaining Future Drug Use and Delinquency

The second question that drives this analysis concerns the relationship between dropping out of school and subsequent drug use and serious delinquent behavior. Does the probability of delinquent behavior increase when an adolescent drops out, as social control theory would argue? Or does getting away from an aversive school environment by dropping out lead to a decrease in delinquency, as strain theory would predict?

Because the other school variables and dropping out can be seen as indicators of a more general construct having to do with difficulties in school, only dropping out is included in the first equation; then the school-related variables are included along with dropping out in the second equation (see Table 4). This strategy allows for an examination of the possibility that any effect of dropout on subsequent drug use is really due to the difficulties that adolescents experience in school and not to their having dropped out of school. We also include prior drug use in the equation, so we are in effect predicting changes in drug use as a function of dropping out and the other variables.

Dropping out of school is significantly related to subsequent drug use even after the effects of prior drug use are entered into the equation. This finding, taken by itself, would support a social control explanation of the effect of dropping out and call into question hypotheses derived from strain theory. In addition to the dropout variable, attachment to parents is found to have a significant negative effect on subsequent drug use. Adolescents who do not get along well with their parents are more likely to use drugs. Males are more likely than females to use drugs, and, as expected, prior drug use is related to subsequent drug use.

In the second set of equations, the school-related variables are entered along with the variables entered in the first equation to determine whether the significant relationship between dropping out and subsequent drug use remains. The findings indicate that when the school-related variables are included in the equation, the effect of having dropped out of school on subsequent drug use is no longer significant. Rather, dropping out of school may be seen as a proxy for other sources of dissatisfaction with school. In the current equation, parental participation with their children in school-related activities decreases the probability of subsequent drug use. The adolescents' own perception of their involvement in school is positively related to drug use. Although this finding appears on the surface to be counterintuitive, it is consistent with other analyses on this sample (Krohn & Thornberry, 1993). The more active adolescents are the ones who are more likely to be using drugs, particularly if their activities are engaged in without parental involvement.

Table 5 presents the results from the analysis predicting subsequent serious delinquency. Again, the strategy of first including the dropout variable without

Table 4.   OLS Regression of Drug Use on Demographic, Family, School, Prior
Drug Use, and Dropout Status Variables

Independent variables	Equation 1			Equation 2		
	Beta	b	S.E.M.	Beta	b	S.E.M.
Demographic						
Male	0.08	0.12^a	0.06	0.03	0.04	0.06
African-American	0.07	0.10	0.08	0.01	0.02	0.09
Hispanic	0.02	0.04	0.10	0.01	0.01	0.11
Underclass	−0.01	−0.02	0.05	−0.04	−0.06	0.06
Family						
Structure						
Single	−0.02	−0.03	0.06	−0.03	−0.04	0.06
Stepparent	0.03	0.08	0.10	0.01	0.04	0.12
Other	−0.01	−0.04	0.10	−0.04	−0.10	0.11
Attachment	−0.10	$−0.22^a$	0.08	−0.08	$−0.17^a$	0.10
Supervision	0.02	0.04	0.07	−0.00	−0.01	0.08
School						
GPA	—	—	—	−0.07	−0.06	0.04
CAT	—	—	—	0.01	0.00	0.00
Commitment	—	—	—	0.02	0.04	0.11
Subject college expectations	—	—	—	0.01	0.01	0.05
Parent college expectations	—	—	—	−0.02	−0.02	0.04
Subject school involvement	—	—	—	0.07	0.06^a	0.04
Parent school involvement	—	—	—	−0.09	$−0.11^a$	0.05
Prior drug use	0.14	0.01^a	0.001	0.25	0.01^a	0.002
Dropout	0.07	0.19^a	0.10	0.04	0.10	0.11
		$R^2 = 0.04$			$R^2 = 0.10$	

$^a p \leq 0.05$ (one-tailed test).

the school-related variables and then entering the school-related variables is followed.

The only variables that significantly predict subsequent serious delinquent
behavior in the truncated analysis are prior serious delinquency and the dummy
variable representing being a male. Males are more likely to commit serious
delinquency, and having committed serious delinquent behavior in the past increases the probability that one will do so in the future. Having dropped out of
school is not related to serious delinquent behavior even when the school-related
variables are not incorporated in the analysis.

When the school-related variables are included in the equation that predicts
serious delinquency, slight changes are observed. Parental supervision becomes

Table 5. OLS Regression of Serious Delinquency on Demographic, Family, School, Prior Serious Delinquency, and Dropout Status Variables

Independent variables	Equation 1			Equation 2		
	Beta	b	S.E.M.	Beta	b	S.E.M.
Demographic						
Male	0.18	0.10^a	0.02	0.16	0.09^a	0.02
African-American	0.06	0.04	0.03	0.06	0.04	0.04
Hispanic	0.06	0.05	0.04	0.08	0.06	0.04
Underclass	0.02	0.01	0.02	-0.02	-0.01	0.02
Family						
Structure:						
Single	-0.02	-0.01	0.02	-0.03	-0.01	0.03
Stepparent	0.00	0.00	0.04	-0.02	-0.02	0.04
Other	0.04	0.03	0.04	0.04	0.04	0.04
Attachment	-0.01	-0.01	0.03	0.01	0.01	0.04
Supervision	-0.05	-0.04	0.03	-0.07	-0.05^a	0.03
School						
GPA	—	—	—	-0.03	-0.01	0.02
CAT	—	—	—	0.01	0.00	0.00
Commitment	—	—	—	0.04	0.04	0.04
Subject college expectations	—	—	—	-0.06	-0.02	0.02
Parent college expectations	—	—	—	-0.08	-0.03^a	0.02
Subject school involvement	—	—	—	0.01	0.00	0.01
Parent school involvement	—	—	—	-0.04	-0.02	0.02
Prior serious delinquency	0.07	0.004^a	0.004	0.06	0.004^a	0.003
Dropout	0.04	0.04	0.04	0.01	0.01	0.04
		$R^2 = 0.05$			$R^2 = 0.07$	

$^a p \leq 0.05$ (one-tailed test).

significantly related to delinquency, indicating that those youths who are less supervised by their parents are more likely to commit serious delinquent behavior. If parents expect their child to go to college, the child is less likely to be involved in serious delinquency. These are minor changes and do not impact the general conclusion to be derived from these findings. Dropping out of school remains unrelated to subsequent delinquent behavior.

It is important to note, though, that dropping out of school never has a negative effect on subsequent delinquency or drug use, as would be expected from a strain theory perspective. Dropping out of school has either a slight positive effect or a neutral effect on these later behaviors.

Discussions and Conclusion

An empirical relationship among dropping out of school, delinquency, and drug use has been confirmed in a number of prior studies. It is not clear, however, just how these three forms of problem behavior are causally related. Indeed, there are three general perspectives that can be adopted.

On one hand, drug use and delinquency may precede dropping out of school. If that is the case, it may be that engaging in such behaviors increases the probability of leaving school prior to graduation. Alternatively, it may be that these behaviors are caused by the same set of predictor variables and are therefore simply concomitant consequences of school, family, and other variables (Fagan & Pabon, 1990).

On the other hand, the causal influence of dropping out of school on subsequent delinquency and drug use is also a source of debate in the prior literature. From a social control perspective (Hirschi, 1969; Thornberry et al., 1985), dropping out of school should lead to an increase in problem behaviors such as drug use and delinquent behavior. Early departure from school weakens the ties that adolescents have with a conventional institution and further frees them from bonds that might have constrained their behavior. Arguments derived from a strain perspective suggest otherwise (Elliott & Voss, 1974). If school is a source of frustration or strain for the youngster, leaving the aversive situation could actually lead to a decrease in drug use and delinquency, rather than an increase.

Finally, adopting a developmental or interactional perspective (Thornberry, 1987), both these processes could be at work. Early delinquency and drug use could place a youngster at risk for dropping out of school, and then the consequences of dropping out could alter later involvement in delinquency and drug use.

This study examined these questions with panel data from a sample of inner-city adolescents. The results are different for drug use than for serious delinquent behavior, and neither set of findings conforms to either a social control or a strain perspective.

The results indicate that earlier drug use is significantly related to dropping out of school, even when a battery of school and family-related variables are incorporated in the equation. Family-related variables are not related to the probability of dropping out, but a number of school-related variables are significant predictors. Adolescents who are experiencing problems in school are more likely to drop out. But even after school-related variables are taken into consideration, prior drug use has an effect on the probability of dropping out. The use of drugs combines with dissatisfaction and lack of success in school to increase the likelihood that an adolescent will drop out.

Given these findings, we might have expected similar results when we replaced drug use with serious delinquent behavior, but this was not the case.

Serious delinquent behavior was not significantly related to dropping out of school. The difference in the findings regarding drug use and serious delinquent behavior may be attributable to the different impact that these behaviors have on the individual's life in general and on schoolwork specifically. The lingering physiological effects of drugs may be a particular impediment to pursuing schoolwork and school-related activities. Drug use can consume much more of the person's time because the effects of the drugs can last long after the period of ingestion. Delinquent acts, on the other hand, tend to be of short duration, with little, if any, lingering physical consequences. These other forms of delinquent behavior may not be as intrusive on the individual's school activities. Thus, drug use would be more likely to lead to dropping out of school than would serious delinquent behavior.

How dropping out of school affects subsequent drug use and serious delinquent behavior is the second question addressed in this study. No support was found for the strain theory hypothesis that removing oneself from an aversive situation would lead to a reduction of aberrant behavior. For both drug use and delinquent behavior, the direction of the relationships with dropping out of school is positive, indicating that if dropping out has any effect, it is to increase, rather than decrease, drug use and delinquent behavior.

More specifically, the relationship between dropping out and delinquency is not significant either when the school-related variables are excluded from or when they are included in the equation. Dropping out is significantly related to later drug use when school-related variables are not included in the equation. This relationship, however, is not significant when the school-related variables are included. Dropping out of school and drug use, therefore, may each be a consequence of problems encountered in school, rather than dropping out of school being a cause of further drug use.

This study provides only an initial estimation of relationships among these variables. It examined the relationship between indicators of delinquent behavior and school dropout over a fairly short time span. Our measure of school dropout was taken when our sample members were between the ages of 15 and 17. Not all students who eventually will fail to complete high school have dropped out by this age; thus, we have assessed only the impact of early departure from school. The impact of not finishing high school on subsequent behavior will have to be examined with additional waves of data.

The short time span also means that what is being assessed is the immediate impact of dropping out on delinquent behavior. There is some evidence to suggest that dropping out of school has a delayed effect on delinquent behavior, rather than an immediate one. Elliott and Voss (1974) focused on the more immediate effect of dropping out on delinquency and found a slight reduction in the probability of delinquency. Thornberry et al. (1985) examined the impact of school dropout over a more extended period of time and found that dropping out substantially increased the probability of delinquency and crime. With the limited time span on which we focused, a positive relationship between dropping out and delinquency and drug use was found. It would therefore be reasonable to expect that extending the follow-up period would produce stronger, more significant results supportive of a social control rather than a strain argument. The dropout would be expected to face continuing economic and social disadvantages, making criminal behavior more attractive. This possibility will be examined with future waves of data from this study.

In sum, the findings suggest that drug use, but not serious delinquent behavior, increases the probability of dropping out of school even after family and school-related variables are taken into account. Dropping out of school is not significantly related to subsequent drug use and delinquency. Neither the social control nor the strain perspective adequately accounts for these findings. It appears that dropping out of school, the use of drugs, and participation in delinquent behavior might form a constellation of problematic behaviors that are, in part, caused by dissatisfaction with school.

References

Agnew, R. 1985. A revised strain theory of delinquency. *Social Forces, 64*, 151–67.

Aston, N. M., & McLanahan, S. S. (1991). Family structure, parental practices and high school completion. *American Sociological Review, 56*, 309–320.

Bachman, J. G., O'Malley, P. M., & Johnston, J. (1978). *Adolescence to adulthood: Change and stability in the lives of young men.* Ann Arbor: Institute for Social Research, University of Michigan.

Barrington, B. L., & Hendricks, B. (1989). Differentiating characteristics of high school graduates, dropouts and nongraduates. *Journal of Educational Research, 82*, 309–319.

Cairns, R. B., Cairns, B. D., & Neckerman, H. J. (1989). Early school dropout: Configuration and determinants. *Child Development, 60*, 1437–1452.

Capaldi, D., & Patterson, G. (1987). An approach to the problem of recruitment and retention rates for longitudinal research. *Behavioral Assessment, 9*, 169–177.

Cohen, A. K. (1955). *Delinquent boys.* New York: Free Press.

Donovan, J. E., & Jessor, R. (1985). Structure of problem behavior in adolescence and young adulthood. *Journal of Consulting and Clinical Psychology, 53*, 890–904.

Dunham, R. G., & Alpert, G. P. (1987). Keeping delinquents in school: A prediction model. *Adolescence, 85*, 45–57.

Ekstrom, R. B., Goertz, M. E., Pollack, J. M., & Rock, D. A. (1986). Who drops out of high school and why? Findings from a national study. *Teachers College Record, 82*, 353–373.

Elliott, D. S., & Voss, H. L. (1974). *Delinquency and dropout.* Lexington, MA: Lexington Books.

Elliott, D. S., Ageton, S. S., Huizinga, D. H., Knowles, B. A., & Canter, R. J. (1983). The prevalence and incidence of delinquent behavior 1976–1980. National Youth Survey Report No. 26. Boulder: Behavioral Research Institute.

Elliott, D., Huizinga, D., & Ageton, S. (1985). *Explaining delinquency and drug use.* Beverly Hills: Sage Publications.

Fagan, J., & Jones, S. J. (1984). Towards a theoretical model for intervention with violent juvenile offenders. In R. Mathias, P. Demuro, & R. Allinson (Eds.), *Violent juvenile offenders: An anthology* (pp.). San Francisco: National Council on Crime and Delinquency.

Fagan, J., & Pabon, E. (1990). Contributions of delinquency and substance use to school dropout among inner city youths. *Youth and Society, 21,* 306–354.

Fagan, J., Piper, E., & Moore, M. (1986). Violent delinquents and urban youth. *Criminology, 24,* 439–466.

Friedman, A., Glickman, N., & Utada, A. (1985). Does drug and alcohol use lead to failure to graduate from high school? *Journal of Drug Education, 15,* 353–363.

Hawkins, J., & Lam, T. (1987). Teacher practices, social development and delinquency. In J. Burchard & S. Burchard (Eds.), *Prevention of delinquent behavior (pp. 241–274). Newbury Park, CA: Sage Publications.*

Hirschi, T. (1969). *Causes of delinquency.* Berkeley: University of California Press.

Hudson, W. (1982). *The clinical measurement package: A field manual.* Homewood, IL: Dorsey Press.

Huizinga, D., Esbensen, F., & Weiher, A. W. (1991). Are there multiple paths to delinquency? *Journal of Criminal Law and Criminology, 82,* 83–118.

Jessor, R., & Jessor, S. (1977). *Problem behavior and psychosocial development: A longitudinal study of youth.* New York: Academic Press.

Kelly, D., & Pink, W. (1971). School commitment and school careers. *Youth & Society, 3,* 224–235.

Krohn, M. D., & Thornberry, T. P. (1993). Network theory: A model for understanding drug abuse among African-American and Hispanic youth. In M. De La Rosa and J. L. Recio Adrados (Eds.), *Drug abuse among minority youth: Advances in research methodology* (pp. 102–128). Washington, DC: U.S. Government Printing Office.

Mensch, B. S. & Kandel, D. (1988). Dropping out of high school and drug involvement. *Sociology of Education, 61,* 95–113.

Peterson, T. (1985). A comment on presenting results from logit and probit models. *American Sociological Review, 50,* 130–131.

Rumberger, R. W. (1983). Dropping out of high school: The influences of race, sex and family background. *American Educational Research Journal, 20,* 199–220.

Thornberry, T. P. (1987). Toward an interactional theory of delinquency. *Criminology, 25,* 863–891.

Thornberry, T. P., Moore, M., & Christenson, R. L. (1985). The effects of dropping out of high school on subsequent criminal behavior. *Criminology, 23,* 3–18.

V

MODERATORS OF THE RELATIONSHIPS AMONG DRUG USE, CRIME, AND OTHER FORMS OF DEVIANCE

In Part IV and elsewhere in this volume, a number of instances are noted in which theoretically informed hypotheses are not confirmed. Further, a number of other situations are apparent in which in some studies a time-ordered hypothesized relationship is confirmed and in other studies the relationship is disconfirmed. For example, Stacy and Newcomb (Chapter 4) and Kaplan and Damphousse (Chapter 8) observe relationships between drug use and later criminal deviance or violence, whereas Brook and her associates (Chapter 3) do not find that drug use predicts aggression or theft/vandalism.

Both the disconfirmation of hypotheses in some studies and the inconsistency in findings across studies suggest the need to consider the conditions that moderate the relationships among variables. Disconfirmation of findings may signify that the theoretical conditions that are presumed to exist for the hypothesized relationship to be observed in fact do not hold, and that if the subjects were selected to reflect the implicit theoretical condition, the relationship would be confirmed. Similarly, inconsistent findings may suggest the need for theoretical elaboration by suggesting further conditions under which the relationship would be observed or fail to be observed.

Part V comprises two studies that consider variables that moderate the hypothesized causal relationships between other deviance-relevant variables. The moderating effects are expressed as interaction terms in multiple regression equations and by comparison of regression effects across groups representing different values of the moderating variable.

In Chapter 8, Kaplan and Damphousse use data collected during two waves (7th grade and young adulthood) of a multiwave longitudinal study of a general population to examine the moderating influence of levels of self-derogation and antisocial personality on the relationship between early drug use and later violence among subjects who were free of violence at the earlier point in time. Consistent with the guiding theoretical framework, the researchers observed a significant main effect of adolescent drug use on later violence, controlling on gender, race/ethnicity, father's education, other forms of deviance, and antisocial personality. Further, this finding was moderated by self-derogation and antisocial personality. Adolescent drug use anticipated later deviant behavior for high self-derogation subjects, but not for low self-derogation subjects. For the latter subjects, the effect of drugs on violence was apparently suppressed by the countervailing effects of antisocial personality. When the interaction of drugs and antisocial personality is entered into the equation, a significant and positive main effect of drugs on later violence is observed, as is a significant negative effect of the interaction term on later violence. Thus, among subjects with low levels of self-derogation, for subjects who have low levels of antisocial personality, drug use leads to higher levels of violence; for subjects who have high levels of antisocial personality, drug use decreases the probability of later violence. Apparently, for subjects who are most prone to violence, the use of drugs has a dampening effect on violence, while for subjects who are least prone to violence, the use of drugs has a disinhibiting effect on violence. These observations raise interesting questions regarding the interaction of drugs and the biochemical and psychodynamic substrate associated with different personality structures.

In Chapter 9, Apospori, Vega, Zimmerman, Warheit, and Gil use longitudinal data from adolescent boys to explore the conditions under which prior deviance leads to drug use. The investigators observe a significant interaction between race/ethnicity and prior major deviance, indicating that prior major deviance had a different impact on drug use among Hispanics, blacks, and whites. Consequently, the interactions between prior major deviance and other predictors are explored for each racial group separately. Different patterns of interaction effects are observed for each group. The authors conclude that the additive linear models are not adequate for studying the relationship between earlier deviance and later drug use. Rather, this relationship is moderated by ethnic factors as well as family, peer, and personality factors. Among the implications of the findings for prevention/intervention programs is the expectation that sources of problem behaviors that should be targeted will vary for different ethnic groups, and indeed the targeted behaviors within each group will be different depending on family conditions, peer relationships, and personality factors.

8

Self-Attitudes and Antisocial Personality as Moderators of the Drug Use–Violence Relationship

Howard B. Kaplan and Kelly R. Damphousse

Introduction

This chapter reports a series of logistic regression models that examine the effect of drug use on violence and the conditions under which the effect on later violence of drug use during adolescence (net of the effect of earlier violence, non-drug/nonviolent deviance, and sociodemographic controls) is relatively strong or weak. We first examine the literature that describes the general consequences of drug use, the putative causal relationship between drugs and crime, and violence as a consequence of drug use. We then introduce the possibility that two variables (self-derogation and antisocial personality) may moderate the drug use–violence relationship and account for apparently contradictory findings regarding this relationship that are reported in the literature.

Theories of Drug Consequences

Though much has been written concerning the *antecedents* of drug abuse, only recently has interest turned to the *consequences* of adolescent drug use (particularly for young adulthood) (Newcomb & Bentler, 1988). Most of the

Howard B. Kaplan and Kelly R. Damphousse • Department of Sociology, Texas A&M University, College Station, Texas 77843.

Drugs, Crime, and Other Deviant Adaptations: Longitudinal Studies, edited by Howard B. Kaplan. Plenum Press, New York, 1995.

current research on consequences focuses on the negative aspects of illicit drug use. Some researchers, however, point to possible positive consequences of drug use (e.g., Kandel, 1978). Kaplan's theory of self-derogation (Kaplan, 1980, 1984, 1985), for example, suggests that adolescents begin to use drugs when they have not met the expectations of themselves and others around them. For such adolescents, "the drug use pattern is expected to contribute to feelings of self-worth by symbolizing attacks on the values according to the standards of which the youth was judged unworthy" (Kaplan, 1985, p. 481). Other possible positive results may include the increased "sociability" of the drug user, who is now the "hit of the party," and the introduction to new peers, who provide acceptance and opportunities for social and material gain.

While the quest for positive outcomes of adolescent drug use remains somewhat untapped, hypotheses regarding the adverse consequences are more readily available. Baumrind and Moselle (1985), for example, suggest that drug use during the pivotal transition stage of adolescence may interfere with identity formation, delaying development of mature adulthood. Newcomb and Bentler (1988) propose that drug use by adolescents accelerates the developmental process by forcing users to prematurely accept adult roles and responsibilities. The "pseudomaturity" experienced by adolescent drug users leaves them poorly prepared for life in the real world, resulting in role performance failure (e.g., in marriage, work) over time. Similarly, Fagan, Weis, Cheng, and Watters (1987) have suggested that drug use during adolescence results in weak development of the skills necessary for analyzing and judging situations that are morally ambiguous or for providing appropriate responses to social cues.

Consequences related to the use of drugs are also suggested by Robins, Darvish, and Murphy (1970), who observe that those who use marijuana during adolescence suffer social consequences such as being less likely to graduate from high school and being more likely to have police records, to drink heavily, and to report violent behavior as adults. A popular theory concerning the consequences of drug use relates to "amotivational syndrome." This condition describes long-term effects of using marijuana, described as a "pattern of apathetic withdrawal of energy and interest from effortful activity" (Baumrind & Moselle, 1985, p. 55). Although these symptoms are common among adolescents in general, the use of drugs is thought to exacerbate the problem. According to Kandel (1978), however, the majority of these conditions occur before the use of drugs. Thus, the relationship might better be seen as spurious, rather than causal.

On balance, though, adolescent drug use is thought to have deleterious effects for young adulthood. The ingestion of drugs impairs the functioning of youths such that they are poorly prepared to function in their adult roles. The developmental process may be slowed down or accelerated (Baumrind & Moselle, 1985; Newcomb & Bentler, 1988). Either outcome results in an inability on the part of the adolescent to deal with the problems inherent in social living. The use of drugs as a coping response leads to dependence on maladaptive coping patterns that preclude functioning in normatively prescribed ways. The end result is an inability to deal with life stress through conventional adaptations and an increased inclination to engage in unorthodox or deviant behavior in order to obtain desired ends.

The use of drugs is also thought to have negative physiological effects on the user, although the extent to which this is the case is still under examination. Different drugs, for instance, are known to have differential effects on the user's mood, including euphoria, depression, and general stimulation. Each of these emotional results of drug use is thought to have differential effects on the behavior of individuals. More specifically, opiates and marijuana seem to have a suppressive effect on aggression, while barbiturates, amphetamines, and cocaine tend to exacerbate aggressive tendencies (Fagan, 1990). Concerning the biological effects of drugs in general on the body, Moyer (1983) has suggested that there are specific areas of the human brain that are affected by substance use that may lead individuals to become, among other things, aggressive.

Association between Drugs and Crime

The "epidemic" (Robins, 1984) increase of drug use and crime among adolescents over the past three decades has resulted in a greater desire for an understanding of the link between the two phenomena. There appear to be two main questions to be answered: First, are drug use and crime correlated? Second, does one cause the other? The former seems much easier to answer than the latter.

Correlation between Drugs and Crime

Clearly, the link between drug use and crimes such as assault and homicide is quite strong. In 1989, for example, one report indicated that over 60% of those arrested for violent crimes had traces of illicit drugs in their urine (Reiss & Roth, 1993). About 10% of all homicides in general are related to drug use, while the percentage is higher in urban areas and increasing overall (Goldstein, 1989). As many as 53% of the homicides in New York during 1988 have been categorized as being drug-related (Goldstein, Brownstein, Ryan, & Bellucci, 1989). Summarizing, then, there exists a great deal of evidence that suggests that criminal activity and drug use are highly correlated. It is more difficult, however, to show how the two concepts are causally related. We examine this problem next.

Causal Relationship between Drugs and Crime

The extant literature suggests that there are at least five ways to explain the empirical relationship between drug use and crime. First, the use of drugs leads to criminal involvement. Lay understandings of the relationship between drugs and crime readily assume that the use of drugs by adolescents is responsible for criminal involvement. Many researchers, while admitting that criminal activity may indeed precede initial drug use, have suggested a causal link between drug use and crime. Speckart and Anglin (1986, 1988), for example, have shown that there is a significant relationship between the *level* of illicit drug use and property crime such that commission of property crime increased as drug use increased and decreased when drug use was discontinued. They, along with others (Ball, Rosen, Flueck, & Nurco, 1981; Nurco, Schaeffer, Ball, & Kinlock, 1984), suggest that the use of drugs influences the level of criminal activity for individuals. A number of other studies suggest that drug use is, for example, causally related to homicide, predatory crime, and other types of crime (Anglin & Speckart, 1988; Chaiken & Chaiken, 1982, 1990; Gold & Moles, 1978; Hunt, 1990; Newcomb & Bentler, 1988; Wish & Johnson, 1984). Drug use may motivate the user to engage in crime or reduce barriers to engage in crimes that are otherwise motivated.

Second, criminal activity leads to drug use. Several researchers have suggested that criminal activity actually precedes, or is concurrent with, drug use. Elliott and Huizinga (1984), for example, concluded that among those who participated in both drug use and delinquency, about half were delinquent before using drugs while the other half initiated both drugs and delinquency in the same year or used drugs first. Along the same lines, Smith and Fogg (1978) reported that those who scored low on an obedience/law-abiding scale were more likely to become involved in drug use. Here, crime is hypothesized to provide the context and opportunity to become involved in drug use. That is, involvement is delinquency allows the individual to come in contact with others who will provide the context, the definitions, and the opportunity to use drugs (Elliott, Huizinga, & Ageton, 1985). Johnston, O'Malley, and Eveland (1978), for example, suggested (p. 155) that "there is no evidence of a lasting impact of drug use on delinquency levels. . . . The nonaddictive use of illicit drugs does not seem to play much of a role in leading users to become the more delinquent people we know them to be. *The reverse kind of causation seems considerably more plausible, that is, that delinquency leads to drug use*" [emphasis added].

Third, both the first and the second interpretation are correct. Drugs dispose individuals to engage in other forms of deviance and reduce barriers to the acting out of deviant dispositions, and participation in other forms of deviance introduces individuals to patterns of illicit drug use while providing settings that are conducive to drug use.

Fourth, delinquency and drug use are to be seen as aspects of general dispositions to deviance. In this case, drugs and other patterns of crime are seen as coincident indicators of a more general construct such as "problem behavior" (Jessor & Jessor, 1977). This orientation is implicit in the inclusion by researchers of drug use items in the makeup of general delinquency scales, suggesting that drug use and other forms of criminal activity are similar. This perspective, of course, ignores the possibility of drugs and crime having any causal effect on each other, since they are treated as alternative operationalizations of the same concept (see Osgood, Johnston, O'Malley, & Bachman, 1988; Robins, 1978).

Finally, drug use and delinquency may be seen as independent forms of deviance that share common antecedents, resulting in a spurious relationship (Watters, Reinarman & Fagan, 1985). Fagan et al. (1987) suggest, however, that while delinquency and drug use may have *some* common antecedents, these antecedents do not fully account for the drug use–delinquency association.

We see, then, that there is a clear correlation between the occurrence of drug use and other delinquent behavior. What is less clear, however, is how the two are causally related. When the assumption of a causal relationship is made, it appears that the issue that causes most concern about the possible drug use–crime relationship is the violent behavior that might result from drug use. We address this literature in the next section.

Violence as a Result of Drug Use

Aggression and violent behavior are among the most salient and feared possible consequences of drug use. Several theories have been proposed that suggest the ways in which drug use may result in violence. Perhaps the most fundamental hypothesized pathway for the effect of drugs on violence is biological. It is thought that drug use damages or at least changes the structure of the brain. This effect may result in an increased likelihood that violent tendencies will be expressed when the opportunity (target) is presented (Moyer, 1983). Marinacci and von Hagen (1972) suggested that alcohol use resulted in damage to the temporal lobe, resulting in susceptibility to violent or antisocial behavior. Fagan (1990) suggests, however, that there is little evidence to support this set of hypotheses. He suggests that if the biological theories were correct, then we would expect less variation in the patterns that we observe. Everyone who used drugs would become violent. Since this is certainly not the case, we must look for answers to the problem along the lines of social context.

The tripartite description by Paul Goldstein (1985) of the relationship between drug use and violence states that drugs are related to violence in three ways: psychopharmacologically, economic compulsively, and systemically. In the first case, he suggests that drugs are related to violence psychopharmachologically such that people have relatively short-term, adverse reactions to drug use (or to the withdrawal from drug use) that cause them to act irrationally or violently. This relationship is also meant to describe violence resulting from drug use when either the perpetrator *or* the victim uses drugs. It also reflects violence that is facilitated by the use of drugs in order to increase boldness or decrease nervousness. The use of drugs in this case is seen to have immediate, direct effects on violence.

Second, drugs can be seen as being related to violence through economic compulsion, where drug users commit economically gainful violent crimes in order to support their drug habits. The violence in this case can be either intended (e.g., planned muggings) or unintended contextual situations that are beyond the control of the drug user (e.g., a victim who resists).

Finally, drug use can be seen as being related to violence systemically such that the patterns of interaction surrounding the drug-use culture often culminate in violence aimed at "protecting turf" or eliminating informers. Such violence may also be the result of conflicts between users fighting over drugs.

Pernanen (1981) theorized that ingestion of intoxicating substances may cause the impairment of cognitive abilities to interpret other peoples' actions. Confusion over the intentions of others may result in violence. Collins (1983) has stated that there are two major variables that influence the causal relationship between drug use and violence. The first is the degree to which an actor is inclined to use violence to settle personal disputes and grievances. The second is the degree to which the actor *believes* that drug use will result in violence. Violence is most likely to occur when both these conditions are present.

Another account of the relationship between drugs and violence posits a "disinhibition" effect (Collins, 1988). That is, the ingestion of drugs (or alcohol) looses an individual from the grasp of internalized social control. He or she therefore becomes more likely to engage in violent or aggressive activities when otherwise disposed to do so, since there is no longer a constraint against expressing aggressive behavior. Zeichner and Pihl (1980) hypothesize that drug use interferes with an individual's ability to recognize the possible adverse consequences of his or her behavior. Another explanation for the motivation to use intoxicating substances was developed by McClelland (1975). He suggested that, especially in the case of males, the use of intoxicating substances offers to the adolescent a degree of power over others. Once intoxication occurs, the desire for expressing power over others may result in acts of violence.

Discussion

Certain findings in the literature have helped contribute to the perhaps premature inclination of researchers to avoid closer examination of the possible causal effects of drug use on crime and the consequences of drug use in general (Kandel, 1978). Kandel, Simcha-Fagan, and Davies (1986) showed that delinquency tended to precede drug use among youths and that drug use among youths is a poor predictor of whether they will commit criminal acts as adults. This general finding has also been suggested by Elliott, Huizinga, and Menard (1989). This tendency is particularly regrettable, since numerous data sets are available that deal with the important transitional period between adolescence and young adulthood, a time when the consequences of drug use are expected to be the most severely experienced (Newcomb & Bentler, 1988). It is also during this period that the circumstances that lead to cessation of drug use and criminality may be more easily studied, since it has been estimated that only 2–6% of adolescent drug use and criminality persists into adulthood (Elliott et al., 1985).

While the theoretical and empirical literature provides cogent arguments for expecting adverse consequences (including crime) of drug use, the presence of such conflicting and ambiguous results and arguments is troubling. Some studies show quite convincingly that drug use causes crime, while others suggest that involvement in crime causes drug use. Still others see drug use and crime as only being spuriously related. This is the case when considering the more particular relationship between drugs and violence (Fagan, 1990).

While some of this ambiguity may be attributed to differences in methodology and sample selection, we believe that the relationship between drug use and criminal activity in general, or violence in particular, may also be a conditional one, involving moderating variables. Baron and Kenny (1986) refer to moderators as qualitative or quantitative variables that affect "the direction and/or strength of the relation between an independent or predictor variable and a dependent or criterion variable" (p. 1174). We suspect that there may be some circumstances or conditions under which the use of drugs during adolescence leads to further involvement in crime or violence. Likewise, under certain conditions, the use of drugs during adolescence may make some adolescents less likely to commit criminal or violent acts.

This suggestion is not unique to us. After observing that the relationship between drugs and crime is strong, Anglin and Speckart suggested that the next step in our quest to understand the relationship between drugs and crime is to ask "what effect do conditional factors have on the overall relationship." What kinds of conditions might these be? Anglin and Speckart (1988) suggest (p. 227) that we should focus on

> *personality characteristics and preaddiction behavioral patterns* . . . that tend to reduce or enhance the degree of the relationship, the variation in the strength of the relationship over the course of the addiction career, and the differential effects of social interventions that are likely to contain the relationship within socially tolerated limits [emphasis added].

Besides those that have been suggested in the work of Anglin and Speckart, several other conditions that may affect the relationship have been suggested. Brook, Gordon, Brook, and Brook (1989) suggested, for example, that there is a differential effect of drug use on delinquency for African-American and white adolescents. In particular, drug use has a larger effect on rebelliousness and tolerance for deviance for whites than for African-Americans. Mexican-Americans, on the other hand, are more likely to use drugs earlier than whites or African-Americans, and Hispanic addicts are more likely to be arrested and spend more time in prison (Desmond & Maddux, 1984). While some are content to treat males and females similarly (Newcomb & Bentler, 1988), others have seen gender as a conditional, moderating variable (Johnson & Kaplan, 1990), since there is evidence that males use drugs and engage in interpersonal violence at differing rates from females (Downey & Moen, 1987). Clearly, we are only beginning to understand the conditional relationships between drugs and violence or crime. Clues to the moderators of the violent consequences of drug use for individuals may be found in the etiology of such use, especially where such explanations may also be used to explain violence. Two such variables are described in the following section.

Theoretical and Empirical Base

Understanding why people engage in drug use may help us better examine and explain why drug use has differential results for different people. When we examine violence as a consequence of drug use, two drug-use etiologies seem especially relevant: self-derogation and antisocial personality. Each of these is thought to lead to drug use *and* to later violent behavior.

For example, the relationship between self-attitudes and deviant behavior in general is well established (e.g., Kaplan, 1972, 1975, 1980, 1985). An important aspect of the theorized relationship is the self-esteem motive, described as motivation to behave in a manner that will minimize experiences of negative self-attitudes and maximize experiences of positive self-attitudes. In this case, self-attitudes refer to the way a person evaluates his or her own behaviors and attributes (either positively or negatively). Self-derogatory attitudes are the result of an inability to defend against, adapt to, or cope with circumstances having negative implications for how a person evaluates himself or herself. As a consequence of experiencing these negative self-attitudes in the context of normative group interaction, the person loses motivation to conform and gains motivation to deviate from the normative expectations (since conforming with these expectations in the past had not resulted in positive evaluation). At the same time, the person becomes motivated to relieve the negative self-evaluation (the self-esteem motive) by engaging in deviant behavior patterns that provide an opportunity to increase level of self-acceptance.

Which particular deviant activity is engaged in is a matter of the variety of opportunities available to the person. Drug use, in particular, is expected to result from negative self-attitudes because of an expectation that such use would lead to the acceptance of the drug user by other drug users or that it would pharmacologically decrease the user's negative self-attitude (Kaplan, Johnson, & Bailey, 1988). Violence, on the other hand, is expected to result among individuals who have high levels of self-derogation, as a reaction against the sources of their self-derogation. Here, the self-derogator "strikes out" at those who reject him or her.

A second risk factor is antisocial personality. Almost by definition, individuals with higher levels of antisocial personality are more likely to engage in violent behavior. They display higher than average involvement in all kinds of violence (Kosson, Smith, & Newman, 1990) and have higher conviction rates (Serin, 1991). This relationship is robust for females as well as for males (Hare, Forth, & Strachan, 1992). Linnoila and his associates (e.g., Virkunna, Rawlings, Tokola, Poland, Guidotti, Nemeroff, Bissette, Kalogeras, Karonen, & Linnoila, 1994) have recently shown that the relationship may be biological in nature. They report that impulsive offenders have lower levels of the serotonin metabolite 5-hydroxyindoleacetic acid in the cerebrospinal fluid (CSF), while nonimpulsive offenders have higher levels than nonoffenders. High levels of testosterone in the CSF are also correlated with aggression.

Many studies have shown a high correlation between drug use and antisocial personality. King, Jones, Scheuer, Curtis, and Zarcone (1990), for example, report that over 50% of their sample of substance abusers were diagnosed as possessing antisocial personality according to the DSM-III-R criteria. They suggest that considering the longitudinal consistency of severe personality disorders and the familial clustering, it is possible that personality psychopathology is an influential factor leading to drug use. Ross, Glaser, and Germanson (1988) found that over 75% of their addiction patients suffered from psychiatric disorders, including antisocial personality, while Khantzian and Treece (1985) found that over 60% of their sample of drug abusers had personality disorders, most of which were antisocial personality. Hesselbrock, Meyer, and Keener (1985) addressed the causal order of the relationship and found that substance abuse almost always followed antisocial personality disorder.

Early psychoanalytical attempts to deal with the etiology of drug use paid particular attention to the pleasure associated with drug use (Yorke, 1970). More recently, Khantzian (1980, 1985) has developed an ego/self-disturbance theory of substance abuse that is related to the relationship between drugs and antisocial personality. While admitting that drug use may exacerbate personality problems, Khantzian believes that people use drugs in an attempt to deal with the terrible problems associated with ego impairments and self-disturbances. As evidence of this, he points to the lifelong difficulties with rage, anger, and aggressiveness experienced by heroin users prior to heroin use. These users reported a decrease in the levels of these feelings of anger and rage. Khantzian (1980) concludes (p. 32) that opiate use is the result of the effectiveness of narcotic drugs to "relieve and to counteract regressed, disorganized, and dysphoric ego states related to overwhelming feelings of rage, anger, and related depression." According to Hendin (1980), adolescence is an especially important time for this kind of "self-medication," as the young person must deal with familial changes inherent in growing up. Such familial difficulties may result in rage directed toward the family, a rage that is so potent and uncontrollable that it frightens the youth. Drugs, particularly marijuana, may be used to help youths quiet the rage.

How is it that drug use lowers levels of anger and aggression? King, Curtis, and Knoblich (1992) suggest a biological reason that drugs may assuage violence, focusing on neurochemical studies involving plasma phenylacetic acid (PAA), a metabolite that has been shown to be negatively correlated with aggressiveness. They show evidence from animal and human studies that suggests that violent subjects have lower levels of PAA in their blood. They suggest that individuals may use drugs to relieve the dysphoria accompanying the aggressive tendencies associated with low levels of PAA. They claim that certain drugs, such as sedatives, act to increase levels of PAA, thereby reducing the aggressiveness and related dysphoria.

Thus, antisocial personality is thought to lead to increased levels of drug use and increased levels of violence (Cadoret, 1992). Ironically, drug use by people with high levels of antisocial personality is described as an attempt to assuage these violent tendencies through self-medication (Hendin, 1980; Khantzian, 1985). There is uncertainty regarding the extent to which such drug use eventually results in lower levels of violent behavior (i.e., the self-medication is successful). On the other hand, those with high levels of self-derogation are more

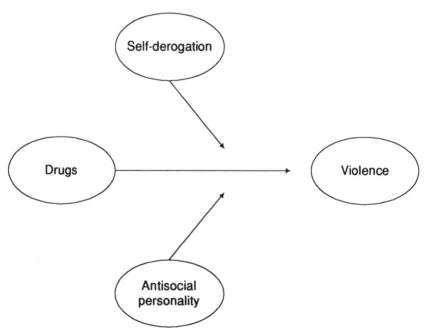

Figure 1. A proposed test of the conditional drugs–violence nexus.

likely both to use drugs (due to the influence of drug-using peers) and to be violent in an attempt to strike out at the instruments of self-derogation (rejecting family members, teachers, society in general) (Kaplan, 1980). We might expect, for example, that individuals who have high levels of self-derogation would experience increased potency on using drugs. This potency is gratifying for people who feel as though they lack importance and power. This newfound "power" might result in increased levels of violence on drug use, as the drug user feels the need to exhibit that power.

To our knowledge, the ways in which drug use interacts with these important variables (self-derogation and antisocial personality) to affect later violence has not been examined. We look at the relationship in the following sections, where we ask the question, "How do levels of self-derogation and antisocial personality moderate the putative causal relationship between drugs and violence?" (see Fig. 1).

Method

The data are provided by subjects who were first interviewed in 1971 (in the 7th grade), Time 1, and reinterviewed between 1980 and 1987 (as young adults), Time 4. The subjects were also interviewed in the 8th (Time 2) and 9th (Time 3) grades. However, these waves were not used in the analysis presented in this chapter. The original panel from which these subjects are drawn is a 50% sample of the 7th graders in the Houston Independent School District in 1971. Of these, 7618 subjects were interviewed at Time 1. Since we were interested in the initiation of violent behavior following 1971, we dropped from the sample those respondents who claimed to have behaved violently prior to 1972. Listwise deletion of cases with missing variables, in cases in which missing variables were not part of a scale, resulted in a usable sample size of 4536 subjects who were interviewed as adolescents and as young adults. When subjects had missing values for variables that were used in the construction of scales, a regression imputation procedure replaced the missing values with predicted values based on the scores of the other variables that made up the scale (see Little and Rubin, 1987). The modal age of the subjects at Time 1 is about 13 years while the modal age of the young adults at the later interview is about 26 years.

In order to examine the possible effects of sample attrition, we examined the intercorrelations of the variables at Time 1 for those who were only in the Time 1 sample and for those who were present for both the Time 1 and the young adult interview. The intercorrelations are so similar that we are confident that the analyses presented here may be generalized to the original cohort. The outstanding differences between the two samples are that the respondents who were only in Time 1 tended to have larger correlation coefficients among some of the variables than those who presented at both Time 1 and Time 4. Our analysis, then, is conservative in nature, since the relationships would have been stronger if the missing respondents had been included in the analyses.

We examine the moderating effects of antisocial personality disposition and self-attitudes on the relationship between adolescent drug use and young adult interpersonal violence by looking at the respondents' self-reported history of drug use and violence.

Variables

Dependent Variable: Interpersonal Violence at Time 4

In the Time 4 questionnaire, the respondents were asked when they first: (1) carried a razor, switchblade, or other knife as a weapon; (2) annoyed, assaulted, or fought other people (strangers) in the street; (3) attacked a person with a weapon or their hands intending to kill or seriously injure the person; (4) took part in gang fights; or (5) took an active part in a riot. Any cases who reported initial acts of violence before 1971 were dropped from the analysis, since we were using the Time 1 measurements made in 1971 as the independent variables. We examined only the respondents who claimed to be violence-free (as we defined it here) for the purposes of this study.

Over 86% of the sample had not engaged in even one of these acts of violence following 1971. This resulted in a dependent variable that was highly skewed. To correct for this problem, we decided to dichotomize the variable to reflect "ever having committed an act of violence" vs. "never having committed an act of violence." While Cleary and Angel (1984) have shown that using OLS regression is acceptable in some analyses using a dichotomous dependent variable, they caution that other techniques are necessary when the probability of success or failure for the variable falls outside the 0.25–0.75 range (see also Aldrich & Cnudde, 1975). Since that is the case in this study, the preferred technique to be used is logistic regression because of the properties of the interval independent variable and its relative ease of interpretation.

Independent Control and Moderating Variables

Adolescent drug use was measured in Time 1 by asking whether the subject had taken narcotics or smoked marijuana during the previous month. These two items were added to form a drug use scale for Time 1 (Drug1) (alpha = 0.713). Socioeconomic status, as a control variable, is operationalized by the level of education achieved by the respondent's father. If the respondent did not know the father's education, the mother's education was substituted. Gender and race/ethnicity were also controlled for in the analyses by including dummy variables representing males, blacks, and Hispanics. Since drug use is so highly correlated with other forms of deviance (e.g., Tonry and Wilson, 1990), we controlled for the relationship by including a summative scale (alpha = 0.575) of nondrug, nonviolent deviant acts reported at Time 1 (Dev1). Respondents were asked whether within the past month they had: (1) taken things worth between $2 and $50 that didn't belong to you; (2) taken little things (worth less than $2) that didn't belong to you; (3) cheated on exams; (4) skipped school without an excuse; (5) broken into and entered a home, store, or building; (6) taken things from someone else's desk or locker at school without permission. This scale is meant to control for deviant tendencies that may result in violence beyond the effect of drug use.

We examined the conditional and moderating effects of antisocial personality dispositions and self-attitudes as measured at Time 1. According to Khantzian (1985), Hendin (1980), and King et al. (1992), individuals with high levels of antisocial personality may be engaging in "self-medication" in an attempt to curb their aggressiveness. At the same time, antisocial personality is known to be related to violence (Hare, 1991; Hare, Strachan, & Forth, 1992). Thus, variation in antisocial personality may result in differential effects of drug use on later violence. Antisocial personality (Anti) is measured using a 13-item scale (alpha = 0.698). These items are face valid indicators or reflections of the respondent's antisocial attitudes: (1) If someone insulted me, I would probably hit him; (2) If you want people to like you, you have to tell them what they want to hear even if it isn't the truth; (3) My family can't give me the chance to succeed that most kids have; (4) If someone insulted me, I would probably think about ways I could get even; (5) Most of the adults I know got what is important out of life without getting an education; (6) If you stick to law and order, you will never fix what is wrong with this country; (7) As long as I stay with the straight life I will never make it; (8) The law is against the ordinary guy; (9) Most of the kids at school do not like me very much; (10) Most of my close friends are the kinds of kids who get into trouble a lot; (11) I was often punished unfairly as a child; (12) A smart lawyer can usually get a criminal free; and (13) I don't care much about other people's feelings. The response to each of these questions is scored 1 ("True") or 0 ("False"), and the summative ranges from 0 to 13.

Self-derogation reflects the self-feelings engendered by an evaluation of self-worth based on past behavior (Kaplan, 1985). The self-derogation (SDR) variable includes the following statements: (1) I don't like myself as much as I used to; (2) I used to be a better person than I am now; (3) I wish I could have more respect for myself; (4) I feel I do not have much to be proud of; (5) All in all, I am inclined to feel that I am a failure; (6) At times I think I am no good at all; and (7) I certainly feel useless at times (alpha = 0.667). For some parts of the analysis, the sample is divided into two groups according to level of SDR. High SDR is defined as having a score of 3 or more on the SDR scale (N =

1852), while low SDR is defined as having a score of 2 or less ($N = 2684$). Our rationale for using this variable is the well-developed link between self-derogation and deviant adaptations (Kaplan, 1972, 1975, 1980, 1986). We suggest that those who have high levels of SDR and use drugs will be more likely to engage in violent behavior.

Analysis and Results

Logistic regression is the preferred technique to be used, since the dependent variable is dichotomous and skewed (Aldrich & Nelson, 1984; Hosmer & Lemeshow, 1989). The analysis was conducted using the statistical package STATA (Computing Resource Center, 1992), which provides maximum-likelihood logit coefficients while automatically checking for identification and collinearity. We estimated a series of logistic regression models to test the effect of drugs on violence, controlling for other variables. Each model has interpersonal violence at Time 4 as its dependent variable and includes the gender, race/ethnicity, and socioeconomic status variables as control variables and the primary independent variable of interest, drug use at Time 1 (Drug1). A base model (including only these five independent variables) was estimated first. Each successive model was estimated and is compared to this first model.

Column I in Table 1 is the baseline model showing a highly significant positive main effect (0.516) of adolescent drugs on later violence, controlling on gender, race/ethnicity, and socioeconomic status [operationalized using father's education (FathEd)]. This finding is contrary to reports in much of the recent literature. For this sample, adolescents who use drugs have a higher probability of being violent later in life, controlling for early involvement in violence. But we know that drugs and deviance are highly correlated. It is possible that the drug use modeled here is really a proxy for deviant behavior in general. If this were the case, it would not be too surprising that drug use (deviance) led to later violence. To test the robustness of this finding regarding the possible relationship between drugs and other forms of deviance, the model in column II was estimated. This model controls for nondrug, nonviolent deviance. The deviance variable is positive and highly significant (0.175), suggesting, as expected, that those who had been deviant at Time 1 were more likely to be violent later on. The inclusion of the deviance variable did not obviate, however, the importance of the drug use variable, which remained positive and highly significant (0.367). Those who use drugs are more likely to become violent later on, even when controlling for the correlate of deviance. Similarly, the drug use–violence relationship exists with the inclusion of the antisocial variable (also known to be highly correlated with violence), as shown in column III. Here, antisocial personality (0.063) is positive and significant, while the drug use variable remains significant, though somewhat smaller in magnitude (0.325). Thus, even taking

Table 1. Logistic Regression Coefficients Showing Effects of Drug Use on Later Violence for the Full Sample[a]

Variables	I	II	III
Male	0.973[b]	0.935[b]	0.897[b]
	(2.647)	(2.548)	(2.453)
Black	0.726[b]	0.737[b]	0.648[b]
	(2.068)	(2.090)	(1.912)
Hispanic	0.707[b]	0.701[b]	0.653[b]
	(2.028)	(2.016)	(1.921)
Fathed	−0.071	−0.062	−0.046
	(0.931)	(0.940)	(0.955)
Drug1	0.516[b]	0.367[b]	0.325[c]
	(1.675)	(1.443)	(1.383)
Dev1	—	0.175[b]	0.131[b]
		(1.191)	(1.140)
Anti	—	—	0.063[c]
			(1.065)
Constant	−2.691	−2.798	−2.989
LL ratio	−1526.22	−1519.37	−1514.71
χ^2	178.140	191.850	201.170
Pseudo-R^2	0.055	0.059	0.062
Cases	4536	4536	4536
Model df	5	6	7

[a]Log-odds are in parentheses.
[b,c]Probability (two-tailed test): [b]$p < 0.01$; [c]$p < 0.05$.

into account the possible mediating effects of deviant behavior and antisocial personality, drug use remains a robust predictor of violence.

We next test the extent to which these findings are the same for individuals with higher or lower levels of self derogation. According to our guiding theory, we would expect that those who have high levels of self-derogation are more likely to behave violently, since they are wont to display anger toward those who are the source of their negative self-attitudes. People with high levels of self-derogation are inhibited from expressing their anger for fear of further driving significant others away, thereby increasing the negative self-evaluation. Thus, the use of drugs by those who are already disposed to violence (because of high self-derogation) may only exacerbate an already bad situation, making violence more likely.

Those who have low levels of self-derogation, however, are inhibited from behaving violently in order to maintain high levels of self-esteem. But if drugs have a "disinhibiting" function, we would expect that drug use might be more likely to lead to violence for those who are inhibited. That is, those who have low levels of self-derogation and are well socialized (low antisocial personality characteristics) are more likely to become violent because their inhibitions are released. On the other hand, those who have low self-derogation and high levels of antisocial personality characteristics may have any violent (antisocial) tendencies assuaged through the ingestion of drugs (Khantzian, 1980, Hendin, 1980).

These hypotheses were tested and are exhibited in Tables 2 and 3. Table 2 shows the baseline model without controlling for deviance (column I), controlling for deviance (column II), and controlling for deviance and antisocial personality (column III) for those subjects who are highly self-derogating ($N = 1852$). In the first three models, the drug variable is positive and significant, suggesting, as expected, that for individuals who are highly self-derogatory, drug use leads to violence, even controlling for nondrug, nonviolent deviance and antisocial personality. Thus, for highly self-derogating individuals, drug use is significantly and positively related to later violence.

In Table 3, we show the same models as in Table 2, except in this case we are looking at the sample of respondents who reported low levels of self-derogation ($N = 2684$). In the base model without controls (column I), drug use has a positive and significant effect on later violence (0.474). This effect remains positive in column II when we add the deviance variable, but it is no longer

Table 2.   Logistic Regression Coefficients Showing Effects of Drug Use on Later Violence for the High Self-Derogation Group[a]

Variables	I	II	III
Male	0.690[b]	0.655[b]	0.620[b]
	(1.994)	(1.926)	(1.858)
Black	0.630[b]	0.650[b]	0.575[b]
	(1.879)	(1.916)	(1.778)
Hispanic	0.608[b]	0.602[b]	0.576[b]
	(1.836)	(1.826)	(1.779)
Fathed	−0.050	−0.049	−0.033
	(0.951)	(0.952)	(0.968)
Drug1	0.504[b]	0.408[b]	0.385[c]
	(1.655)	(1.504)	(1.469)
Dev1	—	0.24[d]	0.099
		(1.132)	(1.104)
Anti	—	—	0.050[d]
			(1.051)
Constant	−2.406	−2.488	−2.696
LL ratio	−697.00	−695.18	−693.74
χ^2	56.980	60.610	63.480
Pseudo-R^2	0.039	0.042	0.044
Cases	1852	1852	1852
Model df	5	6	7

[a]Log-odds are in parentheses.
[b-d]Probability (two-tailed test): [b]$p < 0.01$; [c]$p < 0.05$; [d]$p < 0.10$.

significant (0.292). This suggests that among low self-derogating individuals, drug use is not significantly more likely to result in violence, controlling for nonviolent, nondrug deviance. This finding is even more evident when we examine column III, in which antisocial personality is entered into the model. For those with low levels of self-derogation, and controlling for these variables, drug use is not significantly more likely to result in a higher probability of later violence (0.239).

If we were to leave the analysis here, we would make the same mistake that other researchers may have made, by not examining potential interactions between drug use and other possible moderating variables. In this case, we are interested in the interaction between antisocial personality and drug use. This interaction is tested in the model presented in column IV of Table 3. Here, for those with low levels of self-derogation, there is a significant and positive main effect of drugs on later violence (0.887). There is also a significant and negative effect for the interaction between antisocial personality and drug use on violence (Anti × Drug1) (-0.143). It appears that those who have high levels of antisocial personality *and* use drugs are *less* likely to behave violently. The inclusion

Table 3. Logistic Regression Coefficients Showing Effects of Drug Use on Later Violence for Low Self-Derogation Group[a]

Variables	I	II	III	IV
Male	1.268[b]	1.229[b]	1.189[b]	1.182[b]
	(3.554)	(3.419)	(3.282)	(3.262)
Black	0.803[b]	0.804[b]	0.728[b]	0.719[b]
	(2.233)	(2.235)	(2.071)	(2.053)
Hispanic	0.774[b]	0.796[b]	0.756[b]	0.762[b]
	(2.166)	(2.217)	(2.130)	(2.142)
Fathed	-0.071	-0.052	-0.042	-0.051
	(0.931)	(0.949)	(0.959)	(0.950)
Drug1	0.474[b]	0.292	0.239	0.887[b]
	(1.607)	(1.339)	(1.271)	(2.428)
Dev1	—	0.205[b]	0.165[c]	0.199[b]
		(1.227)	(1.179)	(1.220)
Anti	—	—	0.061[d]	0.081[c]
			(1.063)	(1.084)
Anti × Drug1	—	—	—	-0.143[c]
				(0.866)
Constant	-3.025	-3.153	-3.283	-3.324
LL ratio	-821.20	-817.01	-815.23	-812.29
χ^2	127.120	135.500	139.060	144.940
Pseudo-R^2	0.072	0.077	0.079	0.082
Cases	2684	2684	2684	2684
Model df	5	6	7	8

[a]Log-odds are in parentheses.
[b-d]Probability (two-tailed test): [b]$p < 0.01$; [c]$p < 0.05$; [d]$p < 0.10$.

of this variable is statistically significant according to the statistic G, which follows a χ^2 distribution with 1 degree of freedom (Hosmer & Lemeshow, 1989).

Interaction effects are sometimes difficult to visualize. In order to increase our understanding of the effect, we calculated the effect of drug use on violence for each level of antisocial personality. The results of high, moderate, and low antisocial personality are plotted in Figure 2. As suggested by the negative interaction, drug use by those individuals who have low levels of antisocial personality leads to higher levels of violence. Things change, however, for those who have moderate levels of antisocial personality; there is almost no effect of drugs on later violence. Finally, drug use by those who have high levels of antisocial personality has a lower probability of resulting in later violence.

Discussion

The pattern we have shown here appears to be that drug use during adolescence seems especially to result in later violence among those whom we would least expect to be violent. Specifically, among respondents with low self-derogation, drug use has a greater effect on later violence for those who were relatively well socialized (low antisocial personality). The analysis presented may have an alternative interpretation. It is possible that in cases in which individuals appear to have had their violent tendencies assuaged after using drugs, the *type* of drug itself is responsible for the sedation. Certainly we know that certain types of drugs may have a sedating effect on the behavior of individuals, while others are more stimulating. Those who are violent and use such drugs may be "calmed" through such use. The Time 1 measure of drugs does not allow us to assess this concern, since it is a summed score of marijuana and narcotics use in general. In order to assess the extent to which the *type* of drug used by these adolescents had any bearing on these findings, separate analyses, not presented here, were conducted. At Time 4, each respondent was asked when was the first and last time he or she had used marijuana, LSD, barbiturates, amphetamines, tranquilizers, heroin, other narcotics, cocaine, Quaalude, and freebase. Overall, the analyses show that there are differing rates of drug use among the subgroups being investigated, but these differences are consistent across the spectrum of drugs used. That is, a higher percentage of those who had low self-derogation and high antisocial personality used drugs than any other subgroup (on average, almost 39% had used each particular drug in question). Over 23% on average, of those with high self-derogation and high antisocial personality had used each of the drugs. Not surprisingly, those who had the lowest levels of antisocial personality and low levels of self-derogation were the least likely to use any of the drugs. The analysis showed, however, that while those with low self-derogation and high antisocial personality were more likely to use drugs than any other group, they were *not* more likely to use marijuana and opiates, which might,

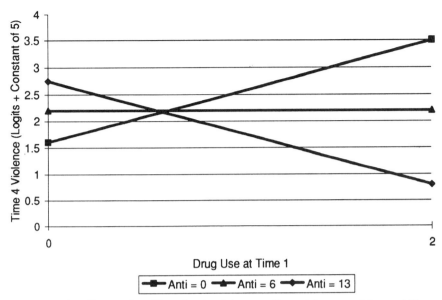

Figure 2. Plot of interaction effect of antisocial personality and drugs on violence at Time 4 for low self-derogation (N = 2684). (ANTI) Antisocial personality level: (0) low; (6) moderate; (13) high.

because of their psychopharmacological properties, explain how the users' violent tendencies might be assuaged.

Conclusion

In this chapter, we suggest that the equivocal nature of the findings surrounding the drug use–violence nexus might be the result of the failure of researchers to examine the conditional relationship between drug use and violence. We examined the conditions under which drug use during adolescence might have a positive effect on criminal activity during adulthood. Specifically, we looked at the long-term effect of drug use on violent activities, controlling for early violence. We suggested that personality dispositions and self-attitudes have important roles to play in this (or any other) drug–crime relationship.

Our results suggest that at least for this sample, there is a main direct effect of adolescent drug use on adult violence, controlling for adolescent violence. This finding is robust even controlling for other types of deviance and antisocial personality. We also showed that there are indeed conditions under which the use of drugs may have a long-term effect on later criminal activity. Not surprisingly, our ability to use adolescent drug use to explain much variance in violence as young adults was not great (pseudo-R^2's were all less than 0.10).

Nevertheless, we were able to show that in general, those groups of individuals that we *least* expected to become involved in violent activities (because of the low levels of antisocial personality and self-derogation) are those who are most directly affected by the use of drugs during adolescence. These well-socialized individuals, who are highly committed to the normative social order, are highly inhibited from displaying aggressiveness. The use of drugs is disinhibiting for these individuals, resulting in their being more likely to be violent later in life. If drugs are indeed disinhibiting, then it makes sense that those who are the most inhibited (as evidenced by high levels of commitment to the normative social order) are at the highest risk of losing such inhibition. Thus, those who are highly committed and still, for whatever reason, use drugs in adolescence are more likely to experience disinhibition and engage in acts of violence later in life. Even though Fagan (1990) has suggested that the disinhibition hypothesis has little support in the empirical literature, we have shown here that the disinhibition principle appears to hold only for those who are *highly* inhibited (i.e., well socialized). Specifically, those who have low self-derogation and low antisocial dispositions are more likely to behave violently when they use drugs. This is reflected in the main effect of drugs on violence for low self-rejecting individuals and in the effect of drugs on violence for subjects who are both low in antisocial disposition and low in self-derogation.

This is also the case for the high self-derogation group, whom we believe to be highly inhibited from acting violently for fear of receiving even more self-rejecting experiences. For this group, drug use also has a positive effect on later violence. High self-derogation subjects are expected to be disposed to engage in violent behavior, particularly when that behavior is directed toward the conventional world, which, in the subject's mind, was the cause of the person's self-rejection. At the same time, the willingness to act out the violent impulse might be inhibited by the tendency of highly self-derogating subjects to be lacking in self-confidence and fearful of adverse consequences of their violent acts (e.g., retaliation, negative social sanctions). However, the use of drugs by self-derogating individuals might mitigate these inhibitions and permit acting out the violent impulses directed toward the conventional world that occasioned distressful self-rejecting feelings.

In some cases, however, the use of drugs by those whom we *expect* to be violent actually lessens the likelihood for violence as an adult. We would expect those individuals who are characterized by low self-derogation in the face of high levels of antisocial personality to be likely to be violent. For these subjects, drug use seems to assuage their violent tendencies. These adolescents who are not inhibited (have high levels of antisocial personality), while still more violent than those who are committed to the social order, are less likely to be violent in young adulthood on using drugs. Specifically, those who are not committed and are not bothered by it (low self-derogation) are significantly less likely to be violent when they use drugs. Those individuals who have "negative" dispositions *and* low self-derogation are obviously comfortable with their disposition. The use of drugs by these individuals has a negative effect on later violence. The violent tendencies seem to be assuaged. The biochemical and psychodynamic mechanisms through which drugs assuage violent tendencies are suggested by the reports of King et al. (1990, 1992) and Linnoila and associates (Virkunna et al., 1994), as well as the reports of Hendin (1980) and Khantzian (1980, 1985), cited above.

In any case, these analyses contribute to the growing body of literature that argues for the specification of moderating variables in attempts to investigate the antecedents and consequences of drug abuse. In this instance, in addition to demonstrating the main effect of drug use on later violence, we were able to show that self-derogation and antisocial personality both had moderating effects on this relationship.

ACKNOWLEDGMENTS. This research was supported by research grant DA02497 and Research Scientist Award DA00136 to H.B.K. from the National Institute on Drug Abuse.

References

Aldrich, J. H., & Cnudde, C. (1975). Probing the bounds of conventional wisdom: A comparison of regression, probit, and discriminant analysis. *American Journal of Political Science, 19,* 571–608.

Aldrich, J. H., & Nelson, F. (1984). *Linear probability, logit, and probit models.* Newbury Park, CA: Sage Publications.

Anglin, M. D., & Speckart, G. (1988). Narcotics use and crime: A multisample, multimethod analysis. *Criminology, 26,* 197–233.

Ball, J. C., Rosen, L., Flueck, J. A., & Nurco, D. (1981). The criminality of heroin addicts when addicted and when off opiates. In J. A. Inciardi (Ed.), *The drugs–crime connection* (pp. 39–65). Beverly Hills: Sage Publications.

Baron, R. M., & Kenny, D. A. (1986). The moderator–mediator variable distinction in social psychological research: Conceptual, strategic, and statistical considerations. *Journal of Personality and Social Psychology, 51,* 1173–1182.

Baumrind, D., & Moselle K. A. (1985). A developmental perspective on adolescent drug use. *Advances in Alcohol and Substance Use, 5,* 41–67.

Brook, J. S., Gordon, A. S., Brook, A., & Brook, D. W. (1989). The consequences of marijuana use on intrapersonal and interpersonal functioning in black and white adolescents. *Genetic, Social, and General Psychology Monographs, 115,* 351–369.

Cadoret, R. J. (1992). Genetic and environmental factors in initiation of drug use and the transition to abuse. In M. D. Glantz & R. W. Pickens (Eds.), *Vulnerability to drug abuse* (pp. 99–114). Washington, DC: American Psychological Association.

Chaiken, J. M., & Chaiken M. R. (1982). *Varieties of criminal behavior.* Santa Monica: Rand Corporation.

Chaiken, J. M., & Chaiken, M. R. (1990). Drugs and predatory crimes. In M. Tonry & J. Q. Wilson (Eds.), *Drugs and crime* (pp. 203–240). Chicago: University of Chicago Press.

Cleary, P. D., & Angel, R. (1984). The analysis of relationships involving dichotomous dependent variables. *Journal of Health and Social Behavior, 25*, 334–348.

Collins, J. J. (1983). Alcohol use and expressive interpersonal violence: A proposed explanatory model. In E. Gottheil, K. Druley, T. Skoloda, & H. Waxman (Eds.), *Alcohol, drug abuse, and aggression* (pp. 5–25). Springfield, IL: Charles C. Thomas.

Collins, J. J. (1988). Suggested explanatory frameworks to clarify the alcohol use/violence relationship. *Contemporary Drug Problems, 15*, 107–121.

Computing Resource Center (1992). *STATA reference manual: Release 3*, 5th ed. Santa Monica: Computing Resource Center.

Desmond, D. P., & Maddux, J. F. (1984). Mexican-American heroin addicts. *American Journal of Drugs and Alcohol Abuse, 10*, 317–346.

Downey, G., & Moen, P. (1987). Personal efficacy, income, and family transitions: A longitudinal study of women heading households. *Journal of Health and Social Behavior, 28*, 320–333.

Elliott, D. S., & Huizinga, D. (1984). *Social class and delinquent behavior in a national youth panel*. Boulder: Behavior Research Institute.

Elliott, D. S., Huizinga, D., & Ageton, S. S. (1985). *Explaining delinquency and drug use*. Newbury Park, CA: Sage Publications.

Elliott, D. S., Huizinga, D., & Menard, S. (1989). *Multiple problem youth: Delinquency, substance use and mental health problems*. New York: Springer-Verlag.

Fagan, J. (1990). Intoxication and aggression. In M. Tonry & J. Q. Wilson (Eds.), *Drugs and crime* (pp. 241–320.) Chicago: University of Chicago Press.

Fagan, J., Weis, J. G., Cheng, Y. T., & Watters, J. K. (1987). Drug use, violent delinquency, and social bonding: Implications for theory and intervention. Final report. Grant No. 85-IJ-CX-0056, National Institute of Justice. Washington, DC: National Institute of Justice.

Gold, M., and Moles, O. C. (1978). Delinquency and violence in schools and the community. In J. A. Inciardi & A. E. Pottieger (Eds.), *Violent crime* (pp. 111–124). Beverly Hills: Sage Publications.

Goldstein, P. J. (1985). The drugs–violence nexus: A tri-partite conceptual framework. *Journal of Drug Issues, 15*, 493–506.

Goldstein, P. J. (1989). Drugs and violent crime. In N. A. Weiner & M. E. Wolfgang (Eds.), *Pathways to criminal violence* (pp. 16–48). Newbury Park, CA: Sage Publications.

Goldstein, P. J., Brownstein, H. H., Ryan, P. J., & Bellucci, P. A. (1989). Crack and homicide in New York City: A conceptually based event analysis. *Contemporary Drug Problems, 16*, 651–657.

Hare, R. D. (1991). *The Hare psychopathy checklist—revised*. Toronto: Multi-Health Systems.

Hare, R. D., Forth, A. E., & Strachan, K. E. (1992). Psychopathy and crime across the life span. In R. D. Peters, R. J. McMahon, & V. L. Quinsey (Eds.), *Aggression and violence throughout the life span* (pp. 285–300). Newbury Park, CA: Sage Publications.

Hare, R. D., Strachan, K. E., & Forth, A. E. (1992). Psychopathology and crime: A review. In K. Howells & C. Hollins (Eds.), *Clinical approaches to mentally disordered offenders*. New York: John Wiley.

Hendin, H. (1980). Psychosocial theories of drug abuse. A psychodynamic approach in D. J. Lettieri, M. Sayers, & H. W. Pearson (Eds.), *Theories on drug abuse* (NIDA Research Monograph 30, DHHS Publication No. ADM 80-967) (pp. 195–200). Washington, DC: U.S. Government Printing Office.

Hesselbrock, M. N., Meyer, R., & Keener, J. (1985). Psychopathology in hospitalized alcoholics. *Archives of General Psychiatry, 42*, 1050–1055.

Hosmer, D., & Lemeshow, S. (1989). *Applied logistic regression*. New York: John Wiley.

Hunt. D. (1990). Drugs and consensual crimes: Drug dealing and prostitution. In M. Tonry & J. Q. Wilson (Eds.), *Drugs and crime* (pp. 159–202.) Chicago: University of Chicago Press.

Jessor, R., & Jessor, S. R. (1977). *Problem behavior and psychosocial development.* New York: Academic Press.

Johnson, R. J. & Kaplan, H. B. (1990). Stability of psychological symptoms: Drug use consequences and intervening processes. *Journal of Health and Social Behavior, 31,* 277–291.

Johnston, L. D., O'Malley, P. M., & Eveland, L. K. (1978). Drugs and delinquency: A search for causal connections. In D. B. Kandel (Ed.), *Longitudinal research on drug use* (pp. 137–156). New York: John Wiley.

Kandel, D. B. (1978). Convergences in prospective longitudinal surveys of drug use in normal populations. In D. B. Kandel (Ed.), *Longitudinal research on drug use: Empirical findings and methodological issues* (pp. 3–38). Washington, DC: Hemisphere.

Kandel, D. B., Simcha-Fagan, R., & Davies, M. (1986). Risk factors of delinquency and illicit drug use from adolescence to young childhood. *Journal of Drug Issues, 16,* 67–90.

Kaplan, H. B. (1972). Toward a general theory of psychosocial deviance: The case of aggressive behavior. *Social Science & Medicine, 6,* 593–617.

Kaplan, H. B. (1975). *Self-attitudes and deviant behavior.* Pacific Palisades, CA: Goodyear.

Kaplan, H. B. (1980). *Deviant behavior in defense of self.* New York: Academic Press.

Kaplan, H. B. (1984). *Patterns of Juvenile Delinquency.* Beverly Hills: Sage Publications.

Kaplan, H. B. (1985). Testing a general theory of drug abuse and other deviant adaptations. *Journal of Drug Issues, 15,* 477–492.

Kaplan, H. B. (1986). *Social psychology and self-referent behavior.* New York: Plenum Press.

Kaplan, H. B., Johnson, R. J. & Bailey, C. (1988). Explaining adolescent drug use: An elaboration strategy for structural equations modeling. *Psychiatry, 51,* 142–163.

Khantzian, E. J. (1980). An ego/self theory of substance dependence: A contemporary psychoanalytic perspective. In D. J. Lettieri, M. Sayers, & H. W. Pearson (Eds.), *Theories on drug abuse: Selected contemporary perspectives* (NIDA Research Monograph 30, DHHS Publication No. ADM 80-967) (pp. 29–33). Washington, DC: U.S. Government Printing Office.

Khantzian, E. J. (1985). The self-medication hypothesis of addictive disorders: Focus on heroin and cocaine dependence. *American Journal of Psychiatry, 142,* 1259–1264.

Khantzian, E. J., & Treece, C. (1985). DSM-III psychiatric diagnosis of narcotic addicts. *Archives of General Psychiatry, 171,* 105–113.

King, R. J., Curtis, D., & Knoblich, G. (1992). Biological factors in sociopathy: Relationship to drug abuse behaviors. In M. D. Glantz & R. W. Pickens (Eds.), *Vulnerability to drug abuse* (pp. 115–135). Washington, DC: American Psychological Association.

King, R. J., Jones, J., Scheuer, J., Curtis, D., & Zarcone, V. (1990). Plasma cortisol correlates of impulsivity and substance abuse. *Personality and Individual Differences, 2,* 287–291.

Kosson, D. S., Smith, S. S., & Newman, J. P. (1990). Evaluating the construct validity of psychopathy on black and white male inmates: Three preliminary studies. *Journal of Abnormal Psychology, 99,* 250–259.

Little, R. J., & Rubin, D. B. (1987). *Statistical analysis with missing data.* New York: John Wiley.

Marinacci, A. A., & von Hagen, K. O. (1972). Alcohol and temporal lobe dysfunction: Some of its psychomotor equivalents. *Behavioral Neuropsychiatry, 3,* 2–11.

McClelland, D. C. (1975). *Power: The inner experience.* New York: Irvington.

Moyer, K. E. (1983). A psychological model of aggressive behavior: Substance abuse implications. In E. Gottheil, K. A. Druley, T. E. Skoloda, & H. M. Waxman (Eds.), *Alcohol, drug abuse and aggression* (pp. 189–202). Springfield, IL: Charles C. Thomas.

Newcomb, M. D., & Bentler, P. M. (1988). *Consequences of adolescent drug use.* Newbury Park, CA: Sage Publications.

Nurco, D. C., Schaeffer, J. W., Ball, J. C., & Kinlock, T. W. (1984). Trends in the commission of crime among narcotic addicts over successive periods of addiction. *Journal of Drug and Alcohol Abuse, 10,* 481–489.

Osgood, D. W., Johnston, L. D., O'Malley, P. J., & Bachman, J. G. (1988). The generality of deviance in late adolescence and early adulthood. *American Sociological Review, 53,* 81–93.

Pernanen, K. (1981). Theoretical aspects of the relationship between alcohol use and crime. In J. J. Collins (Ed.), *Drinking and crime* (pp. 1–69). New York: Guilford Press.

Reiss, A. J., and Roth, J. (Eds.) (1993). *Understanding and preventing violence: Panel on the understanding and control of violent behavior.* Washington, DC: National Academy of Sciences.

Robins, L. N. (1978). The interaction of setting and predisposition in explaining novel behavior: Drug initiations before, in and after Vietnam. In D. B. Kandel (Ed.), *Longitudinal research on drug use: Empirical findings and methodological issues* (pp. 179–196). Washington, DC: Hemisphere.

Robins, L. N. (1984). The natural history of adolescent drug use. *American Journal of Public Health, 74,* 656–657.

Robins, L. N., Darvish, H. S., & Murphy, G. E. (1970). The long-term outcome for adolescent drug users: A follow-up study of 76 users and 146 non-users. In J. Zubin & A. Freedman (Eds.), *The psychopathology of adolescence* (pp. 159–178). New York: Grune & Stratton.

Ross, H. E., Glaser, F., & Germanson, T. (1988). The prevalence of psychiatric disorders in patients with alcohol and other drug problems. *Archives of General Psychiatry, 45,* 1023–132.

Serin, R. C. (1991). Psychopathy and violence in criminals. *Journal of Interpersonal Violence, 6,* 423–431.

Smith, G. M., & Fogg, C. P. (1978). Psychological predictors of early use, late use, and nonuse of marijuana among teenage students. In D. B. Kandel (Ed.), *Longitudinal research on drug use: Empirical findings and methodological issues* (pp. 101–113). Washington, DC: Hemisphere.

Speckart, G., & Anglin, M. D. (1986). Narcotics use and crime: A causal modeling approach. *Journal of Quantitative Criminology, 2,* 3–28.

Speckart, G., & Anglin, M. D. (1988). Narcotics use and crime: A multisample, multimethod analysis. *Criminology, 28,* 197–233.

Tonry, M., & Wilson, J. Q. (1990). Preface. In M. Tonry & J. Q. Wilson (Eds.), *Drugs and crime* (pp. ix–x). Chicago: University of Chicago Press.

Virkunna, M., Rawlings, R., Tokola, R., Poland, R. E., Guidotti, A., Nemeroff, C., Bissette, G., Kalogeras, K., Karonen, S., & Linnoila, M. (1994). CSF bichemistries, glucose metabolism, and diurnal activity rhythms in alcoholic, violent offenders, fire setters, and healthy volunteers. *Archives of General Psychiatry, 51,* 20–27.

Watters, J. K., Reinarman, C., & Fagan, J. (1985). Causality, context, and contingency: Relationships between drug abuse and delinquency. *Contemporary Drug Problems, 12,* 351–373.

Wish, E., & Johnson, B. D. (1984). *The impact of substance abuse on crime rates: Report of the National Research Council panel on research on career criminals.* Washington, DC: National Academy of Sciences.

Yorke, C. (1970). A critical review of some psychoanalytic literature on drug addiction. *British Journal of Medical Psychology, 43,* 141–159.

Zeichner, A., & Pihl, R. O. (1980). The effects of alcohol and perceived intent on human physical aggression. *Journal of Studies on Alcohol, 41,* 265–276.

9

A Longitudinal Study of the Conditional Effects of Deviant Behavior on Drug Use among Three Racial/Ethnic Groups of Adolescents

Eleni A. Apospori, William A. Vega,
Rick S. Zimmerman, George J. Warheit, and
Andres G. Gil

Introduction

Empirical studies have successfully demonstrated the connection between adolescent delinquent behavior and illicit substance abuse (Bachman, O'Malley, & Johnston, 1978; Brook, Whiteman, Gordon, Nomura, & Brook, 1986; Kandel, 1978, 1980; White, Johnson, & Gozansky-Garrison, 1985). However, the specific nature and direction of the relationships continue to be debated (Altschuler & Brounstein, 1991; Elliott, Huizinga, & Menard, 1989; Huizinga, Menard, & Elliott, 1989; Watters, Reinarman, & Fagan, 1985; White, Pandina, & La-Grange, 1987).

The literature indicates that there are three major theoretical propositions offered to explain the relationship between social deviance and drug use. The first suggests that drug use causes crime. Watters et al. (1985) describe this

Eleni A. Apospori, Rick W. Zimmerman, George J. Warheit, and **Andrews G. Gil** • South Florida Youth Development Project, University of Miami, Coral Gables, Florida 33124. **William A. Vega** • School of Public Health, University of California, Berkeley, California 94720.

Drugs, Crime, and Other Deviant Adaptations: Longitudinal Studies, edited by Howard B. Kaplan. Plenum Press, New York, 1995.

approach as the cornerstone of United States narcotics and treatment policy. This policy reflects'the fear that the presence, availability, and nonmedical use of drugs will be followed by both violent and nonviolent criminal acts, affecting the actions of individuals who would otherwise be law-abiding (Epstein, 1974, 1977; Inciardi, 1981; Musto, 1973; Watters, 1983). However, in reviewing the literature on the drug-use-causes-crime hypothesis, Watters et al. (1985) discovered that many studies had found only correlational relationships (Minnesota Department of Correction, 1972; New Jersey State Police, 1971; Ontario Corrections Services, 1973; Roman, 1981; Tinklenberg & Woodrow, 1974), while other studies had focused solely on comparing postaddiction behavior with preaddiction levels of criminal activity (DeFleur, Ball, & Snarr, 1969; McGlouthlin, Anglin, & Wilson, 1978; National Commission on Marihuana and Drug Abuse, 1972, 1973; Nurco, 1976; Stephens & Ellis, 1975; Stephens & McBride, 1976; Weissman, Katsampes, & Giacinti, 1976).

The second perspective encompassed by another body of empirical work suggests that delinquent behavior precedes illicit drug use (Bachman et al., 1978; Inciardi, 1979; Johnston, 1973; Pierce, 1969; Robins & Guze, 1971; Robins & Murphy, 1967). While Huizinga and Elliott (1981) found evidence supporting the second hypothesis, they also found groups of adolescents who became simultaneously involved with delinquent behaviors and drug use, as well as groups who used drugs prior to the onset of delinquent behaviors.

The third perspective, the common-cause model, which a growing number of researchers favor, suggests that relationships, found in both cross-sectional and longitudinal studies, are the outcome of shared etiological antecedents (Akers, 1984; Elliott & Huizinga, 1984; Elliott, Huizinga, & Ageton, 1985; Elliott et al., 1989; Fagan & Hartstone, 1984; Hawkins, Lishner, Catalano, & Howard, 1986; Jessor & Jessor, 1977; Osgood, Johnston, O'Malley, & Bachman, 1988; White et al., 1987). In describing this perspective, Altschuler and Brounstein (1991) examine the clustering of antecedents into categories that describe demographic, social environmental, intrapersonal, and behavioral factors (Flay, D'Avernas, Best, Kersell, & Ryan, 1983; Huba & Bentler, 1980; Jessor & Jessor, 1977; Johnston, Bachman, & O'Malley, 1982; Kandel, 1978, 1980, 1982; Needle, McCubbin, Wilson, Reineck, Lazar, & Mederer, 1986; Perry & Murray, 1985; Stein, Newcomb, & Bentler, 1987; Wingard, Huba, & Bentler, 1979, 1980). However, despite the agreement regarding shared antecedents, there remains inconsistency about which factors are involved, how they operate, the type of delinquency involved (minor vs. serious), the type and level of drug involvement, social and demographic factors (inner city, rural, or suburban; socioeconomic status; and age), and the ability to discontinue illicit use or resist the lure of the drug culture (Altschuler & Brounstein, 1991; Inciardi & Pottieger, 1990; Kleinman, Wish, Deren, & Rainone, 1986; Loeber, Stouthhamer-Loeber, Van Kammen, & Farrington, 1991; Naughton & Krohn, 1988).

The coincident model, a variation of the common-cause model, posits that delinquency and drug use among adolescents are nothing more than coincidental, simultaneous occurrences (noncausal and nonreciprocal) within a cluster of other youth problem behaviors that occur as a result of experimentation during adolescence (Jessor & Jessor, 1977; Kandel, 1978; White et al., 1985). This model focuses more on the meaning of deviant acts than on the cause of such acts. As such, it seeks to understand the social–psychological function of adolescent behaviors in the natural maturational process of defining separate autonomous identities. It is suggested (White et al., 1987) that coincident models may better explain the drug–crime relationship at the lower end of the seriousness scale, while common-cause models are more appropriate for explaining the relationship between serious substance abuse and serious criminal activity.

The first aim of this chapter is to test the common-cause vs. the delinquency-causes-drug-use hypothesis. We hypothesize that the relationship between delinquency and drug use may be partially spurious when social control, differential association, and psychological factors are held constant. This study uses a prospective longitudinal design in which all the putative predictor factors were measured the year before the subjects' report on drug use. The main reason we focus on the deviance-causes-drug-use direction rather than on the drug-use-causes-deviance direction is that the findings from the first wave of data collection from the study on which this research is based showed that 49.5% of our sample of young adolescents reported some type of deviant behavior, while only 4.8% reported drug use. The findings from the second wave of data collection indicate that 62.3% of the adolescents reported some type of deviant behavior, while 10.4% reported drug use. These findings suggest that in early adolescence, deviance appears earlier than drug use. However, this result does not preclude the possibility that in later stages of adolescence or adulthood, drug use may lead to deviance.

Antecedents are grouped into four domains: family factors derived from social control theory and differential association theory, peers' influence factors derived from differential association theory and social control theory, personality factors derived from Kaplan's theory of self-esteem and deviant behavior (Kaplan, Martin, & Robbins, 1985; Kaplan, Johnson, & Bailey, 1986, 1987), and social demographic factors.

The second aim of this study is to explore the conditions under which prior deviance may lead young adolescents to use drugs. Despite the abundance of research on the deviance–drug use relationships, the conditions under which these relationships may hold have not been explored. Given the scarcity of findings in this area, this chapter will examine the interactive effects of variables most likely to influence the relationship between prior deviance and later drug use among adolescent boys. More specifically, questions such as the following are addressed: Can a strong supportive relationship with parents neutralize the effects of prior deviance on later drug use? Are deviant boys whose parents use substances more likely to use drugs than deviant boys whose parents are not substance users? Under what conditions can peers affect the deviance–drug use relationship? Do feelings of derogation make deviant adolescents more prone to drug use? Are lower-class deviant adolescents more likely to use drugs than upper-class deviant adolescents? Are adolescents from disadvantaged racial minority groups more likely to use drugs once they are involved in other types of deviant activities than their counterparts from majority groups?

Methods

Sample

The data presented are from the first two waves of a longitudinal study designed to examine the psychosocial factors associated with adolescent development, with a particular focus on the initiation, cessation, and continuation of drug and alcohol use among adolescent boys. The sample was selected from all 48 public middle schools (6th and 7th grades) in Dade County (Greater Miami), Florida. Following the approval of school officials, including administrators, principals, counselors, and classroom teachers, a total of 9761 consent forms were sent to parents requesting permission to have their children participate in the study. Of this total, 79% were returned; of this number, 83% granted permission. Overall, 6934 students agreed to participate in the study. The overall positive response rate was 71%. Usable data were collected for 6760 students in the fall of 1991.

The multiracial/ethnic characteristics of Dade County are reflected in the composition of the student sample. Of the 4319 students of Hispanic heritage, approximately one half (2192) were born outside the United States. There were 1495 students who identified themselves as black; 62.5% were of African-American heritage, and the remainder were mainly of Caribbean island origin. Non-Hispanic whites comprised about 13% of the sample, and there were 89 students from a variety of other backgrounds.

The decision to focus primarily on boys was made on the basis of two factors: First, limited funding was available to conduct the study. Second, following a review of the available data on the population from which the sample was to be drawn, it was determined that the prevalence rates of substance use among middle-school adolescents were quite low. As a consequence, the size of the sample had to be very large in order to detect with validity and reliability the prevalence and incidence of substance use. Power analyses predicated on expected prevalence and incidence rates indicated that in order for the study to have scientific utility, it would have to focus on only one group, and since middle-school males were found to be at greater risk than their female counterparts, the decision was made to study them. A smaller sample of girls was included in the research, and they are being followed throughout the study.

A questionnaire was administered to students in each of the schools to collect the data. The protocol was developed in both English and Spanish. Several versions of the instrument were developed and tested to accommodate students who had difficulties with reading or language or both. The protocol contained 113 questions, of which 22 were uniquely oriented to students of Hispanic heritage and 10 were designed specifically for blacks. All students were asked a basic core of questions that elicited information on their social, demographic, and cultural backgrounds as well as on a large number of other factors including family patterns and structures, nativity, awareness of prejudice, depression, suicidal ideation and behaviors, self-derogation-rejection, and nonnormative behaviors, including alcohol and drug use. In order to encourage honesty on the part of students, they were assured of confidentiality; they were reminded that there were no student identifiers on their questionnaire; and they were told not to enter their names.

For a subsample of 2992 randomly selected students, the data were augmented by collateral information obtained from their parents/guardians by means of a structured telephone interview. These data included information gathered by means of the Child Behavior Checklist (Achenbach & Edelbrock, 1983).

A second wave of data collection was conducted in the fall of 1992, with 6010 (89%) of the original sample of students completing questionnaires. When the data from the first- and second-wave student questionnaires were matched for those study participants who also had first-wave parent data, information was available on 2377 students.

Measures

A number of scales were developed to conduct this analysis. A detailed description of each scale, including individual questions and Cronbach's alpha statistic, is included in the Appendix.

Two scales were constructed to reflect deviant behavior at Time 1. The first scale contained 7 items measuring minor deviance; the second scale contained 6 items that measure more serious deviance. A scale was constructed to measure alcohol use at Time 1; it contained 6 items focusing on initiation, frequency, and amount of alcohol use and whether alcohol use had caused any problems for the respondent. Use of inhalants and cigarette smoking were measured by single questions at Time 1. To assess maternal and paternal drinking behavior, two scales were constructed of items from the parent questionnaire. Two scales were constructed to measure family pride and family support. The family pride scale contained 7 items from the student questionnaire; the family support scale contained 2 items from the parent questionnaire. Two scales measuring emotional bonding with family members were constructed, one using parent data and one using student data, to examine emotional bonding from both the parent's and the adolescent's point of view. The questions comprising the family pride and support scales and the two emotional bonding scales were adapted from items in the Family Adaptability and Cohesion Evaluation Scales—III (Olson, 1983, 1991).

Peer influence on substance use was measured by two scales, each of which had 4 items. The first measured perceived peer approval of substance use; the second measured perceived peer substance use. Both scales were constructed from items in the student questionnaire. Involvement with and attachment to peers were measured by single items from the student questionnaire. Three derogation scales drawn from the work of Kaplan and his colleagues (Kaplan, 1984; Kaplan, Martin, & Robbins, 1982; Kaplan et al., 1986) were constructed. The first scale, which measures self-derogation, is comprised of 7 items. The second, which measures teacher derogation consists of 4 items. The third, which contains 3 items, measures parent derogation.

Drug use at Time 1 and Time 2 was measured by scales containing self-reported use of six substances during the past 12 months. The race and ethnicity of students were determined by self-reports and from information obtained from the records of the school system. Students were defined as Hispanic if they, or any of their parents or grandparents, were born in a Latin American, Central American, or Caribbean Hispanic country. Socioeconomic status was measured by a scale containing three items from the parent data: father's education, mother's education, and family income.

Results

Zero-order correlations were computed between the Time 1 hypothesized predictors of drug use and Time 2 use of drugs. The results are presented in Table 1. Prior deviance, both minor and major, had the strongest association with subsequent drug use. Prior use of substances had the second strongest association with later use of drugs. Among the peer factors, perceived approval of substance use by peers had the strongest association with use of drugs (Pearson's $r = 0.102$, $p < 0.01$). Two of the personality factors, parent and teacher derogation, had a weak but statistically significant relationship with drug use.

Among the family factors, family pride and emotional bonding reported by students had a weak but statistically significant negative association with drug use. Of the two demographic factors, only race/ethnicity was weakly related to drug use. More specifically, Hispanic students reported more drug use than white students (Pearson's $r = 0.046$, $p < 0.05$), while black students reported less drug use than whites (Pearson's $r = 0.061$, $p < 0.01$).

Table 1.   Zero-Order Correlations between Time 2 Drug Use and Time 1 Drug Use Predictor Variables

Time 1 predictors	Time 2 drug use
Substance use	
Drug use	0.124^a
Use of inhalants	0.117^a
Alcohol use	0.120^a
Cigarette smoking	0.143^a
Deviance	
Minor	0.187^a
Major	0.186^a
Family factors	
Alcohol use by mother (parent data)	-0.002
Alcohol use by father (parent data)	0.020
Family pride	-0.078^a
Family support (parent data)	-0.017
Emotional bonding with family (parent data)	-0.007
Emotional bonding with family (student data)	-0.046^b
Peer factors	
Peer involvement	0.002
Peer attachment	0.071^a
Peer substance approval	0.102^a
Peer substance use	0.083^a
Personality factors	
Self-derogation	0.032
Parent derogation	0.080^a
Teacher derogation	0.088^a
Demographic factors	
Socioeconomic status	0.012
Hispanic	0.046^b
Black	-0.061^a

[a,b]Probability: [a]$p < 0.01$; [b]$p < 0.05$.

In order to assess whether each of these six sets of variables had an impact on later drug use independently of the other five sets, two hierarchical multiple regression coefficients (R change) were computed for each set of the hypothesized predictors. Parenthetically, it should be mentioned that in hierarchical multiple regressions, the control sets of variables are entered first, followed by the set of predictors whose independent direct effect on the dependent variable is estimated. First, a hierarchical multiple regression coefficient (R change) was computed, controlling only for Time 1 drug use. This R change indicated the effect of each set of predictors on Time 2 drug use after the effect of Time 1 drug use was partialed out. Then another hierarchical multiple regression computed an R change for that set of variables, while it controlled for all the other sets of variables. The second multiple R change indicated the direct effect of each set of variables by partialing out the possible effects of the rest of the sets of variables as well as the effects of Time 1 drug use.

The results from the 12 hierarchical multiple regression analyses are presented in Table 2. R change in the first column indicates the effect of each of the sets of hypothesized predictors on later drug use without control for the other five sets. R change in the third column indicates the impact of each set of predictors on later drug use, controlling for all the remaining sets of hypothesized predictors.

As shown in columns 1 and 2 of Table 2, with the exception of the family factors, all the other sets of hypothesized predictors had a statistically significant effect on Time 2 drug use. However, when the effects of the other predictors are partialed out, as shown in columns 3 and 4, peer, personality, family, and social–demographic factors did not have a significant direct impact on later drug use. The only factors that had a statistically significant direct impact on Time 2 drug use were Time 1 use of alcohol/cigarettes/inhalants and Time 1 deviant behavior. More specifically, the results in Table 2 show that the impact of Time 1 use of the substances mentioned above was diminished from 0.163 ($p < 0.01$) to 0.093 ($p < 0.01$) when the other sets of hypothesized predictors were introduced into the regression model. The reduction of the impact of Time 1 use of these substances on Time 2 drug use suggests that some of their shared variance was due to their relationship with the other hypothesized predictors.

As mentioned earlier, the first aim of this research was to test the common-cause vs. the delinquency-causes-drug-use hypothesis. The results from the analysis shown in Table 2 suggest that the relationship between Time 1 deviance and Time 2 drug use was due partially to the direct impact of prior deviance on subsequent drug use ($R = 0.129$, $p < 0.001$) and partially to common antecedents.

Table 2. Multiple Effects of Time 1 Predicting Factors on Time 2 Drug Use

Variables	R change with control for Time 1 drug use		R change with control for Time 1 drug use and all the other scales	
	R	F	R	F
Use of alcohol/cigarettes/ inhalants	0.163	19.480[b]	0.093	4.461[b]
Deviance	0.182	36.415[c]	0.129	12.928[c]
Family factors	0.068	1.754	0.056	0.808
Peer factors	0.132	7.592[b]	0.058	1.309
Personality factors	0.093	6.463[b]	0.043	0.974
Demographic factors	0.062	3.130[a]	0.070	2.574

[a–c]Probability: [a]$p < 0.05$; [b]$p < 0.01$; [c]$p < 0.001$.

The second aim of this research was to explore the conditions under which prior deviance had an impact on later drug use. First, the possibility of interaction between prior deviance and race/ethnicity was explored. The results shown in the first two rows of Table 3 indicated that there was a significant interaction between race/ethnicity and prior major deviance; this finding suggests that prior major deviance had a different impact on drug use among Hispanics and among blacks than it had among whites. On the other hand, the analysis showed that prior minor deviance did not have a different impact on later drug use in different racial/ethnic groups. Given these results, the interactions between prior major deviance and the other hypothesized predictors were explored for each racial/ethnic group separately. The interactions between prior minor deviance and the other predictors were explored for all the racial/ethnic groups combined.

The data presented in Table 3 indicated that among Hispanics, prior major deviance had significant interactions with three of the family factors: paternal use of alcohol, family pride, and family support, and with self, parent, and teacher derogation. Among blacks, prior major deviance had significant interactions with peer involvement, attachment, and perceived substance approval by the peers. For whites, prior major deviance interacted with prior alcohol use and

Table 3. Significant Interactions between Deviance and Other
Predictors of Drug Use

Ethnic group	Interaction	T	Significance
	Hispanic*Major deviance	2.05	0.04
	Black*Major deviance	−2.63	0.008
Hispanics			
	Mjr. dev.*Fath. alcohol use	−2.34	0.02
	Mjr. dev.*Family pride	−3.23	0.001
	Mjr. dev.*Family support[a]	−2.34	0.02
	Mjr. dev.*Self-derogation	4.81	0.000
	Mjr. dev.*Parent derogation	4.53	0.000
	Mjr. dev.*Teacher derogation	2.49	0.01
Blacks			
	Mjr. dev.*Peer involvement	−2.62	0.009
	Mjr. dev.*Peer attachment	−2.72	0.007
	Mjr. dev.*Peer subst. approval	−1.96	0.05
Whites			
	Mjr. dev.*Alcohol use	2.40	0.02
	Mjr. dev.*Peer attachment	2.26	0.02
All			
	Min. dev.*Family pride	−3.99	0.0001
	Min. dev.*Self-derogation	3.80	0.0001
	Min. dev.*Parent derogation	3.17	0.001
	Min. dev.*Teacher derogation	2.69	0.007

[a]Items derived from parent data.

peer attachment. Finally, among all ethnic groups, minor deviance had significant interactions with family pride and the three derogation factors.

In order to understand better the direction and nature of the interactions between deviance and the other predictor variables, multiple regressions were performed to estimate the impact of prior deviance on later drug use under different levels of the variables interacting with deviance. The results from these regressions are shown in Tables 4 and 5.

The first three rows of Table 4 present the effect of prior major deviance on later drug use among the three racial/ethnic groups. Prior deviance had the strongest impact on later drug use among white students and the second strongest

Table 4.   Direction of the Interactive Effects of Major Deviance on Drug Use

Variables interacting with major deviance		Effect of Time 1 deviance on Time 2 drug use				
		b	S.E. b	Beta	T	N
Race/ethnicity	Hispanic	0.420	0.152	0.115	2.763[c]	894
	Black	0.037	0.081	0.039	0.460	227
	White	0.858	0.290	0.220	2.955[c]	277
Hispanics						
Father's alcohol	Low	0.486	0.199	0.125	2.444[b]	630
use	High	−0.285	0.165	−0.130	−1.727	263
Family pride	Low	0.680	0.317	0.180	2.139[b]	230
	High	0.210	0.175	0.058	1.196	663
Family support[a]	Low	0.945	0.448	0.260	2.109[b]	101
	High	0.361	0.162	0.099	2.217[b]	773
Self-derogation	Low	−0.283	0.260	−0.067	−1.091	477
	High	0.757	0.187	0.232	4.051[d]	416
Parent derogation	Low	−0.230	0.178	−0.088	−1.685	575
	High	0.948	0.269	0.243	3.517[d]	318
Teacher	Low	0.224	0.173	0.059	1.303	748
derogation	High	0.769	0.376	0.216	2.044[b]	145
Blacks						
Peer involvement	Low	0.992	0.266	0.721	3.736[c]	42
	High	−0.055	0.077	−0.067	−0.708	184
Peer attachment	Low	0.324	0.117	0.324	2.753[c]	106
	High	−0.100	0.112	−0.110	−0.894	120
Peer substance	Low	0.218	0.099	0.222	2.201[b]	142
approval	High	−0.006	0.152	−0.006	−0.040	84
Whites						
Alcohol use	Low	0.642	0.711	0.095	0.902	141
	High	1.331	0.252	0.528	5.289[d]	135
Peer attachment	Low	−0.210	0.524	−0.043	−0.401	127
	High	1.350	0.385	0.376	3.509[c]	149

[a]Items derived from parent data.
[b-d]Probability: [b]$p < 0.05$; [c]$p < 0.01$; [d]$p < 0.001$.

Table 5. Direction of the Interactive Effects of Minor Deviance on Drug Use

Variables interacting with minor deviance		Effect of Time 1 deviance on Time 2 drug use				
		b	S.E. b	Beta	T	N
All ethnic groups						
Family pride	Low	0.570	0.179	0.168	3.188[b]	522
	High	0.165	0.140	0.049	1.172	906
Self-derogation	Low	0.159	0.190	0.038	0.795	770
	High	0.822	0.288	0.238	2.851[a]	237
Parent derogation	Low	0.090	0.127	0.026	0.710	1062
	High	0.816	0.288	0.236	2.834[a]	237
Teacher derogation	Low	0.132	0.189	0.029	0.697	790
	High	0.383	0.134	0.136	2.853[a]	638

[a,b]Probability: [a]$p < 0.01$; [b]$p < 0.001$.

impact among Hispanic students. However, for black adolescents, prior major deviance did not prove to be a significant predictor of drug use.

Prior major deviance had a different impact on drug use under different condit⁀ ns for three family factors and for the three derogation factors among Hispanic adolescents. The analysis showed that deviance was a significant predictor of drug use under low levels of paternal alcohol use. High family pride neutralized the effect that prior major deviance had on drug use. For Hispanic adolescents with strong family support, the impact of prior deviance on later drug use was not as strong as it was for adolescents with lower family support. Deviance was a significant predictor of drug use among Hispanic boys under high levels of any type of derogation. Low levels of derogation, on the other hand, neutralized the deviance–drug use relationship.

Three peer factors were found to condition the relationship between prior major deviance and later drug use among the black adolescents in the sample. Deviant behavior was a significant predictor of drug use among black students with low involvement and attachment with peers. However, for black boys who were involved with and attached to their peers, deviance was not a significant predictor of drug use. Finally, the analysis indicated that among black adolescents who thought that their peers did not approve substance use, deviance was a significant predictor of drug use. Major deviance did not have an effect on later drug use among black students who thought that their peers approved substance use.

For white students, alcohol use and peer attachment conditioned the relationship between deviance and drug use. In particular, among the students who reported high levels of alcohol use at Time 1, prior deviance was a strong predictor of drug use at Time 2. For the students who reported low levels of alcohol use at Time 1, major deviance did not affect later drug use.

The interactions between minor deviance and other hypothesized predictors are presented in Table 5. As mentioned previously, this research did not find that minor deviance had differential impacts on drug use for the three racial/ethnic groups in the sample. Therefore, the analysis for the conditional effects of minor deviance on drug use was conducted for all of the three groups combined. As presented in Table 5, minor deviance did not have a significant effect on drug use for adolescents with high family pride. Minor deviant behavior is a significant predictor of drug use for adolescents with low family pride. Finally, the results of the analysis suggest that minor deviance did not have an impact on drug use for adolescents with low levels of any type of derogation, while it did have an impact for adolescents with high levels of derogation.

Conclusions

The purpose of the research presented in this chapter was twofold. First, it was designed to test the common-causes vs. the deviance-causes-drug-use hypotheses; second, it was intended to assess the conditions under which deviant behavior may have an impact on drug use. The third major perspective on the delinquency–drug use relationship—that is, that drug use causes delinquency—was not included in that our early findings indicated that among young adolescents, deviant behavior occurs earlier than drug use. However, this circumstance does not preclude the possibility that drug use may lead to other types of deviant behavior in later stages of adolescence or adulthood.

Hierarchical multiple regression analysis showed that the relationship between prior deviance and later drug use was due partly to common causes and partly to the direct impact of deviance on drug use. Although the effect of deviance of drug use was statistically significant, it was not very strong. The reason for this result may be that the hierarchical multiple regressions used to test the two competing hypotheses analyzed additive models that assume that the relationship between prior deviance and later drg use is the same under any circumstances. Moreoever, we recognize that human behavior is too complex to be explained by additive linear models and that more and more nonadditivity is ". . . explicitly stated in substantive discussions of social science" (Costner, 1988, p. 45). Hence the assumption of invariate relationships between deviance and drugs made by prior researchers may not be valid.

Given the lack of research on the conditional effects of deviance on drug use and the highly unrealistic assumption that there are no such conditional effects, this research explored various conditions under which the impact of prior deviant behavior on drug use may vary. That was the second aim of this study.

One of the basic characteristics of the sample is that it includes students from a variety of ethnic/racial and cultural backgrounds. Thus, this study explored the possibility of a differential effect of deviance on drugs among the three major ethnic/racial groups in the sample. The analysis showed that prior minor deviance did not have a differential impact on drug use among the three racial/ethnic groups. However, it was found that the impact of prior major deviance on drug use was different among Hispanic, black, and white adolescent boys, with whites and blacks being the most different in terms of this relationship.

For white adolescents, prior major deviant behavior was found to be the strongest predictor of subsequent drug use. The second strongest predictor was the prior use of inhalants. These findings suggest that drug use among white youth may be the result of a broader prior deviant identity. For black students, prior major deviant behavior was not found to have an impact on later drug use. Teacher derogation and lack of bonding with the family as reported by the student were found to be the strongest predictors of later drug use. From these findings, we can conjecture that for young black adolescents, drug use is not due to a pattern of broader deviant behavior, but rather is a response to adverse types of relationships with significant others such as family members or teachers. Among Hispanic adolescents, prior major deviance was the strongest predictor of subsequent drug use, but it was not as strong as it was among whites. Prior drug use and cigarette smoking, and family pride, were also found to be significantly related to later drug use. These findings suggest that among young Hispanic adolescents, drug use is the result of a prior pattern of broader major deviant behavior and adverse family relationships.

There having been found a differential impact of prior major deviance on later drug use among the three major racial/ethnic groups in the study, the next issue addressed the conditional effects of prior major deviance on drug use within each racial/ethnic group. Among whites, prior major deviance was found to have significant interactions with prior alcohol use and attachment with peers. Prior major deviance was found to be a strong predictor of later drug use among white adolescents who reported high levels of prior alcohol use and strong attachment to their peers. The effect of prior major deviance on drug use was neutralized by low levels of prior alcohol use and low levels of peer attachment.

Although the initial analysis showed that overall prior major deviance may not lead to drug use among young black adolescent boys, further analysis indicated that under certain conditions, major deviance may have an effect on drug use. More specifically, relationships with peers were found to condition the deviance–drug use relationship. Among black adolescents who were more distant from their peers, prior major deviance was related to later drug use. No significant relationship was found between prior major deviance and subsequent drug use among the black youth with ties to their peers. Among the latter group, perceived peer approval of substance use was the only predictor of later drug use. These findings suggest that for young black boys with strong ties to their peers, drug use is not part of a pattern of prior major deviant behavior. In other words, these youngsters use drugs not because they are delinquents in other aspects of their behavior but because they think that their peers approve of it.

The effects of deviance on drug use can be ameliorated under certain circumstances among Hispanics. Low self, parent, or teacher derogation may neutralize the impact of prior deviance on subsequent drug use. Also, high family pride and strong support from the family may deter deviant Hispanic adolescents from using drugs in the future. Another factor that was found to have a significant interaction with prior deviance was paternal alcohol use. Specifically, it was found that among the young Hispanic adolescents whose fathers had low levels of alcohol use, prior deviance was a strong significant predictor of future drug use. On the other hand, no significant relationship was found between prior major deviance and subsequent drug use among those youngsters whose fathers had higher levels of alcohol use. As a matter of fact, those youngsters' prior use of alcohol, which was correlated with their fathers' alcohol use, and their prior use of inhalants were the strongest predictors of their drug use later. These findings suggest that for young Hispanic adolescents whose fathers drink alcohol, drug use is not part of a broader pattern of major deviant behavior. We conjecture that they use drugs because of the favorable attitudes toward alcohol and, perhaps, substance use in general by their fathers.

Minor deviance was not found to interact with race/ethnicity. Therefore, the analyses were performed for the three racial/ethnic groups combined. It was found that minor deviance interacted with family pride and the three derogation factors. Minor deviance had an effect on later drug use when adolescents reported high levels of self, parent, or teacher derogation. Family pride was found to condition the relationship between prior deviance and drug use. In particular, adolescents who had committed minor deviant acts were more likely to use drugs if they had low family pride than their counterparts who had reported high levels of family pride.

Overall, this research indicated that additive linear models are not definitive in studying the relationship between prior deviance and future drug use. The deviance–drug use relationship is a complex phenomenon that it is conditioned by ethnic factors as well as family, peer, and personality factors. The findings of this study have implications for future prevention/intervention programs. The findings suggest that the targeted sources of problem behaviors should be different for different ethnic/cultural groups. In addition, within each ethnic group, for youths with different family conditions, peer relationships, and personality problems, the targeted sources of problem behaviors should be different. However, since this research is the first that studied the conditional impact of devince on drugs using a comparative design, more research on the deviance–drugs relationship should be done along this line and build on these findings, so that future prevention/intervention programs will be based on solid theoretical and empirical grounds.

ACKNOWLEDGMENT.   This research was supported by research grant DA05912 from the National Institute on Drug Abuse.

Appendix: Items and Alphas for Scales

Minor deviance (alpha = 0.73):
>   Taken $2 or less when you weren't supposed to?
>   Gotten angry and broken things?
>   Taken between $2 and $50 when you weren't supposed to?
>   Carried a weapon?
>   Started a fist fight?
>   Taken things from someone else's desk or locker when you weren't sup-
>   posed to?
>   Damaged or destroyed property on purpose that didn't belong to you?

Major deviance (alpha = 0.77):
>   Taken part in gang fights?
>   Used force to get money or expensive things from another person?
>   Broken into and entered a home, store, or building?
>   Taken a car for a ride without the owner's permission?
>   Taken something worth more than $50 when you weren't supposed to?
>   Beaten up someone for no reason?

Alcohol use scale (alpha = 0.86):
>   Number of days used alcohol during the past 12 months
>   The last time you drank alcohol; how many drinks did you have?
>   How often do you drink enough to feel pretty high or drunk?
>   In which grade did you first drink alcohol?
>   In which grade did you first get drunk at least once a week?
>   Has your use of alcohol ever caused any problems for you?

Cigarette smoking:
>   Have you ever smoked cigarettes?

Maternal substance use (parent data) (alpha = 0.52):
>   In a typical month, how many days would you say you drink alcohol?
>   When you drink, how many drinks do you usually have?

Paternal substance use (parent data) (alpha = 0.65):
>   In a typical month, how many days would you say your spouse drinks al-
>   cohol?
>   When he drinks, how many drinks does he usually have?

Family pride scale (student data) (alpha = 0.87):
>   Family members respect one another.
>   We share similar values and beliefs as a family.
>   Things work out well for us as a family.
>   We really do trust and confide in each other.

Family members feel loyal to the family.

We are proud of our family.

We can express our feelings with our family.

Family support scale (parent data) (alpha = 0.64):

Family members ask each other for help.

Family members consult other family members on their decisions.

Emotional bonding with family (student data) (alpha = 0.75):

Family members feel very close to each other.

Family togetherness is very important.

Emotional bonding with family (parent data) (alpha = 0.63):

Family members feel very close to each other.

Family togetherness is very important.

Peer substance approval (alpha = 0.88):

How do you think your close friends feel about people who:

a. smoke cigarettes?

b. smoke marijuana (pot, grass, weed)?

c. use cocaine (coke)?

d. drink beer, wine, liquor (alcohol)?

Peer substance use (alpha = 0.89):

How many of your close friends do you think:

a. smoke cigarettes?

b. smoke marijuana (pot, grass, weed)?

c. use cocaine (coke)?

d. drink beer, wine, liquor (alcohol)?

Peer involvement

I keep from getting involved with other kids.

Peer attachment:

How many of your private thoughts and feelings do you think you can share
with your very best friend?

Self-derogation scale (alpha = 0.82):

I don't like myself as much as I used to.

At times I think I am no good at all.

I wish I could have more respect for myself.

In general, I feel that I am a failure.

I certainly feel useless at times.

I used to be a better person than I am now.

I feel I do not have much to be proud of.

Teacher derogation (alpha = 0.81):

Some of my teachers are usually not interested in what I say or do.

My teachers feel that I am a failure.

My teachers do not like me very much.

My teachers usually put me down.

Parent derogation (alpha = 0.72):

My parents do not like me very much.

My parents have put me down for a long time.

My parents are usually not very interested in what I say.

Drug use Time 1 (alpha = 0.85) and **drug use Time 2** (alpha = 0.90):

How many times have you smoked pot during the past 12 months?

How many times have you used cocaine other than crack during the past 12 months?

How many times have you used cocaine during the past 12 months?

How many times have you used angel dust during the past 12 months?

How many times have you taken uppers or downers during the past 12 months?

How many times have you taken tranquilizers during the past 12 months?

Socioeconomic status (parent data) (alpha = 0.70):

Father's education

Mother's education

Family's income

Race/ethnicity:

Hispanic

Black

White

References

Achenbach, T. M., & Edelbrock, C. (1983). *Manual for the child behavior checklist and revised child behavior profile*. Burlington, VT: University Associates in Psychiatry.

Akers, R. L. (1984). Delinquent behavior, drugs and alcohol: What is the relationship? *Today's Delinquent, 3*, 19–47.

Altschuler, D. M., & Brounstein, P. J. (1991). Patterns of drug use, drug trafficking, and other delinquency among inner-city adolescent males in Washington, D.C. *Criminology, 29*, 589–622.

Bachman, J. G., O'Malley, P. M., & Johnston, L. D. (1978). *Adolescence to adulthood: Change and stability in the lives of young men—Youth in transition*. Ann Arbor, MI: Institute for Social Research.

Brook, J., Whiteman, M., Gordon, A. S., Nomura, C., & Brook, D. W. (1986). Onset of adolescent drinking: A longitudinal study of intrapersonal and interpersonal antecedents. *Advances in Alcohol and Substance Abuse, 5*, 91–110.

Costner, H. L. (1988). Research methodology in sociology. In E. F. Borgatta & K. S. Cook (Eds.), *The future of sociology* (pp. 84–112). Newbury Park, Ca: Sage Publications.

DeFleur, L. B., Ball, J. C., & Snarr, R. W. (1969). The long-term social correlates of opiate addiction. *Social Problems, 17*, 225–234.

Elliott, D., & Ageton, A. R. (1976). *Subcultural delinquency and drug use*. Boulder: Behavioral Research Institute.

Elliott, D. S., & Huizinga, D. (1984). *The relationship between delinquent behavior and ADM problems*. Boulder: Behavioral Research Institute.

Elliott, D. S., Huizinga, D., & Ageton, S. S. (1985). *Explaining delinquency and drug abuse*. Beverly Hills: Sage Publications.

Elliott, D. S., Huizinga, D., & Menard, S. (1989). *Multiple problem youth: Delinquency, substance abuse, and mental health problems*. New York: Springer-Verlag.

Epstein, E. J. (1974). Methadone: The forlorn hope. *The Public Interest, 36*, 3–13.

Epstein, E. J. (1977). *Agency of fear: Opiates and political power in America*. New York: Putnam Press.

Fagan, J., & Hartstone, E. (1984). *Dilemmas in juvenile corrections: Treatment interventions for special problem youth*. San Francisco: URSA Institute.

Flay, B., D'Avernas, J. R., Best, J. A., Kersell, M. W., & Ryan, K. B. (1983). Cigarette smoking: Why young people do it and ways of preventing it. In P. Firestone & P. McGrath (Eds.), *Pediatric and adolescent behavioral medicine* (pp. 132–183). New York: Springer-Verlag.

Hawkins, J. D., Lishner, D. M., Catalano, R. F., & Howard, M. O. (1986). Childhood predictors of adolescent substance abuse: Toward an empirically grounded theory. *Childhood and Chemical Abuse, 11*, 11–48.

Huba, G. J., & Bentler, P. M. (1980). The role of peer and adult models for drug taking at different stages in adolescence. *Journal of Youth and Adolescence, 9*, 449–465.

Huizinga, D. H., & Elliott, D. S. (1981). *A longitudinal study of drug use and delinquency in a national sample of youth: An assessment of causal order*. Boulder: Behavioral Research Institute.

Huizinga, D. H., Menard, S., & Elliott, D. S. (1989). Delinquency and drug use: Temporal and developmental patterns. *Justice Quarterly, 6*, 419–455.

Inciardi, J. A. (1979). Heroine use and street crime. *Crime and Delinquecy, 25*, 335–346.

Inciardi, J. A. (1981). *The drugs–crime connection*. Beverly Hills: Sage Publications.

Inciardi, J. A., & Pottieger, A. E. (1990). Kids, crack and cocaine. *Journal of Drug Issues, 20*, 181–194.

Jessor, R., & Jessor, S. L. (1977). *Problem behavior and psychological development: A longitudinal study of youth*. New York: Academic Press.

Johnston, L. D. (1973). *Drugs and American youth: Report from the Youth in Transition Project*. Ann Arbor, MI: Institute for Social Research.

Johnston, L. D., Bachman, J. G., & O'Malley, P. M. (1982). *Highlights from student drug use in America, 1975–1981*. National Institute on Drug Abuse. Washington, DC: U.S. Government Printing Office.

Kandel, D. (1978). *Longitudinal research on drug use: Empirical findings and methodological issues*. New York: Hemisphere Halsted.

Kandel, D. (1980). Drug and drinking behavior among youth. *Annual Review of Sociology, 6*, 235–285.

Kandel, D. (1982). Epidemiological and psychosocial perspectives on adolescent drug use. *Journal of the American Academy of Child Psychiatry, 21*, 328–347.

Kaplan, H. B. (1984). Pathways to adolescent drug use: Self-derogation, peer influence, weakening of social control and early substance abuse. *Journal of Health and Social Behavior, 25*, 270–289.

Kaplan, H. B., Martin, S., & Robbins, C. (1982). Application of a general theory of deviant behavior: Self-derogation and adolescent drug use. *Journal of Health and Social Behavior, 23*, 274–294.

Kaplan, H., Martin, S., & Robbins, C. (1985). Toward an explanation of increased involvement in illicit drug use: Application of deviant behavior. *Research in Community and Mental Health, 5*, 205–252.

Kaplan, H., Johnson, R., & Bailey, C. (1986). Self-rejection and the explanation of deviance: Refinement and elaboration of a latent structure. *Social Psychology Quarterly, 49,* 110–128.

Kaplan, H., Johnson, R., & Bailey, C. (1987). Deviant peers and deviant behavior: Further elaboration of a model. *Social Psychology Quarterly, 50,* 277–278.

Kleinman, P. H., Wish, D. E., Deren, S., & Rainone, G. (1986). Multiple drug use: A symptomatic behavior. *Journal of Psychoactive Drugs, 18,* 77–86.

Loeber, R., Stouthhamer-Loeber, M., Van Kammen, W., & Farrington, D. P. (1991). Initiation escalation and desistance in juvenile offending and their correlates. *Journal of Criminal Law and Criminology, 82,* 36–62.

McGlouthlin, W. H., Anglin, D., & Wilson, B. D. (1978). Narcotic addiction and crime. *Criminology, 16,* 293–316.

Minnesota Department of Correction (1972). *Survey of drug use among institutionalized juvenile boys at Red Wing.* Minneapolis: Minnesota Department of Corrections.

Musto, D. (1973). *An American disease: Origins of narcotic control.* New Haven: Yale University Press.

National Commission on Marihuana and Drug Abuse (1972). *Marihuana: A signal of misunderstanding.* Washington, DC: U.S. Government Printing Office.

National Commission on Marihuana and Drug Abuse (1973). *Drug use in America: Problem in perspective.* Washington, DC: U.S. Government Printing Office.

Naughton, M. J., & Krohn, M. D. (1988). Assessments of the home environment and early adolescents' intentions to smoke cigarettes. *Journal of Early Adolescence, 8,* 169–182.

Needle, R., McCubbin, H., Wilson, M., Reineck, R., Lazar, A., & Mederer, H. (1986). Interpersonal influences in adolescent drug use—The role of older siblings, parents and peers. *International Journal of the Addictions, 21,* 739–766.

New Jersey State Police (1971). *Drug abuse and crime in New Jersey.* Trenton: State Law Enforcement Planning Agency.

Nurco, D. (1976). Crime and addiction: Methodological approaches to correct for opportunities to commit crime. In R. Shellow (Ed.), *Drug use and criminal behavior* (pp. 489–508). Washington, DC: National Technical Information Services.

Olson, D. H. (1983). *Families: What makes them work.* Beverly Hills: Sage Publications.

Olson, D. H. (1991). Commentary: Three-dimensional (3-D) circumplex model and revised scoring of FACES III. *Family Process, 30,* 74–79.

Ontario Corrections Services (1973). *A survey of drug use among wards prior to admission to training school.* Ontario: Ontario Corrections Services.

Osgood, D. W., Johnston, L. D., O'Malley, P. M., & Bachman, J. G. (1988). The generality of deviance in late adolescence and early adulthood. *American Sociological Review, 53,* 81–93.

Perry, C. L., & Murray, D. M. (1985). The prevention of adolescent drug abuse: Implications from etiological, developmental, behavioral and environmental models. *Journal of Primary Prevention, 6,* 31–52.

Pierce, J. I. (1969). Delinquency and heroine addiction in Britain. *British Journal of Criminology, 9,* 108–124.

Robins, L. N., & Guze, S. (1971). Drinking practices and problems in urban ghetto populations. In N. Mello & J. Mendelson (Eds.), *Recent advances in studies of alcoholism* (pp. 825–842). Washington, DC: U.S. Government Printing Office.

Robins, L. N., & Murphy, G. E. (1967). Drug use in a normal population of young Negro men. *American Journal of Public Health, 57,* 1580–1596.

Roman, P. M. (1981). Situational factors in the relationship between alcohol and crime. In J. J. Collins, Jr. (Ed.), *Drinking and crime* (pp. 143–151). New York: Guilford Press.

Stein, J. A., Newcomb, M. D., & Bentler, P. M. (1987). A 8-year study of multiple influences on drug use and drug use consequences. *Journal of Personality and Social Psychology, 53,* 1094–1105.

Stephens, R. C., & Ellis, R. D. (1975). Narcotic addicts and crime: Analysis of recent trends. *Criminology, 12*, 474–488.

Stephens, R. C., & McBride, D. C. (1976). Becoming a street addict. *Human Organizations, 35*, 87–93.

Tinklenberg, R. R., & Woodrow, K. M. (1974). Drug use among youthful assaultive and sexual offenders. In S. H. Frazier (Ed.), *Aggression: Proceedings of the 1972 annual meeting of the Association for Research in Nervous and Mental Disease*. Baltimore: Williams & Wilkins.

Watters, J. K. (1983). *U.S. heroin addiction policy, 1914 to 1983: Research report*. Rockville, MD: Treatment Research Branch, National Institute on Drug Abuse.

Watters, J. K., Reinarman, C., & Fagan, J. (1985). Causality, context and contingency: Relationships between drug abuse and delinquency. *Contemporary Drug Problems, 12*, 351–373.

Weissman, J. C., Katsampes, P. L., & Giacinti, T. G. (1976). Opiate use and criminality among a jail population. *Addictive Disease, 1*, 269–281.

White, H. R., Johnson, V., & Gozansky-Garrison, C. (1985). The drug–crime nexus among adolescents and their peers. *Deviant Behavior, 6*, 183–204.

White, H. R., Pandina, R. J., & LaGrange, R. L. (1987). Longitudinal predictors of serious substance abuse and delinquency. *Criminology, 25*, 715–740.

Wingard, J. A., Huba, G. J., & Bentler, P. M. (1979). The relationship of personality structures to patterns of adolescent substance use. *Multivariate Behavior Research, 14*, 131–143.

Wingard, J. A., Huba, G. J., & Bentler, P. M. (1980). A longitudinal analysis of personality structure and adolescent substance use. *Personality and Individual Differences, 1*, 259–272.

VI

EMERGING ISSUES IN LONGITUDINAL RESEARCH ON DEVIANT BEHAVIOR

Taken together, the eight studies previously considered suggest that by building on their strengths and taking into account their weaknesses, it is possible to anticipate (1) that research on the causes and consequences of deviance will increasingly focus on relationships among diverse patterns of deviance and (2) the forms that such research will take. In Chapter 10, I address these issues by considering contemporary themes and emerging issues in longitudinal research on the relationships among patterns of deviance.

10

Contemporary Themes and Emerging Directions in Longitudinal Research on Deviant Behavior

Howard B. Kaplan

The themes and directions that characterize contemporary research on deviant behavior are foreshadowed in the organization and substance of this volume. These characterizations refer, respectively, to the theoretical frameworks that guide the research and the methodological approaches to the estimation of theoretically informed causal models.

Theoretical Integration

Increasingly, research on the causes and consequences of deviant behavior is guided by integrated theoretical frameworks. Theoretical integration is occurring in two ways. First, more specific explanatory constructs are being subsumed under more general constructs. Second, theoretical frameworks are including a greater number of general explanatory constructs than had been included in the past.

Howard B. Kaplan • Department of Sociology, Texas A&M University, College Station, Texas 77843.

Drugs, Crime, and Other Deviant Adaptations: Longitudinal Studies, edited by Howard B. Kaplan. Plenum Press, New York, 1995.

Generality of Constructs

It is becoming more and more apparent that causal models may be expressed more parsimoniously. The literature on psychosocial antecedents of drug abuse and other deviant adaptations suggests that numerous specific predictors may be incorporated within a much smaller number of constructs. These constructs include experiences of failure and rejection, the inability to assuage distressful self-feelings associated with such experiences and to forestall subsequent experiences of this type, and the opportunities to learn and perform behaviors that are socially defined as maladaptive patterns of coping, including patterns of substance abuse and other deviant adaptations. Under experiences of failure and rejection, as one example, may be subsumed the experiences of school failure, belonging to a minority group, perceived parental rejection, the possession of stigmatized physical features, and being fired.

The generality of constructs has important implications for the testing of theoretical models. Because each construct subsumes a number of more precisely stated concepts, it is possible to express that construct in terms of the measures that the more diverse concepts subsumed under that construct have in common. Without this procedure, it would be more difficult to determine the meaning of any given variable. The more concrete or specific the variable, the greater the number of meanings that may be attached to it. Thus, indices of economic deprivation and minority status may reflect intrinsically disvalued life circumstances or the absence of personal goals and social resources that might permit the achievement of personally valued goals. Any specific index of self-derogation or concomitant subjective distress may reflect both the experience of distressful life circumstances and the absence of conventional (or unconventional) mechanisms that might forestall or assuage the experience of self-rejection resulting from adverse life circumstances; any such index would also reflect motivation to seek alternatives (including deviant adaptations) to conventional adaptive patterns that have failed to facilitate self-enhancing attitudes.

Any specific deviant pattern may reflect prior histories of stress-inducing circumstances that are adapted to by the deviant patterns, the absence of conventional coping mechanisms and related personal and social resources that might have permitted the individual to deal with stress-inducing life circumstances without adopting the deviant pattern, circumstances that facilitate the deviant pattern, including social learning experiences in delinquent groups, the absence of conventional bonds, and socially disapproved circumstances that induce social rejection and consequent psychological distress to which the individual adapts via substance abuse or other deviant patterns. Thus, outbursts that are thought to indicate psychopathology may reflect simultaneously the absence of socially acceptable coping patterns, histories of subjectively distressful adverse life circumstances that disposed to psychopathology, and subjectively distressful consequences of psychopathology. Even when a temporal relationship between, for example, association with drug-using peers and degree of substance abuse is unequivocally established, the relationship may be accounted for in terms of normative endorsement of the patterns, opportunities to engage in the patterns, accessibility of drugs, and social learning processes.

Because an explanatory construct may be expressed in terms of a number of more specific concepts and measures, and any particular measure may be interpreted in terms of a number of explanatory constructs, latent variable methodology (see Chapters 4 and 6) has proved to be quite useful in distinguishing between the meaning that a particular measure shares with other diverse indicators of a particular construct and other meanings the measure might have.

Inclusive Theoretical Frameworks

Increasingly, more inclusive theoretical frameworks guide contemporary research on the relationships among patterns of deviance and their correlates. Constructs that in the past represented narrow theoretical approaches are now joined by representative constructs from diverse explanatory approaches in the context of broader paradigms. It is no longer unusual, for example, to observe, in the same model, constructs reflecting stressful experiences, vulnerability, labeling, social learning, and social control factors. Ultimately, it is to be expected that the integrated approach presented in Chapter 1 will guide much of the research on the relationships among deviant behaviors, other antecedents and consequences of these behaviors, and the variables that mediate or moderate these relations. In such integrated approaches, the etiological models address the disposition to engage in the deviant pattern, acting out the deviant pattern, and changes in level of engagement in the deviant pattern (Kaplan, 1984).

Disposition to Engage in Deviant Patterns

The disposition to adopt a deviant pattern is a function of both the group's attitude toward the pattern and the nature of the subject's attitude toward the group. The disposition to use illicit drugs, for example, may or may not be congruent with the shared values of membership/reference group(s). The person with a history of self-enhancing experiences in the membership/reference group(s) that endorse(s) or use(s) illicit drugs associates the motivation to use drugs and the norms endorsing drug use with acceptance by the group members. Given a history of self-devaluing experiences, however, the individual is less disposed to conform to the shared values of the group (including perhaps illicit drug use). In the more usual case, in which the group norms proscribe illicit use of drugs and drug use is incompatible with the group values, the person is not disposed to use drugs, particularly when past conformity has been rewarded with acceptance by the group members. When the experiences in such a group have been essentially self-devaluing, however, the person is more disposed to use drugs and is attracted to values that contradict those of the group. Thus, a person becomes disposed or motivated to use drugs in any of three ways: (1) by socialization in groups that endorse drug use; (2) by attraction to groups that endorse illicit drug use; and (3) by loss of motivation to conform and becoming motivated to deviate from conventional group values because of past self-devaluing experiences in such groups.

Acting Out Deviant Dispositions

Acting out deviant dispositions depends in large measure on available opportunities to engage in the behavior and on the meanings associated with the act and the perceived consequences of the act. Continuing with the example of illicit drug use, if one is disposed to use drugs, opportunities (a supply of drugs is available and there is occasion for use) increase the likelihood that one will use drugs. Similarly, if disposed to use drugs, one is more likely to do so if one anticipates relatively few self-devaluing outcomes and relatively more self-enhancing outcomes. The outcomes might relate to material rewards, attitudes of others, relief of physical or psychological distress, or any of a number of valued outcomes. Whether particular outcomes are interpreted positively or negatively depends on such variables as the person's history of self-enhancing/self-devaluing experiences in the group. Less directly, the onset of illicit drug use is the outcome of determinants of disposition to use drugs, opportunities to act out dispositions, and anticipation of the consequences of drug use.

Changes in Level of Involvement

Changes in the level of involvement in the deviant act following initiation of the deviant response are a function of the circumstances surrounding initial use. These circumstances include the variables that influence initiation, that result from initial involvement in the pattern, and that reflect changes in the person's psychosocial situation. Certain of these circumstances (alone or in combination) will increase involvement, whereas other circumstances will decrease level of involvement.

Illicit drug use, for example, generally increases given three conditions: (1) if the person associates need satisfaction with the illicit drug use; (2) if the subject experiences a weakening of the motive that ordinarily acts to constrain illicit drug use; and (3) if the opportunities for illicit drug use remain constant or increase. Need satisfaction depends on the self-evaluative significance of perceived traits, behaviors, and experiences (particularly the responses of highly valued others). Illicit drug use satisfies the person's need for positive self-evaluation in a number of ways: It permits the youth to avoid conventional standards that measure his or her failure, it allows the youth to conform to the expectations of a positive reference group (e.g., drug-using peers), and it validates earlier drug use or the resulting deviant identity.

The motives that ordinarily constrain deviant impulses are reflected in the self-evaluative significance of internal and external social controls. These controls are weakened if accompanied by an absence of visible adverse consequences of earlier illicit drug use and by decreased attraction to conventional values. These characteristics result from (1) the ongoing processes that influence the disposition to use illicit drugs and (2) the rejecting responses of conventional groups following initial drug use. The reciprocal rejection between the youth and conventional society increases the attraction to and interaction with peers who use drugs, thus providing ongoing occasions and opportunities for drug use.

Conversely, illicit drug use is less likely to increase if (1) the drug used does not appear to satisfy the needs that stimulated the initial response, (2) delinquent behavior stimulates threats to the satisfaction of other needs (such as those associated with continuing emotional commitment to conventional morality or fear of formal sanctions), and (3) changes in the person's needs or in the available conventional opportunities to satisfy those needs render illicit drug use superfluous.

Estimation of Causal Models

Increasingly, the estimation of causal models is occurring in the context of research designs that (1) use longitudinal frameworks, (2) employ multigeneration observations, and (3) focus on the relationships among multiple patterns of deviance.

Longitudinal Research

Research on deviant behavior is increasingly characterized by longitudinal research designs not only because in general such designs permit establishing temporal relationships between deviant behaviors and their hypothesized antecedents and consequences, but also because they permit the incorporation and testing of insights from the developmental and life-course perspectives.

Longitudinal research on deviant behavior permits the testing of dynamic models that take into account the interaction and mutual influence of the varied risk factors at different developmental stages and in different social contexts. As Glantz (1992, p. 401) observes with reference to drug abuse:

> A developmentally oriented drug abuse etiology model emphasizes the origin of the risk for drug abuse as evolving, particularly during the maturational period of the individual. The factors constituting the risk are not constant but developed through the interactions of the individual with his or her environment and in the context of that individual's progression through the stages and maturational tasks of growing up. Vulnerability develops, and in this sense it is not just a set of static, predisposing antecedent factors, but rather a dynamic process. No single vulnerability factor is the "cause" of drug abuse by itself; instead, it is a contributive component in an interactive system that leads to emergent factors that in turn interact and evolve. Any single risk factor must be understood as having its etiological influence in the context of many other factors with which it interacts over time, probably developing through a number of transformations eventually leading to a heightened vulnerability to drug abuse. Thus, a given factor may have a different contributive effect at different developmental periods. Similarly, a factor's contribution will vary in the context of the particular other factors with which it interacts. Particular combinations of characteristics and circumstances interacting over time will differentially predispose an individual to, or protect him from, vulnerability to drug abuse.

Longitudinal research also permits investigation of the influence of later stages in the life course on the adoption of and changes in the level of involvement with deviant behaviors. Following a cohort of subjects into later stages of life permits documentation of changes regarding the loss, addition, or redefinition of social roles and the consequences of these role changes. Not the least significant of these role changes relates to the presence and maturation of the subjects' children. The addition of interview data from later decades of life permits examination of the effects of role strain experienced at earlier stages in conjugal family and work careers on later adaptations, including deviant patterns. The experience of stresses at early stages in adult careers may be expected to interact with perceived inadequacies during childhood and adolescence in influencing the nature and effectiveness of conventional and deviant adaptations to stress. It is widely accepted that parental behavior influences child behavior. However, it is not widely understood how the parent affects the child and when the seed of those influences is planted.

Specifically, the parent is the outgrowth of his or her own earlier dynamics in early adolescence and before. If parental behavior represents a strong influence on the deviant behavior of children, then it becomes important to understand the antecedents of the parental behavior. A more abundant literature exists on the influence of parental responses on child behavior than on the experiences of the parent-as-adolescent influence on later parental responses, and thus as indirect influences on the responses of the next generation.

Findings indicating the relevance of age of mother for second-generation outcomes specifically suggest the need to examine child-rearing patterns of subjects who do not form families until the fourth decade of life. The testing of the parental generation during the third and fourth decades of life will permit determination of the degree to which parental responses to the children are stable and the extent to which parental responses and experiences (including those relating to deviant patterns) are variable due to changes in the demand characteristics associated with the stage of development of the child or other changes in the parental environment (Roberts, Block, & Block, 1984). The life-span approach to the study of drug abuse permits linking stages in personal development to second-generation outcomes.

Multigeneration Research

Numerous studies are available that investigate either the linkage between early adolescent traits, behaviors, and experiences and attributes, behavior, and experiences observed at later stages in the life cycle, or relationships between the attributes, behavior, and experiences of the parental generation and outcomes for the second-generation children. Less common, however, are studies that demonstrate the association between substance abuse, other deviant adaptations, and their correlates for one generation during a specific developmental stage (such as early adolescence) with comparable variables and relationships for second-generation children observed at the same developmental stage, or studies that attempt to decompose that relationship in terms of later stages of development (including stages of early and later parenthood) of the first-generation and common antecedents of the two generations. Such studies should appear with greater frequency in the future.

Multigeneration research has two major advantages in studies of the antecedents and consequences of deviant behavior. First, when subjects from different generations are tested at comparable developmental stages, the parallelism between first- and second-generation subjects during the same developmental stage (e.g., early adolescence) permits the comparison of levels of response (e.g., level of involvement in drug abuse) and relationships between variables (e.g., the association between more or less positive parent–child relationships and engaging in substance abuse and other deviant adaptations). The examination of correlates of substance abuse, for example, for early adolescence in the first and second generations will permit some assessment of the effects of historical changes on the relationships between a deviant pattern, its hypothesized antecedents, and its consequences. Interviews with the children of drug abusers and nonabusers at the same developmental stages (e.g., early adolescence and as young adults) as their parents were when they were first studied permits examining the stability of the theoretically informed models that were tested in longitudinal context on the first generation.

A second advantage, as suggested above, is that the observed relationship between patterns of deviance for two successive generations may be explained. Models may be tested that show that first-generation deviant patterns have consequences for later child-rearing patterns that, in turn, affect the deviant adaptations of the second generation subjects. Alternatively, the common deviant patterns may be accounted for in terms of the common circumstances faced by both generations, including those associated with particular developmental stages.

Relationships among Patterns of Deviance

Deviant patterns take many forms, including failure to perform conventional roles such as being part of the work force and engaging in parenthood at appropriate times in the life cycle, illicit drug use, childhood hyperactivity, difficult temperament during infancy, depressive affect, severe self-derogation, disvalued social identities, rebelliousness, school rejection, interpersonal violence, and theft. These forms of deviance and so many others increasingly are being interpreted in terms of the latent constructs that are used as explanatory factors in research on the antecedents and consequences of any particular form of deviance. At the same time, explanatory constructs are themselves being interpreted as forms of deviance where they had not been so interpreted in the past.

The end result is that studies of the antecedents and consequences of deviance are more and more taking the form of studies of the relationship among patterns of deviance. As the studies that constitute the greater part of this volume illustrate, patterns of deviance may be common outcomes or causes of other patterns of deviance, a particular pattern may be uniquely associated with another pattern of deviance, and patterns of deviance may mediate or moderate the relationships between multiple modes of deviance. The explanation of deviance is coming to depend to a much greater extent than was hitherto recognized on the understanding of the causal relationships among multiple patterns of deviance.

ACKNOWLEDGMENTS.   This work was supported by research grant DA02497 and Research Scientist Award DA00136 to the author from the National Institute on Drug Abuse.

References

Glantz, M. (1992). A developmental psychopathology model of drug abuse vulnerability. In M. Glantz & R. Pickens (Eds.), *Vulnerability to drug abuse* (pp. 389–418). Washington, DC: American Psychological Association.

Kaplan, H. B. (1984). *Patterns of juvenile delinquency.* Beverly Hills: Sage Publications.

Roberts, G. C., Block, J. H., & Block, J. (1984). Continuity and change in parents' child-rearing practices. *Child Development, 55,* 596–597.

Author Index

Subject Index